<u>Note</u>

This book is a record of all the information and data on the small band of Apache Indians who are located in that part of the Sierra Madre of Mexico which lies on the border line between the states of Chihuahua and Sonora.

The first entry starts in 1927, which was the beginning of my knowledge of these Apaches, and the following entries go on in the order in which the information, clippings, photographs, and etc. were collected.

A good bit of the material, especially in the newspapers, is somewhat exaggerated, but where personal information was obtained as much care as possible was taken to get reliable material. Some of the data relates to former times, during the Apache Wars, and to remains found in caves or other sites which have been inhabited by Indians, whether Apaches or not.

Grenville Goodwin

Feb. 7, 1931

Tucson, Arizona

Grenville Goodwin and Neil Goodwin

# The Apache Diaries: A Father-Son Journey

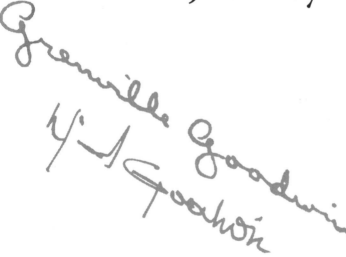

University of Nebraska Press:

Lincoln and London

Publication of this volume was assisted by The
Virginia Faulkner Fund, established in memory
of Virginia Faulkner, editor-in-chief of the
University of Nebraska Press.

Page i: The first page of the diary.
Frontispiece: Grenville Goodwin, Tucson, about 1930.
Courtesy Arizona Historical Society. Negative B#29902.

Library of Congress Cataloging-in-Publication Data
Goodwin, Grenville, 1907-1940.
The Apache diaries : a father-son journey / Grenville
Goodwin and Neil Goodwin.
    p.    cm.  Includes bibliographical references and index.
ISBN 0-8032-2175-4 (cloth: alk. paper)  1. Western Apa-
che Indians – History.  2. Western Apache Indians –
Social life and customs.  3. Goodwin, Grenville, 1907-
1940 – Diaries  I. Goodwin, Neil.  II. Title.
E99.A6  G646  2000    979′.004972–dc21    99-047666

*This book is dedicated to*
*Margot and Seth,*
*and to*
*the people whose story it tells*

FOR SPIKE,

JUST THINK — IF YOU HAD GONE
TO THE GRAY, YOU MIGHT HAVE
GONE ON OUR RECENT TRIP TO
MEXICO. .... YOU'RE ALWAYS
ELIGIBLE THOUGH — HOPE YOU
ENJOY —

6/18/2000

# Contents

List of Illustrations     viii

Acknowledgments     xi

Overture     xiii

Prologue     1

PART ONE

1. A Stolen Child     19
2. Phantom Apaches     24
3. To Rescue His Son     26
4. Geronimo's People?     31
5. Menace in the Mountains     36
6. Double Revenge     51

PART TWO

7. Crossings     61
8. Pulpit Rock     68
9. The Caves     74
10. Apaches and the Bavispe Valley     76
11. Enemy People     99

PART THREE

12. Taking Stock     109
13. The San Carlos Connection     114
14. Close Encounters     122
15. An Apache Camp     135
16. Booty     150
17. Apache Gold     153
18. The Hidden Camp     161
19. A Refuge in the Espuelas     169
20. The Smugglers     184

PART FOUR

21. Echoes of Mexico at San Carlos          191

22. Carmela          206

23. Are There Any Left?          212

24. Fugitives and Descendants          223

Epilogue          237

APPENDIX ONE

Historical Chronology          245

APPENDIX TWO

The Chita Hueca Camp Description          251

APPENDIX THREE

The Espuelas Camp Description          255

Notes          259

Index          275

# Illustrations

PHOTOGRAPHS AND DRAWINGS

*Following p. 58*

1. Grenville Goodwin, Turkey Hill Pueblo, 1929.
2. The Apache captive, Lupe, about 1940.
3. Francisco Fimbres and posse, Nácori Chico, 1930.
4. Barney Burns and Norberto Aguillar Ruiz, Nácori Chico, 1996.
5. Rodolfo Rascón, Estolano Madrid Fimbres, Norberto Aguillar Ruiz, Nácori Chico, 1996.

*Following p. 106*

6. Pulpit Rock, 1996.
7. Petroglyphs in the caves in El Paso Púlpito.
8. Grenville Goodwin and his first deer, El Paso Púlpito, 1930.
9. The church at Bacerac, 1930.
10. The church at Bacerac, 1996.
11. Nelda, Lola Barela, Barney, Huachinera, 1996.
12. Bavispe, 1996.

*Following p. 188*

13. The Apache Kid.
14. Guadalupe Quesada, 1976.
15. Margot at the upper Apache camp, Sierra las Espuelas, 1997.
16. Chita Hueca Apache camp—group of dwellings.
17. First house, main camp, Sierra Chita Hueca, 1931.
18. House types, Apache Rancheria, Chita Hueca.
19. Circular piece of iron, Chita Hueca camp, 1931.
20. Articles found at the Chita Hueca camp in 1931.
21. Small leather bottle from Apache camp, 1926.
22. Neil, Sierra las Espuelas Apache Rancheria, 1997.

23. Seth and Kathy, Rancho la Cabaña, 1995.

24. Main Apache camp at Sierra las Espuelas, 1997.

25. Sierra las Espuelas Apache Rancheria — complete plan.

26. House, Sierra las Espuelas, 1997.

27. Bill Curtis, Apache camp in the Sierra las Espuelas, 1931.

28. House, Apache camp, Sierra las Espuelas, 1931.

29. Sierra las Espuelas Apache Rancheria — plan, main camp.

30. Sierra las Espuelas Rancheria — plan, main corrals on ridge.

31. Neil, Sierra Las Espuelas Apache camp, 1997.

32. Sierra las Espuelas Rancheria — plan, small pens in canyon below ridge.

33a – d. Drawings, house types, Apache camps, Sierra las Espuelas.

*Following p. 236*   34. Yanozha, Chappo, Fun, and Geronimo, Cañon de los Embudos, March 1886.

35. The Apache captive, Julio Medina, 1950.

36. The Apache captive girl, Bui, 1932.

37. Carmela Harris, Los Angeles, about 1935.

38. Carmela Harris, Los Angeles, about 1948.

39. Jan and Grennie, Santa Fe, 1937.

40. Grennie with Neil Buck and his family, Santa Fe, 1938.

41. Neil Buck, San Carlos, about 1951.

42. Barbara Buck King, San Carlos, 1997.

MAPS

1. Arizona, New Mexico, Sonora, and Chihuahua — xvi

2. Travels of Grenville and Neil in Mexico — xvii

# Acknowledgments

*There are many people without whom this book would not have been possible, but chief among them is Barney Burns, a tireless, resourceful and inspiring collaborator, companion, and dear friend.*

*It was through Barney and his friend Tom Naylor that I came to know Nelda Villa, without whom we might never have met and gained the trust of so many welcoming and generous people in the villages of Sonora and Chihuahua. Raised in the Sierra Madre among pioneering Mormon and Mexican families, Nelda grew up surrounded by much of the history this book attempts to set forth, and her willingness to share it with us has proven a priceless gift. The tragic and untimely death of Tom Naylor deprived us all of a good friend and a brilliant mind. Tom was in on the beginning of my search with Barney and Misse Smith, and, though gone, he has, in a way, always been with us.*

*Throughout this enterprise, Margot, with her great Irish heart and her nearly infallible instincts, has taught me the meaning of trust. She has braved the elements, not only of the Sierra Madre but also of my own singlemindedness, with grace, generosity, and patience. When my son, Seth, travels with us in Mexico, it is, in some ways, like having my father there. They look alike, and Seth is closer by far in age and temperament to my father when he did this work than I am. I am doubly grateful to Seth, for he has introduced us all to Kathy, who brings us her own high Irish heart and sunny nature and adds her trail craft and outdoor culinary arts to Seth's. Happily for us all, and most happily for themselves, they were married in the summer of 1999.*

*There are so many people on both sides of the border who opened their doors and eventually their lives to us. Any time they speak, the story told in this book gathers strength. Of all the people we have spoken to, either briefly or at length, I want to single out for special thanks: Berle Kanseah, Mildred Cleghorn, Ruey Darrow, Jeanette Cassa, Francisco Zozaya, Rodolfo Rascón, Ola Cassador, Mike Davis, Barbara Buck King, Cline Griggs, Estolono Madrid Fimbres, Norberto Aguillar Ruiz, Pedro Urquijo, Beula Fenn MacNeil, Manuela Chafino, Ann McGarrell,*

Tony Levario, Charles Walter Swanson, Herman Hatch, Maurice Whetten, Elvin Whetten, Alvah Fenn, Lloyd Davis, Miguel Cruz, and the Muñoz family.

My agent, my good and old friend Ike Williams, believed in this story almost before I did, and Gary Dunham has been an invaluable editor. There are many scholars, researchers, and historians upon whose experience, wisdom, and friendship I have leaned heavily: Diana Hadley, Charles Kaut, Keith Basso, Becky Orozco, Alden Hayes, Bill Hoy, Bernard Fontana, Alan Ferg, Philip Greenfeld, John Welch, Mr. and Mrs. Morris Opler, Edwin Sweeney, Alan Radbourne, Seth Pilsk, Jay Van Orden, Dale Brenneman, Lori Davisson, Jose Isabel Gamez, Gloria Valdez, Nick Houser, Dale Giese, Karl Laumbach, Marc Simmons, Henrietta Stockel, Cynthia Hayostek, Virginia, Bill, and Imelda Wallace, Aïda Desouches Gabilondo, the Gabilondos—owners of the Santa Anita Ranch, Carlos Borunda of the Divisidero Ranch, and Robbin Bell at Peace River Films.

Most of the people who have spoken with us had ancestors who were part of the conflict about which this book is written. To those people I am especially grateful for believing that this story should be told, and for helping us to tell what is, in reality, only a small part of it.

What they know would fill a library: Roque Barceló, Agustín Barceló, Tomas Barceló, Lola Barela, Rose Belvado, Sandra Belvado, Chato Bluth, Mack Bluth, Harrison Bonito, Cliff Bowman, Quinn Boyd, Enriquez Burgos, Miguel Burquez Ramos, Antonio Burquez Renteria, Rodrigo Chafino, Manuel Coronado, Macidonia Cruz, Ryne Dasila, Chester Davis, Isabel Enriquez, Lavine Fenn, Cruz Fernandez, Pedro Fimbres, José Fuentes Gutierrez, José Jesús Fuentes, Dr. Roy Hatch, Ether Haynie, Ramon Jordan, Thelma Kindelay, George Lane, Don Chano Leyva, Ed Maddox, Billy Martineau, Virginia Martinez Cuevas, Arturo Martinez Tapia, Annie McNeil, Floyd McNeil, Miles Miller, Gregoria Molina Barela, Fernando Montaño, Ralph Morrow, Benjamin Murrieta, Heraclio Olivas Renteria, Jesús Pedregón Ramos, Juan Portillo, Walter Ramsey, Rufino Reyes, Simón Rodríguez Mendez, Ramón Rodríguez, Alberta Rope, Manuel Ruiz, Rafaela Ruiz, Carlisle Russell, Emiglia Samaniego, Natalia Samaniego, Douglas St. Clair, Russell Taylor, Pedro Toscano, Clarence Turley, Marion Vance.

# Overture

Imagine this.

Imagine that you live in Piños Altos and that it is 1927. The Sierra Madre rises all around you. The mountains are said to be safe now, but it was not always so. Until 1886, when the Apache Geronimo finally surrendered, the mountains were places of fear. Now almost all the Apaches are gone. Ten years ago your father and your cousins, the Fimbres family, cleared some land in the mountains and built cabins there.

You have two brothers, and your twin sister is Maria; you do everything together with her. Your father is Reyes, a farmer. You are twelve years old, and this is all you have ever known.

There is someone else. There is Lupe, an Apache woman.

Lupe has lived with your family for five years. When she was about fifteen she was captured by your father and some others trying to recover cattle stolen by Lupe's people, the wild Apaches who still live in the mountains. No one ever sees them.

Lupe has chosen to stay with you because it is too dangerous for her to return to her people. She tried it once, and they said they would kill her if she ever came back. So she takes care of you and your sister. She is Apache, but she is now of your family.

She says there are Apaches always watching. She says that you and your sister and your father and mother and brothers are never alone. The Apaches hide and watch what you do, she says. She is afraid. She says her uncle, Apache Juan, is a bad man.

Having the Apaches in the Sierra is like having a phantom by your side who sees your every move and could do something to you at any moment, but who is invisible to you. Only Lupe knows when they are there. She says she can smell them, and whenever she does she gathers you and the other children up and brings you inside. Lupe has a sixth sense, a gift, an awareness that gives her sight where you are blind. She has learned your language and your ways; she has been baptized in the church by the priest, but still she is alien—all the more so because she will not tell you about her other life, and now you are afraid to ask because it makes her angry.

One day your father, Reyes, is in his cornfield, watching for the wild turkeys that eat his corn. There is a small hut in a corner of the field. He goes in to watch for turkeys and finds a stranger asleep in the hut. Reyes takes the man's rifle and removes the cartridges, then wakes him up. The man is sleeping soundly because he is ill with fever. Reyes asks him who he is, what he is doing there. The man says he is resting. They talk; then after a while the man tells Reyes to be very careful; he may be in grave danger.

The man may be American. He is tall and blond but speaks very good Spanish. He says there are Apaches always nearby. The man knows this because he visits their camp sometimes, and trades with them. They do not harm him. He says they hide in the bushes and behind rocks and watch everything. They are led by a man named Juan who is very bad. The man in the hut tells your father that Juan watches you and your sister and all the other children. This man says the children should never be left alone because of what Juan might do. He says he thinks Juan might want the children.

In the mornings Lupe is always awake first. She makes paper-thin tortillas outside, slinging them around her hands and her forearms until they are right. She cooks them in seconds on a hot sheet of iron. This day you know her mind is elsewhere, because now she burns one, now another. She is watching the ridges to the east where the Sierra Madre rises. Then she goes all still, turns into the drifting air, her eyes closed, narrowing all awareness to a single faculty of sense, studying, searching in the dark behind her eyes for some meaning, for a faint whiff. A slight shake of head, shrug of shoulder and she resumes cooking. You wonder what it was, but don't ask. Lupe says she'll go out this day and look for palmilla for weaving baskets. She has planned this since last week. The time is right, and she says it's safe.

You and your sister and your two Fimbres cousins beg to go along. You take a blanket and some food because it is a long walk and you want to stay out until tomorrow. You love to do this. There is a cave you know about that you love to sleep in.

You find the cave; then while you are gathering palm leaves in the afternoon, you see Lupe stop and stiffen. She looks at the ground for a long time. then says this to you and the others:

"Here is where five Apaches stood and waited for a long time yesterday. Here is where they stood their rifles on the ground while they waited. I can also smell them. We have to go home."

You and your friends do not want to. You are having an adventure; you want to spend the night in the cave. You are not worried; if there are Apaches, they would not do anything bad. They don't bother people any more. Lupe is only a servant and cannot make you go home against your will. Lupe is very afraid and says she will not spend the night out, and even though you decide to stay, she goes home, saying your parents will come for you and bring you back. Though you would not say it to her face, you and your friends think her superstitious — an Indian. Your parents do not come. Like you, they think Lupe is afraid for no reason. You spend the night in the cave.

Nothing happens to you.

But the next day you find that there has been a murder and a kidnapping on the road up from the valley. Maria Dolores Fimbres is dead, and her son, little Gerardo Fimbres, is captured. In your village nothing will ever be the same again.

Lupe had reason to be afraid. Descended from a long line of warriors, including Geronimo, Victorio, Juh, Cochise, and Mangas Coloradas, her people had been making their enemy's blood run cold for 250 years in northern Mexico.

In 1927 they could still do it. The Apache Wars were not over yet.

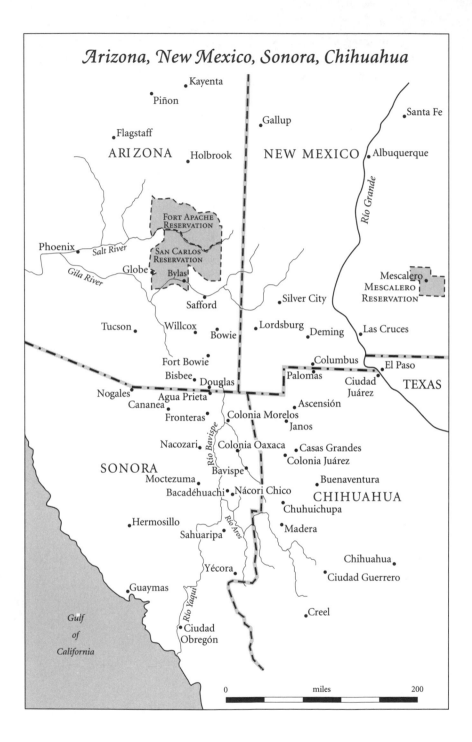

# Arizona, New Mexico, Sonora, Chihuahua

Kayenta

Piñon

Flagstaff

ARIZONA    Holbrook

Gallup

Santa Fe

NEW MEXICO    Albuquerque

*Rio Grande*

FORT APACHE
RESERVATION

Phoenix    *Salt River*

*Gila River*    Globe    SAN CARLOS
RESERVATION

Bylas

Safford

Silver City

Mescalero
MESCALERO
RESERVATION

Tucson    Willcox    Lordsburg    Deming    Las Cruces

Bowie

Fort Bowie    Columbus

Bisbee    Palomas    El Paso

Nogales    Douglas    Ciudad    TEXAS
Juárez

Agua Prieta

Cananea    Ascensión

Fronteras    Colonia Morelos

Janos

Nacozari    Colonia Oaxaca    Casas Grandes

*Rio Bavispe*    Colonia Juárez

SONORA    Bavispe    Buenaventura

Moctezuma    Nácori Chico    CHIHUAHUA

Bacadéhuachi

Chuhuichupa

Hermosillo    *Rio Aros*    Madera

Sahuaripa

Chihuahua

Yécora    Ciudad Guerrero

Guaymas    Creel

*Rio Yaqui*

Gulf
of
California    Ciudad
Obregón

0    miles    200

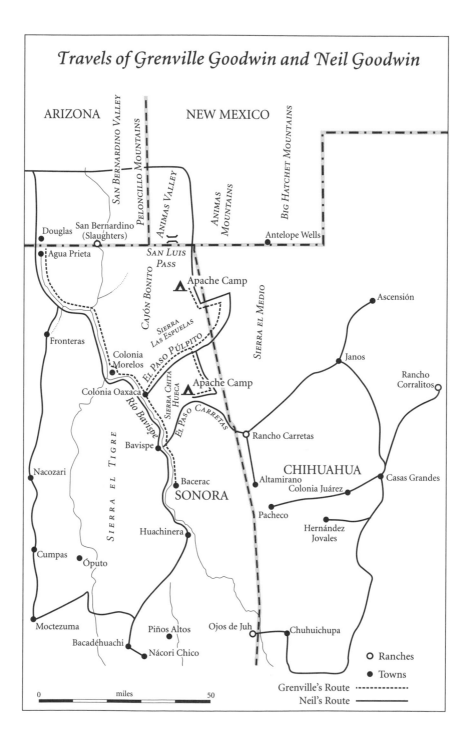

# Travels of Grenville Goodwin and Neil Goodwin

ARIZONA

NEW MEXICO

San Bernardino Valley

Pelloncillo Mountains

Animas Valley

Animas Mountains

Big Hatchet Mountains

Douglas

San Bernardino (Slaughters)

Antelope Wells

Agua Prieta

San Luis Pass

Cajón Bonito

Apache Camp

Fronteras

Sierra Las Espuelas

Sierra el Medio

El Paso Púlpito

Ascensión

Colonia Morelos

Janos

Rancho Corralitos

Colonia Oaxaca

Sierra Chita Hueca

Apache Camp

El Paso Carretas

Río Bavispe

Rancho Carretas

CHIHUAHUA

Sierra el Tigre

Bavispe

Nacozari

Altamirano

Casas Grandes

Bacerac

Colonia Juárez

SONORA

Pacheco

Huachinera

Hernández Jovales

Cumpas

Óputo

Moctezuma

Piños Altos

Ojos de Juh

Chuhuichupa

Bacadéhuachi

Nácori Chico

0        miles        50

○ Ranches

● Towns

Grenville's Route ----------

Neil's Route ——————

# THE APACHE DIARIES

# Prologue

Two hundred fifty miles north of Piños Altos, and a world apart, my father's life would soon be touched by these events, as would mine and my own son's. My father was beginning his life's work as an ethnographer among the Apaches, and it started with Lupe's people.

MY FATHER

I never knew my father. A tumor killed him soon after I was born. Though I can recite an abundance of biographical fact, what died with him is lost to me forever.

I sometimes imagine that if I were to hear the sound of his voice just once, all the details I have collected would, like a backwards-running, slow-motion film of a shattering mirror, suddenly coalesce into a perfect whole—alive at last.

In an attempt to make his image whole I have undertaken this book. It is an exploration, and, like all explorations, and all journeys, I begin it without any certainty of where it will lead—all the more so because it is an exploration of two mysteries. One is my father. The other is a mystery that he once tried to solve himself: who are Lupe's people, the phantom Apaches of the Sierra Madre?

In 1927 a small band of these people, still locked in a centuries-old conflict with the Mexicans, ambushed the Fimbres family near Nácori Chico, Sonora. They killed Maria Fimbres, the wife, and kidnapped her three-year-old son, Gerardo. Her husband's pursuit of revenge was soon making headlines throughout the Southwest.

In 1930 my father entered the Sierra Madre to find out what he could about these Apaches before they were exterminated, and he recorded this compelling experience in a diary. There it waited, essentially lost, like an old treasure map, until, in 1962, I found it again, incomplete and enigmatic. It was a tale of murder and kidnapping and a lost people. I took up the hunt—my father's unfinished mission—and this is the story of completing the mission and of my encounter with the father I never knew.

If anything, my father is more elusive than the "phantom tribe." Sometimes he's with me, sometimes out of sight, but, like a wolf, he is always there, covering ten miles for every one of mine. There will be times when he'll circle close, an incandescent presence in the brush; then he'll be gone.

Although my father was only thirty-three when he died in 1940, he had published several papers and two books about the Western Apache. Soon after his death, his great friend, the anthropologist Edward Spicer, wrote that my father's landmark monograph, *The Social Organization of the Western Apache*, was "one of the most detailed and best-documented studies of Indian social organization."[1] Twenty years later Spicer noted how my father's stature had grown:

> To Grenville Goodwin we owe most of what understanding we have of the way of life of the Western Apaches. The abundant literature on the Western Apaches, inspired in great part by the spectacular forays of Geronimo and his predecessors, is largely a literature of the men who fought the Indians and participated in the final relentless round-ups. It is not a literature from which emerges a view of the values by which Apaches lived. But for the work of Goodwin we would have lost all opportunity to participate in the Apache world.[2]

My father's friend and colleague Morris Opler considered him to be "one of the most gifted and effective field anthropologists in the history of the discipline."[3]

Most of my father's anthropological colleagues praised him generously, but I have heard that some could never forget that he was an amateur, without formal training or degrees: gifted, but an amateur nonetheless. I have heard that some felt he got too close to his subjects, lost his objectivity, recorded material that could not be used because it was either too private or possibly was compromised by subjectivity.

I have also heard that he is considered one of the most enigmatic and romantic figures in American anthropology.

THE APACHES

My father went to work among the Apaches at a time when little was known about them, except to the Apaches themselves. A few talented and observant soldiers and reporters such as John Bourke, Britton Davis, Charles Lummis, and John Cremony had written about them as adversaries.[4] Pliny Goddard, whose work was published between 1906 and 1920, was one of the first anthropologists to write about the Apache.[5] The linguist Harry Hoijer had recently begun to work with Apache and other Athabascan languages.[6] Morris Opler was beginning his work at the Mescalero Apache Reservation.

Other anthropologists had been working on the neighboring Pueblos and on the Navajos for a generation already, and the field was crowded with such pioneering scholars as Elsie Clews Parsons (Puebloans), Frank Cushing (Puebloans), Father Berard Haile (Navajo), Washington Matthews (Navajo), Gladys Reichard (Navajo), Clyde Kluckohn (Navajo), Robert Young (Navajo), and Mary Wheelwright (Navajo). But the Western Apaches were virtually unstudied. The anthropologist Alfred L. Kroeber wrote in 1931: "In terms of precise knowledge, the Apache are, with the possible exception of the Ojibwa, the least known surviving North American group."[7]

And yet "Apache" has, for over one hundred years, been one of the most iconic, and, in the popular mind, infamous of all Native American tribal names. It is by now an all-too-familiar irony that "*Apache*" was a name bestowed by others. They did not call themselves "Apache," but simply: Nde, (pronounced "n-déh"), the People. Not knowing their name was just the beginning of our ignorance about them.

During the nineteenth century, European-Americans never came to understand the Apaches as fellow human beings because they were always *the enemy*. The wars between the U.S. government and the Apaches lasted from 1861 until 1886, longer than any other Indian conflict within the United States. Those 25 years of strife produced a flood of print and cinematic fiction in the United States that swept around the world. But those years pale in comparison with the 250 years during which warfare persisted in Mexico. Never more than a few thousand, the Apaches of what is now northwestern Mexico and the southwestern United States beset the northward Spanish advance from the date of first contact, probably in the early 1600s. As a people, the Apaches were never Christianized, never urbanized, never colonized, never enslaved, never broken. The vulnerable outposts and caravans of the Spanish colonial frontier made easy marks for the highly mobile Apaches, who raided mercilessly for goods and livestock. Some historians believe that the Spanish presence in northern Mexico helped to give birth to the Apache practice of raiding.[8]

In the early nineteenth century there were reliable reports of Apache raids in the district of Guerrero, southwest of Chihuahua City and about two hundred and forty miles south of El Paso.[9] During the late eighteenth century they may have raided as far south as the state of Durango, Mexico, some four hundred miles south of El Paso.[10]

Of course, Apaches were not the only raiders. Farther east, in Texas, the Kiowas and the Comanches took a serious toll as well.

No one who was not Apache entered the heart of Apacheria unbidden, but the Apaches were careful, it seems, not to drive the Spanish away altogether. The Apaches tolerated a certain level of settlement on the borders of their vast mountain and semidesert domain, because these settlements were a source of highly desirable items obtainable only through raiding.[11] Periods of relative peace between the Spanish and the Apaches punctuated the long years of vicious warfare, but the warfare endured, and it reached levels of astonishing ferocity on both sides. By the late nineteenth century, as the Apache Wars came to their dramatic conclusion, both sides were steeped in blood and loathing, and the memory of this prison of hate lingered long after the fighting was over.

Before settlement on American reservations in the 1870s and 1880s the Apaches lived as small, highly mobile, seminomadic bands of families or small groups of families scattered over an area extending about two hundred miles north and at least two hundred miles south of the present international border. It extended from what is now central Arizona eastward across much of New Mexico and well into west Texas. Never acting as a united tribe, and rarely even forming large groups, the Apaches were hunters, gatherers, warriors, and raiders. They practiced little animal husbandry, though some were subsistence agriculturists, growing corn and squash.

There were three main Apache groups: the western, the central, and the eastern. The Western Apaches, all in Arizona, were my father's field of study. They consist of five subdivisions: Northern Tonto, Southern Tonto, Cibecue, White Mountain, and San Carlos. The Central Apaches consist of three subdivisions: Chiricahua, Jicarilla, and Mescalero, and the Eastern Apaches consist of two subdivisions: Lipan and Kiowa Apache.

Of these, it was the Chiricahua that were the most notorious because of their prolonged resistance to U.S. army control. Mangas

Coloradas, Cochise, Victorio, and Geronimo were all Chiricahua. Among the Chiricahua there arc three subdivisions: the Ch'uk'ane nde, the Chihé nde, and, farthest south, the Ndéndaa'i, meaning "enemy people," or "people who make trouble." [12] Some translate Ndéndaa'i as "white man Apaches" or "Indian-white man" because of their intermixture with local Mexican populations. Some sources add a fourth division, the Bedonkohe, though there is some disagreement as to whether they are a separate division or a band within one of the divisions. [13]

Many believed that the Sierra Madre Apaches were descended from Ndéndaa'i Chiricahuas who were not swept up in the final campaigns of the Apache Wars of the 1880s. The Sierra Madre Apaches subsisted in small bands, groups, or family units isolated from one another and from Mexican society. Scattered over a huge area, about seventy-five miles wide and two hundred miles long, directly south of Arizona and New Mexico, there may well have been as many as a hundred people in 1900, but their numbers steadily declined thereafter. They raided ranches for livestock and occasionally robbed and killed people caught alone and unprotected in the mountains, but they were on the brink of extinction, going against the march of time and the odds of survival. Between 1900 and 1920 they seem to have kept a relatively low profile, but in the early 1920s the Sierra Madre Apaches began to make their presence known as increased development in the remote mountains brought them into more frequent contact with loggers, ranchers, and miners. By the end of that decade the Apaches were big news throughout the border region; they had become legends in their own time.

THE MYTHOLOGY

In the classic western movie, *Fort Apache*, a young West Pointer played by Henry Fonda speaks disdainfully of the Apaches he has just seen outside the fort. The seasoned Indian fighter played by John Wayne warns him: "If you saw them, they weren't Apaches."

For Mexicans, the most terrifying thing about the Apaches was their stealth. Attacks came without warning. Even after Geronimo surrendered in 1886 and all or nearly all of the four-hundred-plus Chiricahua Apaches under U.S. government control were sent far away to prison in Florida, the knowledge that some Apaches remained in the Sierra Madre kept most Mexicans out of the mountains for another generation.

The Mexican folklore surrounding the Apaches of the Sierra Madre is at times operatic in its drama, and certain themes and characters appear again and again. There are stories about an old woman who is surprised alone in the mountains while gathering food. She is captured (in many of the versions, by being roped) and fights like a wildcat, snarling, scratching, and biting until she is subdued and brought in. She always dies in captivity—sometimes by falling from the roof of a jailhouse, sometimes by ramming her head into the stone wall of a jail cell. Sometimes she is even a man in disguise.

There are stories of a young girl, captured alone in the mountains and kept tethered by a rope to a tree like a wild animal, or locked in a room where she makes heartrending animal calls at night. Sometimes, in an act as determined as it is desperate, she tries to bite through a vein in her arm so as to bleed to death. She, too, often ends up in a jail cell where she refuses to eat anything and starves herself to death.

Always there are stories of Apaches watching from hiding, peering through the windows, making bird calls at night, throwing rocks from places of concealment. Every town has this story: A woman is cooking over a stove, and suddenly an Apache face appears at a window. As fast as thought, the woman slings a skillet of hot grease through the window at the terrifying apparition.

There is a recurrent story of a beautiful young white woman who is killed during one of the many raids on Apache camps, her blue eyes vividly remembered. She lived, perhaps as a captive, or even as a "renegade," among the Apaches, sharing her fate with theirs. In some versions she is pregnant at the time of her death; in others she wanders into a village, wounded and in need of help. She never recovers.

The persistent suspicion that there are American or Mexican renegades or outlaws among or in collusion with the Apaches is a powerful theme in the folklore on both sides of the border. The possibility that there may be such traitors among the Apaches who have stolen Mexican children is a betrayal beyond imagining. There is something at once grotesque and compelling in such a metamorphosis: a being who was once "one of us" and is now "one of them."

Curiously, a benign version of this transmutation is part of the mythology surrounding my father as well. He went to live among the Apaches at such a young age—he was barely twenty—that they shaped him more than his own family did. My mother wrote of him: "He rebelled violently against his background and eastern culture he was brought up in. He never wanted any of his friends to know anything about his family and their wealth. He was very shy with his own kind, but perfectly at ease with simple people."

My father was a privileged Easterner who escaped into the West and rejected his high-born origins. In the 1920s, long after the frontier was gone, the West was still a place to make a fresh start. In our family there are stories hinting that my father was rootless, rebellious, alienated . . . but also charismatic: a beloved infidel. It is hard to imagine a more discrepant product of the staid, patrician Hartford, Connecticut, establishment than Grenville Goodwin.

Walter Lippincott Goodwin, my father's father, was what, in the gilded age, might have been called a "sportsman." He was the scion of a family business empire built on insurance and railroad fortunes. He was a Connecticut state legislator and was fond of polo, race horses, fox hunting, shooting, and the late Victorian good life.

His passion, though, was horses. He had estates in Saratoga, New York, and Middleburg, Virginia: one for the racing season and one for the fox-hunting season. He owned a stable of thoroughbreds and was an avid shooter and angler. He made sure that each of his sons learned to ride a horse and handle a gun—skills that, in some ways, made my father's Sierra Madre adventure possible.

My father's parents were divorced in 1917—a time when divorce was rare and scandalous. His mother, Elizabeth Sage Goodwin, (after her second marriage to Meredith Hare, Elizabeth Sage Hare) counted herself among the movers and shakers of the New York avant-garde intelligentsia. She was one of the organizers of the New York Armory show of 1913, and the granddaughter of one of the founders of Cornell University. Hers was not a world of lightweight socialites, but my father rejected what he saw as the upper-crust pretense of this milieu. But at the same time he fashioned his own world from much of what his parents offered: scholarship and learning, an appreciation of culture and history and the natural world. Although he grew up in a family where art was enshrined, he respected only craftsmanship and science, drawing the line at art, which perhaps he thought frivolous.

Two of my father's brothers, as well as his father and two of his uncles, went to Groton and Yale. Grennie, as my father was often called, went to Groton himself at the age of fourteen but loathed it and lasted only a few months. Long interested in progressive education, his mother sent him to an experimental boarding school in Lake Placid, New York, but he was soon stricken with tuberculosis. The hot, dry climate of the West was the TB cure of choice in those days. So in 1922, at the age of fifteen, my father was sent to rough it and recover at the Mesa Ranch School, a spartan boarding school in Mesa, Arizona.

His mother had already discovered the Southwest and had a hunch that Grennie would take to it. She had a pied-á-terre in Santa Fe, where she maintained a high profile in a world peopled by the likes of Elsie Clews Parsons, Edward Weston, Georgia O'Keefe, Ansel Adams, Mabel Dodge, Maurice Sterne, Tony Luhan, Robinson Jeffers, and Frieda Lawrence. Later she would live for periods of time in Colorado Springs, where, in the late '20s and early '30s she was involved in the founding of the very progressive Fountain Valley School and Colorado Springs Fine Arts Center.

Only dormant, apparently, my father's tuberculosis returned at the end of his second year at the Mesa Ranch School. Though he had to come home, he had fallen in love with the Southwest. Its cultural and natural setting was what first drew him in, and then he was drawn deeper by its way of life—a way of life, he thought, that might one day be his as well.

Grennie's mother next placed him in an upstate New York sanatorium where he spent a year successfully recovering from TB, at which point he entered The Gunnery School, a private boarding school in Washington, Connecticut. He spent his summers in Santa Fe with his mother and brothers, and immediately after graduation in the summer of 1927 returned to the Southwest and never lived in the East again.

One of his first undertakings that summer was an extended camping trip on the Navajo Reservation, during which he explored its many cliff dwellings and visited its remote trading posts to collect classic Navajo weavings and jewelry. It was then that he met the Bureau of Indian Affairs (BIA) policeman John Hoffman, who was the first to tell him about the Sierra Madre Apaches. In his diary he noted the meeting in detail, never realizing how it had nudged the trajectory of his life. Grennie had many interests, and he wanted to pursue them all—archaeology, natural history, anthropology, Spanish Colonial history. He spent two years exploring these fields, certain, it seems, that in one of them he would find his life's work.

One thing Grennie knew for sure: he wanted to live close to nature and in the out-of-doors. At first he thought he might have a future in forestry, so in the fall of 1927 he signed on at a lumber camp at McNary, Arizona, on the northern edge of the Fort Apache Reservation. But TB had weakened him, and the demands of the lumberjack life were more than his constitution could withstand. He lasted only a couple of months, but living and working with White Mountain Apache logging crews gave him his first prolonged contact with the Apaches. The next year he split between extensive travel in the West and work as a park ranger at Frijoles Canyon in New Mexico's Bandelier Monument—a region rich in cave dwellings and prehistoric sites.

It appears that by the end of the summer of 1928 he had reached an important decision to pursue a growing interest in archaeology. He moved to Tucson to be near the University of Arizona and its preeminent archaeologist, Byron Cummings, whom he had met while at the Mesa Ranch School. During the school year of 1928–29 he had a student card. Though he took no courses, he had, I suspect, somehow apprenticed himself to Cummings.

Always ready to drop everything for adventure, it wasn't long before Grennie had left Arizona to join a cousin, Douglas Burden, for the winter in Ontario, to work on a film about the Ojibwe Indians.[14] The trip to Canada was perhaps Grennie's first chance to practice ethnography in the field. As was his habit, he kept beautifully organized notebooks: one of them has page after page of Algonquin words and phrases; another is an illustrated inventory of woodcraft, hunting practices, and handmade artifacts such as snowshoes, birch-bark baskets, animal traps, knives, and canoes.

The following summer Grennie was back in Arizona with the Archaeology Summer School run by Byron Cummings to help excavate the Turkey Hill Pueblo near Flagstaff. At the end of the summer he enrolled as a freshman at the University of Arizona for the academic year 1929–30.

The 1927 Francisco Fimbres attack/murder/kidnapping had received little or no publicity in American newspapers until, in the fall of 1929, a large-scale manhunt and punitive expedition was organized with a base of operations in Douglas, Arizona. Suddenly the Fimbres tragedy and the Sierra Madre Apaches were receiving national newspaper coverage in the United States. It was irresistible. Grennie slipped away from classes at the University of Arizona and made for Douglas to interview those involved in the manhunt and to gather newspaper articles.

He spent the Christmas of 1929 at Coolidge on the San Carlos Reservation, passing his time at a local trading post, and beginning to make friends among the Apaches. Bert Rufkey, the manager of the trading post, told him that he had heard about the Sierra Madre Apaches from the people on the reservation, who knew them all too well.

During the following summer, while at Fort Apache, Grennie heard that the Sierra Madre Apaches would sometimes roam as far north as the reservation to raid for horses and women, and by November he had resolved to go to Mexico in search of these people. My father, just a freshman at the University of Arizona, had irreversibly entered the gravitational field of this epic story and had begun a diary to record his experience.

THE DIARY

In 1962 I was helping my mother gather and sort through my father's raw field notes for the publication of *Western Apache Raiding and Warfare*.[15] We came to a box of notebooks, and as we went through them, she set one volume aside, saying that I might be interested in it. She had kept all of his field notes, knowing they were an invaluable scholarly resource, as well as a legacy for me. I had read *Social Organization of the Western Apache* and had studied the notes we were now organizing. I found that the more he became, in his writing, a vessel of Apache culture, the more opaque as a person he seemed to me. I cherished his collection of Indian artifacts that I grew up with, but somehow I was never able to penetrate my father's writings or experience.

What my mother had set aside was the Sierra Madre diary. I began to read it and could not put it down. It was more than a thrilling story: here was my father for the first time, clearly visible through his somewhat awkward, deadpan prose. I was twenty-two, about the same age as he had been when he wrote it. Both of us were barely out of boyhood.

The diary is a big, leatherbound scrapbook. Pasted onto its pages are lined sheets of paper with his handwritten entries, photographs, watercolor drawings, maps, diagrams, and clippings. There may well have been a set of original field notes, but they have disappeared, as have all but one of his photographic negatives. The first entry was made in August 1927 and the last one on November 9, 1931, at the end of his last trip to Mexico.

The story told in the diary is rich with drama and the promise of adventure, and I wanted to be a part of it. Beginning in 1976 I began to follow in my father's footsteps, traveling to northern Mexico and the American Southwest.

As I follow, I imagine my father talking directly to me. He does not tell me who he is. He just says, "Follow me, and we will do this thing together."

But the diary is more than a personal narrative. It is the only serious attempt to investigate and describe the Apaches of the Sierra Madre. My father was the sole ethnographer to visit, survey, and inventory their campsites. The diary is a description of an Apache way of life hitherto unknown to any but the Sierra Madre Apaches themselves.

Among the specific instructions in my father's will for the bequest of possessions and collections, one thing stands out vividly in my mind. Among all his field notes, manuscripts, and ethnographic collections, the Sierra Madre diary alone was to remain always in possession of the family, and was never to be given to an archive or museum. It was his way of saying that it was a treasured experience—perhaps unlike any other in his life.

STRUCTURE, POINT OF VIEW

I thought the diary should be published. It was an important piece of ethnography and history, and it was a powerful story. From a personal point of view, it was something my father began that I could finish—perhaps the only such project of all those left undone at his death. The diary was fragmentary and truncated, and it needed a great deal of work to provide context and missing pieces. Even then, finding the missing pieces would not be enough to give the project its shape. The work needed to be made more universal, more dramatic, and it needed a coherent organization. In short, the diary needed to come to life.

As I explored Mexico and the American Southwest, sometimes with others, sometimes alone, I began to keep a diary of my own. Eventually I realized that a book could be built from a dialogue between our two diaries. My father was there first, found the way, broke the ground. His diary records the stories when they were fresh, told by the people who were involved. My diary is another voice, a counterpoint to my father's, separated from his by fifty years of time. With our two voices combined, his entries would provide a point of departure, introduce a subject or a story, and, I hoped, my entries would finish the story, elaborate on the subject, speculate, interpret, or entertain.

My father's entries appear in chronological order, just as he wrote them, so as to preserve the integrity of the timeline of his experience. My entries are selected from diaries written over a period of twenty years and are inserted in the book out of chronological order wherever they best respond to my father's entries. For that reason, there is no reason to date my entries, though occasionally I will refer to the year or the season if they are of substantive importance to the narrative.

I also had to devise a way to advance the story beyond the abrupt end to his diary on November 9, 1931, when he finished his second trip to Mexico. As my mother and I continued to sift through his papers, we found Sierra Madre Apache material that took us from 1931 almost to the end of my father's life. It makes a fainter trail to follow than the one left by the diary, but it is a trail nonetheless—enough to provide a narrative spine and thematic threads for the continuing story of violence, captured children, and, most compelling for me, the possibility of descendants of those Apaches surviving to this day.

TRAVELS AND RESEARCH

To maintain the balance between my father's voice and mine, I have condensed much of my own experience in Mexico so that only the distilled essence of what I have learned is here. My companions in this enterprise and I made our first research trip in 1976, followed by others in 1978, 1987, 1988, 1994, 1995, 1996, 1997, and 1999. During these journeys, we conducted dozens of interviews with Mexicans and Mormon elders on both sides of the border. They live the raw life of the north Mexican outback. They are leathery, funny, welcoming, and grave. When we tell them what we're doing, that my father was once here, they look at us with unusual interest, invite us to settle in and talk story. Through a process of comparing these oral histories with each other, and with my father's diary and the very patchy written record, it is often possible to reconstruct sequences of events.

The written record is not only patchy, it is also extremely unreliable. As a whole the subject is so sensational that it has given birth to the worst kind of lurid and inaccurate writing, beginning with the original newspaper reports, on which much of what has been written since draws heavily. Only after a thorough review of what has been written on the subject and after exhaustively recording oral histories can the story be told with any certainty of its accuracy. Because my father's diary was recorded soon after the events, it is very reliable, and it provides a good baseline for checking dates and facts, though the few inaccuracies in the diary are noted. I have changed none of the diary's original text, except for spelling out abbreviations, correcting misspellings, and paragraphing long entries. I have eliminated a handful of very short, trivial entries. The Apache camp descriptions in the diary are edited for readability, and the full texts of these descriptions are in the appendices.

Like my father, I travel with friends who know Mexico well. Chief among them is a close friend, an archaeologist/historian named Barney Burns who has become a full and indispensable collaborator in this project. He holds a Ph.D. in archaeology, lives in Tucson, and is widely traveled in northern Mexico and the American Southwest. He is every bit as extraordinary in his own way as my father's guide, Bill Curtis, was. Barney has, on more than one occasion, had to talk his way out of potentially terminal encounters with both Mexican federal police and the much more dangerous drug traffickers that infest the Sierra Madre. Barney doesn't speak perfect Spanish, but, it turns out, that serves us well. He plays the clown with Mexicans we meet, disarming and charming them. People talk to him readily. They open up and answer his questions. They show him family photographs, tell him about children's birthdays and pet animals—and they tell him things they would never tell a stranger. He never gets lost. I wouldn't dream of crossing the border without him.

Nelda Villa is a Mexican historian of Mormon background who lives in Colonia Juárez and who frequently joins us. Her wide personal connections, native Spanish, and quiet sweetness put everyone we meet at ease. My wife, my north star, Margot, is with us often, though never often enough, as are my son Seth and his wife, Kathy Doherty.

The diary is a legacy, an endless family adventure—a gift from my father, in lieu of himself. When he did all this work, he was a proto-father, in many ways not the man I would have known had he lived. In this form he has been there all my life, like a ghost at the dinner table. I am so accustomed to this presence that the idea of actually coming face to face with him moves me beyond words to an inner threshold that I still feel utterly unprepared to cross.

As I try to imagine a palpable Grenville, I often wonder if he would have wanted me to bother to try and understand him, saying simply: "Don't look for me. I'm not there, not real. Only the Apaches are real."

He was half my age when he began his quest for the Sierra Madre Apaches, but he did it with a professionalism and confidence beyond his years. He did it, moreover, without recording so much as a single personal reaction or moment of introspection—strange for someone who twice came face to face with his own mortality in the form of tuberculosis, but, of course, a perfect pre-adaptation for a career in ethnography. I find it maddening. It seems to put him out of my reach, and it makes me realize how different we are in important ways. Yet, with his thoroughness, he is my eyes and ears. He is all of my five senses.

At the very least, the search is real.

# Part One

## First Page, Grenville's Diary

**NOTE**

*This book is a record of all the information and data on the small band of Apache Indians who are located in that part of the Sierra Madre of Mexico which lies on the border line between the states of Chihuahua and Sonora.*

*The first entry starts in 1927, which was the beginning of my knowledge of these Apaches, and the following entries go in the order in which the information, clippings, photographs, etc. were collected.*

*A good bit of the material, especially in the newspapers, is somewhat exaggerated, but where personal information was obtained, as much care as possible was taken to get reliable material. Some of the data relate to former times, during the Apache Wars, and to remains found in caves or other sites which have been inhabited by Indians, whether Apaches or not.*

*Grenville Goodwin*
*Feb. 7, 1931*
*Tucson, Arizona*

# 1

# A Stolen Child

**August, 1927, Piñon Trading Post, Navajo Res., Arizona, Grenville's Diary**

*Met Mr. Hoffman at this place. He was a former sheriff at Columbus, New Mexico, and is now chief of police on the Navajo Reservation.[1] He says that in the Sierra Madre, south of the U.S. border, there is a band of about 30 Apaches who are still in a primitive condition. They live entirely in the mountains, and are unmolested by the Mexicans, who fear them. Occasionally they come in to trade at some small town for ammunition, etc., but go right out again. They will not bother Americans, but do not hesitate to rob or kill a Mexican if caught in the mountains unaware.*

*Mr. Hoffman says that one time while on a trip in the Sierra Madres, just south of the border, he ran into their camp. The Apaches were friendly, and he stayed with them 3 days while his horses rested up. They took good care of his horses, each day he asking them where the horses were, and the Apaches telling him. These people wore the old time clothes, gee string and all. When Mr. Hoffman wanted to leave, they brought him his horses and gave him a message to take back to Apaches at San Carlos.[2]*

**Neil's Diary, Mount Kisco, New York**

It's 1962, the first time I have read this. It is a diary, an old leatherbound volume from a box of my father's field notes that my mother and I have been going through. It is a rainy November weekend north of New York City, and when I read this first page, I am riveted and cannot put the book down. There are handsome, lovingly drawn maps and diagrams, dozens of photographs and newspaper clippings, and 120 pages of my father's immaculate, impossibly small handwriting.

I am twenty-two, only two years older than my father was when he wrote the opening entry, and a kind of longing awakens in me.

Questions crowd my mind. These are hidden, fugitive, secret people, going against the grain of history even more than the intractable Geronimo did, and in 1927 my father was reaching for them. This fragment calls to me powerfully, and I want to find and follow all its loose ends, but the trajectory of my life already feels determined and aimed in a far different direction.

I devour the pages. The story begins to take shape, and I love its incompleteness because that makes it a gift from my father. It's as if he is talking to me for the first time. I've never heard his voice; he's never beckoned me before, but now . . . this.

As I read this diary I sense the beginning, the outline of a journey — at first in my father's footsteps, and then beyond, to places he never went. My mother said that before he died he used to talk to me in Spanish, saying how we would lurk together in the bushes, how we would be *muy coyote*. I wonder: is there still a way, could this be it?

I think he had a feeling that this was a story whose end he might never reach, not because as he wrote this he knew he would die young, but because he sensed that his work among the Apaches in Arizona would be monumental, overwhelming, taking all of his time, leaving none for those in Mexico.

By 1927 he had already made a beginning, and he collected information about these elusive people from a variety of sources. As he came to understand the Apaches on the reservations, the ones living in the wild in Mexico became less abstract. They were Apaches, not unlike his friends in Arizona, but they were doomed by isolation and defiance and by the overwhelming odds against them and by the deep and abiding hatred between themselves and the Mexicans.

I wonder: this was not all that long ago. Could there be any of these people left alive?

### Thanksgiving, 1929, Cave Creek, Arizona, Grenville's Diary

*We stayed at John Hands' place over the weekend and while there a piece came out in the* Arizona Daily Star *about Fimbres and the Sierra Madre Apache.*[3] *On returning to Tucson, I secured the clipping and also previous articles which had come out in the* Star *concerning these Apaches; namely in 1928–1929.*

### Neil's Diary, Nácori Chico, Sonora

This is the town where it all began: the Fimbres kidnapping, the killings, the manhunts. This is the town where Lupe, the Apache woman, had lived since her capture in about 1915. Members of the Fimbres family were among those who caught her. The kidnapping has made this a marked town.

Since I first read the diary in 1962 the story has never been far from my mind. It has loomed like unfinished business, but always out of reach — so far from my life as a New England–bound architect.

Finally, resolve and opportunity came to me, deriving partly from a career change from architecture to documentary filmmaking. In between producing natural history films for public television, I have found the time to begin making research trips to Mexico and the Southwest. My first was in 1976. It is now 1999, and this is my sixth trip.

With me now are my son Seth, twenty-nine, historians Barney Burns and Nelda Villa, and a close friend — architect and writer Don Metz. We are 175 miles south of the Arizona-Sonora border in the tiny, ancient mountain village of Nácori Chico, talking with elders who were here as children in 1927, and who knew the people involved. The Fimbres affair was a sensational event: murder, kidnapping, and gunfights in the Sierra Madre. Details have been lost, and conflicting versions have evolved through decades of telling and re-telling. In fact, the series of events have now become myth, cloaking the characters in degrees of heroism, cowardice, or villainy they never had. But with the help of people who were there, we can reconstruct the essentials.

It is October 15, 1927. Francisco Fimbres and his wife Maria Dolores Fimbres are going from their home in Nácori Chico to the settlement of Piños Altos, the site of a gold mine forty kilometers into the Sierra Madre.

Each is on horseback: he carrying their two-year-old daughter, Vicki, and Maria Dolores their three-year-old son, Gerardo. Maria is pregnant with the couple's fourth child. The infant, Soledad, has been left at home. Six miles from Nácori Chico, Maria's horse begins to tire, so Francisco gives her his to ride so she won't have to walk. He continues on foot with her horse, carrying the little girl. They have a rifle. It is in a scabbard on Francisco's horse, now ridden by Maria. She and Gerardo move ahead of Francisco. Not far from the place where they had changed horses, the trail takes a hairpin bend to the right around a sharp ridge. Maria approaches the bend.

Apache women rush from hiding. They grab the reins of Maria's horse and pull her down, stab her with knives, slit her throat, drop her body into the ravine by the trail. They take three-year-old Gerardo with them and disappear. It happens fast and with hardly a sound. Francisco sees it all, and is unable to prevent it. He is unarmed, and he has the baby.

He knows that if he had tried to help they all might have been killed. There are times later when he might well think that would have been better.

### Neil's Diary, Douglas, Arizona

Pedro Urquijo is a gentle and benign old Mexican who lives on a quiet, tidy street in the border town of Douglas. He was born eighty-five years ago, close to Nácori Chico.

The Urquijo family moved to Douglas and, after the attack, Francisco Fimbres used to stay with them, and he patiently answered young Pedro Urquijo's questions about the attack.

Pedro says, "Francisco Fimbres was about one hundred feet behind on the trail. Apache women attacked his wife, stuck her many times with a knife, rolled her over the edge and ran off with the boy."

Pedro asked Francisco Fimbres, "Did you have a gun?"

"Yes, but it was on Maria's horse."

"What did you do then?"

"I had the baby, and I hid the baby in some bushes and rode my horse to where some cowboys were, just below the road to get help. They looked everywhere right away for the Apaches and for the boy, but they were nowhere."

Pedro says that Francisco Fimbres always wore a black hatband and a black armband after that, and that he was obsessed with revenge.

For two years, accompanied by friends and relatives, Fimbres combs the Sierra for the Apaches and his son without ever seeing them. On a cold January day in 1929, while in the Sierra Madre, Fimbres encounters Gilberto Valenzuela, a candidate for the presidency of Mexico, and Ricardo Topete, senator from Sonora, who are traveling through a rugged pass to cross the mountains from Chihuahua to Sonora. They make camp, and during the course of the night Fimbres tells his story. These influential men are deeply moved and soon have persuaded the governor of Sonora and the mayors of the border towns of Douglas, Arizona, and Agua Prieta, Sonora, to come to the aid of Fimbres.

The local authorities decide to mount a large-scale punitive expedition into the Sierra to exterminate the Apaches.[4] The story is picked up by local newspapers, and soon Los Angeles and New York papers are covering the sensational drama. Before long international attention is focused on the manhunt and Fimbres's mission of revenge.

## 2

# Phantom Apaches

**Christmas, 1929, Coolidge, San Carlos Res., Arizona, Grenville's Diary**

*We stopped at Bert Rufkey's trading store here, and he knew of the Sierra Madre Apache.[1] He said that they used to come up on the reservation here occasionally. His opinion was that they would never be caught.*

**Neil's Diary, Douglas, Arizona**

Who are these people? As much as I want to know the unvarnished truth, folklore is irresistible, and it has a truth of its own. I have started asking around in southern Arizona to see if anyone remembers the Sierra Madre Apaches. Virtually everyone does, and they want to talk. When I listen to a story, the storyteller and his culture are revealed. Because these Apaches are shrouded in mystery, the cultural perception of events is as telling as the events themselves. In fact the cultural perception becomes one of the events, part of the story.

I'm in the B and P Palace Bar Billiard Hall in Douglas. My father stopped here in 1930.

This is a famous old border watering hole in what was once a boom town built around an immense Phelps-Dodge smelter that has, since 1904, processed copper ore from mines on both sides of the border. Copper has fallen on hard times now, and with it, Douglas. Main street has a half-deserted look, but some of the buildings suggest there was once a golden age here.

By ten in the morning most of the chairs in the B and P are occupied by men watching the pool games. The early regulars have already bellied up to the bar. The room is dark, with high ceilings, lights hanging low over the pool tables. Dusty mounted heads of elk, mountain lions, bighorn sheep peer out of the gloom from high on the walls.

The man behind the bar this morning is Russell Taylor. He is a regular conspirator; he sits on a low counter behind the bar and leans sideways towards me, his elbow on the bar talking *sotto voce.*

Russell says that the first he knew of the presence of Apaches was in 1923 when a small group entered the Animas Valley from Mexico with a one-year-old heifer and a two-year-old bull. He remembers that one was trailing a piece of rope and they were both branded— one with an "O" on the left hip. He said they were found running loose. The Apaches had apparently used the cattle as pack animals but had turned them loose as soon as they had outfitted themselves with horses. One of the brands belonged to the Palomas Land and Cattle Company, an immense Mexican ranch running along the border nearly all the way from El Paso to the Sonora line—a distance of some one hundred twenty-five miles.[2]

Russell grew up in the Animas Valley of New Mexico. He left, a young man, in 1940. He says that in the early days there was not much evidence of the Apaches, but they started to make themselves noticed following the 1923 visit. He said it was thought they were moving back and forth between the reservations and Mexico.

In 1946 or '47 when he was working for the Palomas Land and Cattle Company the presence of Apaches was well known. The foreman tolerated them and told his men to leave them alone, allowing the Apaches to take a few head a year to eat.

Russell continues. What he says is mostly myth, but embedded in the myth are facts I will come to recognize. I find them recorded in my father's diary, in clippings and in later interviews. Russell tells about kidnapped Apache children, about cowboys capturing old Apache men or women, about strongholds deep in the Sierra Madre and about seeing moccasin tracks himself.

I listen to it all, savoring the texture of the stories, but I don't really know who these people were. They are a mythical people, a phantom people, to some an outlaw people.

In 1929 and 1930, most Americans thought that on this continent there were no more like them, and that's the thing that drove the journalistic feeding frenzy and gave the Francisco Fimbres affair national publicity.

# 3
# To Rescue His Son

**February, 1930, Douglas, Arizona, Grenville's Diary**
*Stopped in at* Douglas Daily Dispatch *office, and was referred to Chief of Police Leslie Gatliff for information concerning the Sierra Madre Apache. Went to the police station where I found Mr. Gatliff who was most kind in giving information.*

*He said the expedition would start the last of March or first of April, but that he would write me when sure. I never heard from him. Their idea was to cut tracks into the mountains, and if possible surround these Apaches, and bring them back to the San Carlos Res. They are extremely wild, and about 30 years ago he and his party roped one of the Apache old women, who they came on unexpectedly, and who fought like an animal to get away. The country is very unsettled, extremely rough, and game is plentiful.*

*Mr. Gatliff says there is a white man with these Apaches, who he thinks may be Judge McComas' boy, taken in 1883, somewhere between Silver City and Lordsburg, and who was never found. He would like very much to catch these Apaches if for nothing else than to determine if this were true. If so the white man is completely Apache now.*

**Neil's Diary, Anadarko, Oklahoma**
The fate of six-year-old Charley, kidnapped following the ambush and murder of his parents, had been one of the great mysteries of the Apache Wars. There is much folklore and some good evidence of a white man — with red hair, like Charley's — among the Sierra Madre Apaches. Who it may have been no one knows, but it was not Charley McComas. For many years only the Chiricahuas knew what happened to him, and it was a closely guarded secret, though by now it is well documented.[1]

Margot and I are with Ruey Darrow, the chairwoman of the Fort Sill Chiricahua–Warm Springs Apache Tribe. Both her great aunt and her father were members of the band that captured Charley McComas, and she is repeating to us what they told to her.

On March 27, 1883, Chiricahua warriors on what is called "Chatto's Raid" ambushed Judge Hamilton C. McComas, a New Mexico territorial judge, and his family near Lordsburg, New Mexico. The Apaches killed the judge and his wife and, with Charley as a captive, vanished across the border into the Sierra Madre. On May 20 General George Crook, guided by Western Apache scouts, crossed the border, marched over one hundred miles through the Sierra Madre, and attacked the stronghold of the Chiricahuas. Unknown to Crook, Charley McComas was there, a prisoner. During the attack, a Chiricahua woman was killed, and her enraged son, a man called Speedy, turned on Charley and struck him a fatal blow to the head with a rock.

Ruey Darrow says that her great aunt was there, and, while fleeing the soldiers, saw Charley lying on the ground, barely alive. She tried to carry him to safety but was forced to abandon him or face death herself in the battle. His body was never found by Crook's soldiers.

## Grenville's Diary, cont'd.

*It is not generally known, but one of the Apache men was killed by 2 or 3 fellows this winter.*

*While here, I got all the papers on this Apache expedition.*

## Neil's Diary, Douglas, Arizona

Francisco Fimbres is desperate and bent on revenge after two years of futile pursuit. He has scoured the mountains and found only cold trails and campfires, never the Apaches. However, reinforcements appear to be on the way, for the expeditionary force is taking shape under the sponsorship of officials on both sides of the border.

Although nominally under the command of a Mexican military officer, Colonel Carillo, the force is really an ad hoc group of heavily armed irregulars. It is to be made up largely of non-Mexican soldiers of fortune who want to strike a blow in the last battle of the Apache Wars, the last of the great manhunts. A circular is printed with invitations to enlist, and it is widely distributed. The *Douglas Daily Dispatch* runs almost daily articles, and the story is picked up by wire services and printed in New York and California papers. Francisco Fimbres becomes a media star. He's portrayed as an heroic figure, and his many futile expeditions into the Sierra Madre are detailed. The romantic and chivalric appeal is as irresistible as it is shameless. Just listen to what the eager applicants write to the organizing committee. . . .

—Have you room for a fellow who has done two hitches in the marine corps and one in the navy? I never fought Indians, but I have chased Spicks all around Haiti and Nicaragua, and was in the landing and occupation at Vera Cruz. I guess I'll have the guts to chase these birds.

—If you contemplate going in after those Indians soon I shall count it a very great privilege to join you. I have hunted big game in many parts of America, but I am sure shooting at an Apache Indian would give me a greater thrill than any I have heretofore shot at.

—I have traveled all over the globe. I have seen a bit of life and I have fought men of all colors, so I would like to become one of your expedition for I love action.[2]

According to the newspapers, from hundreds of respondents, twenty-five heroes are chosen for combat with the savage Apaches.

On closer inspection there is an underbelly, an unspoken agenda to this "humanitarian mission." Running side by side with articles about the rescue are articles in the *Douglas Dispatch* promoting opportunities for tourism, hunting, fishing, prospecting, and development in the Douglas–Agua Prieta area. This tragedy is going to be good for business. Like everyone else in the country, the promoters of the expedition are desperate for any economic opportunity, for the stock market has just crashed, taking with it the price of copper, the coin of the realm in Douglas.

When the expedition comes to the attention of the U.S. State Department and the Mexican federal government, officials envision a heavily armed, trigger-happy gang of adventurers and opportunists on the loose in Mexico. The U.S. Consul in Douglas summons the organizers to explain themselves.

In a recently uncovered series of official State Department documents summarizing this meeting, the expedition's organizers do an abrupt about-face, in an attempt to salvage the enterprise.[3] They substitute the commercial agenda for the rescue operation. They insist that the intention was never to launch a paramilitary incursion onto Mexican soil to save Gerardo. Their intention was rather to introduce American businessmen and sportsmen to Mexican opportunities.

The government of neither country is convinced of this explanation or of the integrity of the organizers, and the inevitable happens.

### April 6, 1930, Tucson, Arizona, Grenville's Diary

*The Fimbres Expedition has been called off by request of the Mexican Government, its purposes not being entirely commercial.*

### Neil's Diary, Douglas

My father does not say what is going through his mind at this time, but the Francisco Fimbres affair and the Sierra Madre Apaches may well be distracting him from his studies at the University of Arizona, where he is a freshman, for his is an uneven performance. According to his transcript, he's getting straight A's in ethnology, scraping by in everything else, and he's failing English.

While spending Thanksgiving with John Hands the previous November, he would have heard not only about the Fimbres attack. Hands would have told him all about the murder of his brother Alfred by "renegade" Apaches on March 28, 1896. It had happened outside the very house in which Hands served my father dinner. The small band was tracked back into Mexico, where their camp was attacked, a youth killed, at least one man shot in the leg, and two children kidnapped. The survivors disappeared into Mexico and presumably never returned—possibly joining the people who eventually attacked the Fimbres family.[4]

What my father heard from Bert Rufkey at his trading post at San Carlos at Christmastime must have whetted his appetite even more, so that by February of 1930 he has decided that this story is important enough to come down to Douglas himself to interview Police Chief Gatliff and collect clippings.

From what Navajo police officer John Hoffman and others have said, and from the newspaper reports, Grennie must wonder if the Sierra Madre Apaches represent a pre-reservation form of culture. If so, they would be living history, a "lost people," a once-in-a-lifetime opportunity for an ethnographer of the 1930s. A heady thought.

One thing he knows: time is of the essence. Even though the Douglas Expedition is off, there's still Fimbres, bent on bloody revenge. Governor Elias of Sonora decides to give what aid he can to Fimbres and the people of Nácori Chico. He puts up three hundred pesos, thirty new Mauser bolt-action rifles with plenty of ammunition, and—a license to kill.[5]

In March 1930, only days after the cancellation of the "punitive expedition," Francisco Fimbres and other Mexicans from Nácori

Chico head into the mountains after the Apaches for perhaps the tenth time in two and a half years. In spite of all the searching, he and his men have made no contact with the Apaches since the day of the kidnapping, October 15, 1927.

Like everyone else, my father knows next to nothing about the Sierra Madre Apaches, but he is gaining knowledge about reservation Apaches in Arizona. As soon as the school year is over, he goes into the field, spending much of the summer of 1930 on the San Carlos and Fort Apache Reservations. He is working part time at a trading post, getting to know people, learning the language, and going to ceremonials. He is one of the few ethnographers the Western Apaches have ever seen.

# 4
# Geronimo's People?

**August 1930, Cibecue, Fort Apache Res., Arizona, Grenville's Diary**

*Got talking with an Apache Police here, and he said that sometimes in summer some of Geronimo's people come up from Old Mexico and run horses off the reservation. These had been seen in the summer of 1929 by an Apache, a friend of his, but were wild and would not stop to talk. He only saw them from a distance, but they appeared to be dressed in modern clothes.*[1]

## Neil's Diary, Fort Apache

I try to imagine what it must have been like to hear from an Apache that "Geronimo's people" have been up from old Mexico as recently as one year ago. It must have had an electrifying effect, for when my father used to talk to my mother about these people, she told me that is how he referred to them: "Geronimo's people."

For the Western Apaches on the reservations of San Carlos and Fort Apache, Geronimo had always been trouble. He was a Chiricahua Apache, and although they speak closely related languages and share a very similar culture, Western Apaches and Chiricahuas had separate traditional homelands and a poor opinion of one another. The Chiricahuas named Tonto (Western) Apaches derisively: "The Brainless Ones."[2]

In 1876 the Chiricahuas had their own reservation in the Chiricahua Mountains of southeastern Arizona, but were wrenched from it and forced to move to the desert of San Carlos, with its hated heat. It was only a matter of time before dissatisfied Chiricahuas broke for freedom in Mexico. Because Geronimo was a capricious, intractable instigator of the outbreaks, his name has become inseparable from the legend surrounding the final, violent years of the Apache Wars.

In the blistering Sierra Madre summer of 1886, at the end of the last outbreak, Geronimo led a group of thirty-five men, women, and children and for five months eluded pursuit by five thousand American soldiers and even more Mexican soldiers. It was an astonishing feat of cunning and endurance, and, more than anything else, it made Geronimo's reputation. Hounded constantly, but never caught, he and his people finally surrendered on September 4, 1886, because they were tired of life on the run. Geronimo and all the Chiricahuas were sent as prisoners of war to indefinite exile, first in Florida, then in Alabama, and finally in Oklahoma. So, in 1929, the Sierra Madre Apaches were, in all likelihood, not "Geronimo's people" at all.

If not Geronimo's people, who were they?

Six from Geronimo's band were known to have slipped back into Mexico just before surrender. There was the legendary Apache outlaw, the Apache Kid, who fled to hiding in Mexico in the late 1880s. But there were many others besides these seven Apaches left in Mexico in 1886. Among them were almost certainly bands of Ndéndaa'i, the southernmost of the Chiricahua groups, scattered in the Sierra Madre, who may never have known U.S. reservation life and who managed to avoid the Geronimo-obsessed military dragnet of 1886.

Asa Daklugie, son of the great Ndéndaa'i Apache warrior, Juh, testified before a land-claims hearing on May 13, 1950. When asked if some of the Chiricahuas escaped from the army after they surrendered in 1886, he said, "I don't think so. Small bunch in Mexico that never came out." [3]

Since that time they had built hidden camps, stolen cattle, and exchanged acts of brutal murder with the Mexicans. But as far as my father is concerned, they remain faceless and nameless, until, in 1932, he befriends an old Western Apache scout named John Rope. Grennie spends hours listening as John Rope tells him the story of his life, and then one day, the old Apache says, in his matter-of-fact way, that he used to know a couple of the Sierra Madre Apache personally. "When the Chiricahua were taken away by the government in 1886, two of the men were never caught. One was called Natcułba•ye, and the other one was called Adiłnadzi•d. The latter was shot through his left thigh. I guess these two men are still living down in the Sierra Madre, if they are not dead." [4]

Six years after that, Grennie visits the Mescalero Apache Reservation, where he meets some of the Chiricahua who live there, among them Sam Kenoi and Sam Haouzous, who tell him that they knew one of these men, as well.

## July 4, 1938, Mescalero, Grenville's Diary

*Allan Houser's father,[5] now living in Oklahoma, says he was about six-teen years of age when the Chiricahua were sent to Florida in 1886, claims that he knew the chief of the people who remained in the Sierra Madre at this time and never came in. This chief's name was 'adiɬna'idzi·d,[6] and he was the leader of all the people who remained out. He was a middle-aged man at the time so he must be too old to be chief now, or dead, he says. Sam Kenoi also knew this to be true. Allan Houser's fa-ther says that now the chief must be the son of the man. He had a son at that time, whom he also knew. This son would now be a man of fifty or sixty, and might be the present chief.*

## Neil's Diary, Fort Apache

My father was to hear the name of Adiɬnadzi·d at least one more time that year. The old scout, Sherman Curley, said that in 1896 he served with an army unit in hot pursuit of Sierra Madre Apaches across the border. They attacked a small camp very close to the border, and Curley recognized Adiɬnadzi·d, describing him as an old man who, though wounded in the leg, was able to escape.[7] Curley had reason to recognize the man. Adiɬnadzi·d had once been a prominent mem-ber of Naiche's band, and had served as an army scout himself in 1885 before joining one of the outbreaks. Adiɬnadzi·d is thought to have been with Geronimo in September 1886, but, instead of cross-ing the border to surrender, he and five others slipped away and re-mained in Mexico. The man identified by the army as the leader of this group was Natcuɬba·ye—possibly a variant phonetic rendering of Mal-shua-pie, listed as a member of Geronimo's band in the 1884–85 census.[8] A third possible member of the group was Satsi-nistu, the brother-in-law or nephew of Naiche. Indeed, military ac-counts say that Naiche waited on a small hill looking back for a lag-ging relative before he crossed the border to surrender to General Miles in September of 1886.[9] An article in the August 20, 1890, edi-tion of the *Tombstone Epitaph* lists Na-pi-a and El-cha-nache as pos-sible members of the band. The article identifies Adiɬnadzi·d and Natcuɬba·ye as well, claiming that the latter easily passes for Mexi-can and slips into villages where he gathers the latest news and learns of likely targets for attack.

In addition to the outbreaks by Ndéndaa'i Chiricahuas, there were at least two outbreaks from San Carlos and Fort Apache in the 1890s, though how many were involved is unknown.[10] These people almost certainly joined Apache bands already in Mexico, and may well have been joined by others slipping away from American reservations at later dates. Other native people, such as Yaquis, might have joined them, as well as white renegades, outlaws, and, later, revolutionaries who just wanted to live outside the law—not hard to do, even today in the Sierra Madre.

My father is careful not to romanticize the Sierra Madre Apaches, but I often wonder if he secretly relishes the idea that there are still a few "untamed" Apaches—as the Mexicans called them. By the end of the summer of 1930 he is getting to know Apaches and Apache culture well. He goes to at least two puberty ceremonies and writes detailed descriptions of them. These rituals are beautiful, sensual, and primal in their power. He feels Apache culture beckoning. The University of Arizona pales by comparison, and he decides to skip the 1930 fall term and go to Mexico to see for himself, and perhaps even to meet with the Sierra Madre Apaches.

Earlier in the summer he had spent a month and a half at Goulding's Trading Post on the Navajo Reservation, and while there he made a new friend who for a short time was part of the plan.

### Nov. 10, 1930, Navajo Res., Kayenta, Arizona, Grenville's Diary

*Propositioned Bullets Hardy about going down into the Sierra Madre to find out about these Apaches. He seemed inclined to go, so I started out to get the latest news at Douglas, which I was to send him, and if satisfactory, arrange to meet him someplace in Dec., and go on down.*

### Neil's Diary, Fort Apache

Like pot shards in an old midden, names like this are scattered through my father's diary. Some I trace, and they come to life out of old records and people's memories. Of Bullets Hardy there is no sign, though his name suggests he might have been remembered for a long time and by many. All I have found is that "Hardy" is a common Navajo name in the Kayenta area of the Navajo Reservation. Kayenta is the nearest town to Goulding's Trading Post, where my father spent the early summer of 1930, and Bullets must have been someone in whom my father placed much confidence and trust. More than that, though, he must have been an old Mexico hand, perhaps a Navajo with Apache relatives, or one who spoke Apache and Spanish fluently. One thing is clear. My father is Mexico-bound.

## 5
# Menace in the Mountains

**Nov. 14, 1930, Douglas, Arizona, Grenville's Diary**

*Went to Douglas Dispatch office and looked up all news since May 1930. There were three articles of which I got the clippings.*

*Now went to Mr. Gatliff's house and told him what I wanted to know. It would be almost impossible to come in contact with these Apaches, he says, they being so wild. But there would be a chance to see their camps, etc. The country should be studied as there are many ruins in the locality. However, it would not be safe for one to go alone, either because of danger of accident or from harm by Indians or Mexicans. He admitted that a good deal of false information had come out in the papers, but that the reports of the wildness of the country, and the plentiful game were true, and that the Apaches were really there, and actually in a wild state.*

*The report of the killing of two Apache women and a man in April, 1930 was also true, as he had received a personal letter from Fimbres, stating the facts of the incident. The lost cave, in which Apache material had been found, he did not know the location of, but supposed it was somewhere east of Nácori Chico.*

**Neil's Diary, Douglas, Arizona**

It has been eleven months since my father last spoke with Chief Gatliff. This is the first time he has interviewed anyone familiar with the details of the case since February, just prior to the cancellation of the punitive expedition. Now Gatliff confirms that when Francisco Fimbres went back into the mountains on his own manhunt in March, he finally encountered some Apaches and killed three of them. But that's all my father records. No indication that this was the revenge that Fimbres sought, or that Gerardo, now a captive for three years, was recovered. Gatliff only repeats what he hears from others. What Grennie really needs now is someone with firsthand experience.

**Grenville's Diary, cont'd.**

*However, he told me of a Mr. Bill Curtis who had found an Apache storage cave in the Sierra Espuela, southeast of Douglas. He advised me to go see him to get further information, as he had brought some of the material found out with him.*

*Concerning the Fimbres Expedition, which was to have gone out in the Spring, Mr. Gatliff said they had intended to take 2 or 3 Apaches from San Carlos if possible.[1] He was kind enough to outline, on my map of Sonora, an area which he described as being seventy-five miles wide and two hundred miles long, from the border, just east of Douglas, running south as far as the Aros River, and covering the main part of the Sierra Madre.*

*In this area, the Apaches lived, from time to time moving their camp, and usually staying on the west slope of the mountains. The area between the loop of the Rio Bavispe, where the Sierra el Tigre lies, they have stayed out of since the opening of the Tigre mine. Most of the place names shown on the map were mere ranches.*

*On going to Mr. Bill Curtis' house found he was not home, but returned later and met him there. He turned out to be a Mormon, one who had come south from Utah in the '90s to the New Mormon Mexican settlements. In 1916 he was Gen. Pershing's chief of scouts on the latter's Villa expedition.[2]*

*I told him what my errand was and he gave me a lot of valuable information. He has a ranch down in the Sierra Madre, southeast of Douglas, which has brought him in close contact with these Sierra Madre Apache. Fimbres and other parties concerned in these affairs are well acquainted with him. About the storage cave they found, he related the following.*

*About 4 years ago, he and another man were up in the S. Espuela, when they ran into one of the Apache men. This fellow was by himself, and mounted, being dressed in the old-time way. He ran for it; and would not stop to parley. On riding a little further up a canyon, blue birds commenced to fly up out of the brush in its bottom somewhat further. Taking this as a sign that other members of the band were the cause of the birds' being disturbed, Curtis and his party got out of the mountains in a hurry. Later on, gathering up 15 men, and arming themselves, they came back and picked up the trail of the Apaches, following* them for several days, and coming on 5 successive camps, just recently evacuated. Right at the crest of the S. Espuela they came on several caves used for storage by the Apaches. One or two of these were sealed with mud and rock, which they tore out, finding much Apache material stored. Inside were some moccasins; a pair of buckskin breeches, women's dresses of cloth, several four-strand, twisted, rawhide riatos [ropes] of various sizes, a good many tanned cowhides, some big balls of tallow, a burden basket, a dish basket, and a pitched water bottle, a buckskin saddle bag, several saddles, one of which bore the brands of all the local ranches cut into it, two cowhide shirts, arrows of two kinds, one of mountain willow, and of cane with separate hardwood point, sometimes tipped with a nail, one or two bows of mountain willow hardened by fire, backed with sinew, shaped in 2 demi arcs, and strung with sinew, and finally a flat stick about 12 in. long which had on it paintings of horses, cattle, deer, etc., done with great skill.

In one of the houses of this Apache camp by the caves was found a sort of rawhide shot or powder bottle, sewn with heavy yellow thread. He showed me this bottle, one of the rawhide ropes, a saddle bag sewn with sinew, several pieces of tanned cowhide which had much the same texture as buffalo skin, and a calf hide bag. This last had been skinned over the head, the tail and legs tied up with sinew, the hair left on the outside, and tanned on inside. This was full of acorns when found, but since the acorns were dumped out, and the hair has been eaten off the outside by moths.[3] In the way of food were found stores of squawberries; acorns, acorn flour; roasted mescal; dried meat; etc.

The party looted the caves, bringing back much material, but the objects which Mr. Curtis showed me were all he has left. He used the cowhides to make pack bags of, which he has at his ranch now. Several parties have since been up to these caves so that they are now probably well stripped.

At different places Curtis has found the camps of these Apaches. They build brush structures of various shapes, and sometimes even put up a crude rock-mud wall. Their basketry is crude and bears designs in 2 colors, red and black. At one place in a mountain valley the ground was marked off by stakes as if for some game. A meat drying camp was located also, where much meat had been dried on pole frames still standing. At this place there was a crude sledge made with 2 half circles of poles for skids, and sticks laid between them, with a handle in front and behind for the purpose of pushing or pulling the meat from camp to drying racks.

Nowadays the boys only use bows and arrows as the men are able to obtain guns and ammunition through stealing. That they are able to obtain useful articles in some way or other is shown by the finding of a pair of field glasses of U.S. Army type which had been lost by the Apaches in a cornfield, near a Mexico town on the west side of the Sierra Madre, while raiding it.[4]

The costume worn by the men he described as being a gee string, moccasins with rawhide soles and buckskin uppers which came as far as the knee, and a headband of buckskin painted red. In cold weather a shirt, or jacket with sleeves, on which they leave the hair, tanning the inside only, is worn. The women wear buckskin, or, if possible get cloth to make dresses of. He said he has seen quilts stolen by these Apaches which have been stripped of their lining to be used for dresses, the cotton batting left lying upon the ground.

One instance occurred in which the Apaches raided a burro train of tobacco. They stripped the cloth wrapping off the tobacco, and left the latter lying there, only taking the cloth.

### Neil's Diary, Douglas, Arizona

I can picture Bill Curtis, the master storyteller, enthralling my father with what must have been hours of narrative, and giving a clearer picture of the Apaches' way of life than anything he has yet heard. Some of what Bill tells him can still be heard today along the border, and for that matter among the children of some of Bill's brothers and sisters with whom I have spoken. A nephew, James Dowdle, confirms that his uncle Bill did accompany General Pershing's 1916 punitive expedition against Pancho Villa, who had raided Columbus, New Mexico. Bill was not chief of scouts, nor does his name turn up in a search of federal personnel records or payroll records, but that apparently is not unusual for those who went along as unofficial scouts, mule skinners, teamsters, or packers, as Bill may well have done.[5] Bill's self-promotion to chief of scouts notwithstanding, what he had to say about the Sierra Madre Apache has the ring of truth and corresponds well with what I have discovered myself.

My friend Barney Burns and I find the Bill Curtis story of the attack on the burro train carrying tobacco etched in the memory of many elders in the Rio Bavispe villages. People tell us that it happened in about 1920 and that two packers named Jesús Pedregón and Leonardo Olivas were killed. We never expect to learn much more than that, but in 1996 one ninety-two year old man says that Pedregón had a son, also named Jesús, now living in Douglas, Arizona, and with almost no trouble we find him and his own son at home watching football on television.

We have yet not met anyone who has lost such a close relative to the Apaches, and we do not know how touchy a subject this might be—what old wounds it might open. There is between the two men a solemnity from which hardly a ray of levity or well-being escapes. It is as if they have both been overwhelmed by the murder of their father/grandfather and have never been able to leave its shadow.

The murder of Jesús Pedregón and his companion, Leonardo Olivas, sounds unspeakably ferocious. It happened on September 10, 1923, while they were carrying a load of tobacco and corn from Bavispe over the mountains, via the long, tortuous Carretas Pass to Casas Grandes in Chihuahua.

They were too poor to buy a firearm for protection.

It would have been a journey of several days, and they would have stopped as guests at ranchhouses along the way. The Carretas Pass would have been the most dangerous part because of its many blind curves, steep walls and drop-offs, but they crossed without incident and were on the long, gradual descent to the Carretas Plains on the other side of the mountains when they were attacked.

They were shot from ambush, from above. Jesús was killed with one shot, Leonardo with three. Then they were mutilated. Their attackers skinned the men's thighs and then laid back the thigh muscle and left them that way. The attackers scattered the tobacco and the corn on the ground, taking only the cloth wrapping.

Because of the mutilation and the theft of the cloth, Jesús Junior believes, as did Bill Curtis and many others, that his father was killed by Apaches, though not everyone is so sure. Neither I nor others much more knowledgeable have ever heard of Apaches practicing this kind of mutilation. To complicate the matter further, our friend the historian Nelda Villa interviewed an Olivas descendant in Casas Grandes who said that the two men had with them a pet wolf, others say simply a big dog, and that it had been eating the bodies when they were found. Others say the dog was guarding the bodies and would let no one approach them.[6]

I wonder if one of the many blood feuds born of the Mexican Revolution could have led to this killing. Jesús Pedregón was running guns and ammunition during the Revolution in about 1918 or 1919, and it would not have been the first time that a political score was settled in blood. As we continue to gather folklore, we hear that a saddle and horse belonging to Olivas was recovered at the village of San Miguel following the killings. The neighboring towns of San Miguel and Bavispe were on opposite sides during the Revolution, and there are those who believe someone in San Miguel may have been responsible for the ambush.[7]

Whoever committed these murders, they were probably not Mexican bandits, as nothing but the cloth sacks were stolen: not the corn, nor the tobacco, nor the burros. The killers probably intended to terrorize those who found the bodies. They could have been Apaches, or they could have been people who wanted the Apaches to be blamed.

These valleys, remote and often beyond the law, have seen their share of violence. Mexico was ravaged by chaos and civil war during the most brutal part of the revolutionary period between 1910 and 1920, and instability continued throughout the following decade. Against this lawless backdrop, Apaches as well as bandits and other predators may have felt emboldened, so it is not always possible to assign responsibility for the atrocities that marked this period. And if the murderers were Apaches, there is certainly no way of knowing if the same group who attacked the Fimbres family seventy-five miles to the south also attacked Pedregón and others closer to the border.

### Grenville's Diary, cont'd.

*Mr. Curtis claims these Apaches will not bother a white man as much as the Mexicans, and will not fight unless the odds are in their favor. However a while back an American out by himself was shot twice by them. He was mounted and made a run for it, but getting off to open a gate, was too weak to remount and died there. A party sent out to find him, tracked him to the gate and found his body there.*

*At another time the Apaches carried off a small Mexican boy, taking him to the mountains where their camp was. Here they stripped him of his clothes, giving him Indian ones instead. The Apache women were very good to the boy. However he managed to get away in the night, and make his way back to his home.*

## Neil's Diary, Colonia Juárez, Chihuahua

If he had had time, my father might well have been able to find this boy in 1930 and ask him to tell all he remembered about his few days with the Apaches. It would have been a vivid memory, full of the simple detail that could help bring these elusive people to life. Grennie did not find him, but to me the idea that there might be someone still alive who'd had actual contact with the Apaches is compelling.

It turns out that the story of this little boy's capture is still told in the towns of the Sierra Madre. I first hear it in Colonia Juárez with Barney Burns and Nelda Villa. It is her hometown, a largely Mormon community. Its trim lawns and plantings, brick houses, driveways with basketball hoops, and towheaded kids give the place a suburban American feel.

We're talking with two very knowledgeable Mormon elders, Herman Hatch and his brother, Dr. Roy Hatch. They grew up in the mountains, and they speak English with a soft southwestern cowboy drawl, inserting local words and place names in perfect unaccented Spanish. There are many other stories told in the villages of the Sierra Madre of stolen children. Such kidnappings have been occurring for hundreds of years, and there must be no greater horror for a Mexican family. Roy and Herman both knew the Mexican boy that Bill Curtis told my father about.

The year is 1928, and the boy's last name is Dórame. He is out alone and is surprised and caught by Apaches near the sawmill at Pacheco, a very remote mountain village, about one year after Gerardo Fimbres's capture. After a short period of time, the Apaches decide to trust the boy to go out and bring in the horses. He selects the best horse and scatters all the others, riding as fast as he can for home. Other versions of the story say that one of the old Apache ladies feels sorry for him, unties him, and tells him to go home.

The boy finds his way to a remote mountain ranch. Wearing buckskin clothing and moccasins that the Mexicans call "*tewas*" he walks out of the brush at the edge of a field on a ranch belonging to the Villa and the Mendoza families. The men are plowing; they see him, take him in, and finally deliver him home to Pacheco.

Herman remembers that he and this boy used to play together as children in the 1930s, but the two men have long since lost touch with the boy—can't even remember his first name. We follow other leads and find only that the boy and his family have long ago moved away, leaving no trace.

### Grenville's Diary, cont'd.

*Lupe, of whom accounts were given in the papers is pretty much Mexicanized now, and weaves excellent straw sombreros. She was caught by a party of Mexicans who were trailing the Apaches. The Mexicans, being closer than they thought, ran onto them, and routed the Indians. But as they started to run, the mule which Lupe was riding bucked her off. She crawled into some brush, trying to hide, but the Mexicans saw her and brought her back a captive. After she had been with Fimbres family for about a year, Fimbres let her go back to her people in the mountains at her request. However in a couple of days she came back, saying her people would not take her back, and that her brother had threatened to kill her, saying she was no longer one of them. She has remained with the Fimbres family ever since.*

### Neil's Diary, Colonia Hernández Jovales, Chihuahua,
### Home of Muñoz Family

After leaving the Nácori Chico area, Lupe lived in this village for a time. In 1950 she married a Mexican, Perfecto Muñoz, who already had a son, Roberto, from a previous marriage. After Lupe's stepson Roberto married and Perfecto died, Lupe stayed here and helped raise Roberto's nine children. Now in their thirties and forties, most of them are at home today as we arrive. They are full of stories about Lupe, the Apache captive.

Lupe would become angry when asked about her life before capture—not because of bitterness over being kidnapped, but because she did not want to be thought of as an Apachita, an Indita. They all knew what she was, knew she was different, and they adored her all the same.

She had learned to make excellent Mexican food: big tortillas, fruit preserves, cookies for the kids for after school. When they had been scolded by their own parents the children could always come into Lupe's busy kitchen for treats, diversion, and comfort.

She was renowned as a seamstress and as a weaver of straw hats and baskets. She could vault onto a horse and ride bareback all day. Whenever she went from village to village, or from ranch to ranch, she never used roads or trails; she simply struck out through the bush. When the children were with her they would ask her if she wasn't afraid of getting lost. She was never lost; she always knew the way. She had the uncanny knack of knowing when someone was coming on a mountain trail.

"I can feel them through the ground," she would say. And the travelers would appear.

The only thing she said to her step-grandchildren about her capture was that, when she was locked in a room at first, she felt like a young turkey: nervous, panicky, ready to bolt through any opening. She was used to eating only roots and could eat none of the Mexican food. She had a brother, she said, a mother, a sister. Eventually she put it all behind her, severed all ties, all memories, keeping only the scars and the instinct—that sixth sense by which she navigated the mountains and knew when her people were near.

### Neil's Diary, Nácori Chico, Sonora, home of Rafaela Ruiz

Lupe also lived for a while in the home of the Ruiz family in Piños Altos, in the mountains east of Nácori Chico. Reyes Ruiz was one of the men who captured Lupe, and Rafaela, his daughter, vividly remembers Lupe and her fear of her own people.[8]

Doña Rafaela is sweet and gracious, and well past the age of eighty. The front room in her house in Nácori Chico has whitewashed walls and a polished concrete floor, and on the wall is a large calendar illustrated with scenes of Switzerland. She sits in an easy chair, low to the floor, positioned so she can see out the door to the Sierra Madre rising starkly beyond the fields of wheat. Rafaela's ten-year-old granddaughter, who doesn't yet know that she is beautiful, leans softly into her grandmother, only half hearing what we say.

There is an elegance and grace in the way Rafaela holds herself, sitting gathered and erect in her chair. She talks to us of the years that Lupe spent with her family in Piños Altos in the early 1920s.

Lupe tells Rafaela's father, Reyes, that she is afraid of Apache Juan, the leader of her band, that he is bad and that he kills people. As Rafaela is growing up, the name "Apache Juan" is known to all. At night, when all the houses are locked and no one is in the village streets, Apache Juan sometimes rides his horse through the town at a dead run, calling out, "Yo soy Indio Juan." It terrifies the people and he knows it and he does it for pleasure.

While at Piños Altos Lupe can always tell when the Apaches are near, because she can smell them. She becomes agitated and tells everyone to keep their children indoors. Sometimes, while out in the bush with the children gathering food, she stops, suddenly alert, and hurries the children home, knowing her people are close, watching. The only times that the Mexicans see the Apaches are when the Apaches show themselves on purpose. What they do not know is that concealed Apaches are almost always watching them.

Lupe says that before she was captured her people would watch the town of Nácori Chico and Piños Altos and the ranches so often that they came to know the inhabitants and could describe them by their idiosyncrasies: this one limps, this one always walks very fast, this one always wears such and such a hat. As she tells them this, they recognize their neighbors and themselves from Lupe's descriptions. Until Lupe is captured and lives among them, the Mexicans have no idea they are so closely watched.

Lupe lives with different Mexican people, and she is always accepted as a member of the family. Cayetano is Francisco's uncle; she calls him "brother." When Francisco's son is kidnapped Francisco turns to her, desperate for advice. No one is able to name a credible motive for the attack on him and his family. Some think it was a case of mistaken identity; some say Apache Juan had Maria Dolores Fimbres killed just because it pleased him.

Some say it was revenge for the kidnapping of Lupe herself, many years earlier, and that it was Lupe's mother who slit Maria's throat and stole Gerardo: a child for a child.

Lupe advises Francisco Fimbres against pressing the pursuit of

Apaches while they have Gerardo. She tells Francisco that as long as there is a chance that Gerardo is still alive, Francisco must be patient and wait until they have become attached to him. They will then be much less likely to do him harm.[9]

By November of 1930 the barrooms, bunkhouses, and town plazas all along the border and deep into Sonora and Chihuahua are awash in the latest news of Fimbres and the Apaches. My father records what he reads and what Bill Curtis and others tell him—the extraordinary along with the mundane—in the same deadpan voice. So, when, on November 14, he hears the following startling news, he records it in his diary without comment. When I read it, then re-read it, I ache with impatience to know everything—Bill must know more, must have said more. They must have talked about it at great length, but this is all my father writes.

### Grenville's Diary, cont'd.

*Bill Curtis said that the report of Fimbres' boy being taken to the graves of the three Apaches killed in April, and there left dead is true, as well as that one of the Apache women whose head was cut off was the mother of Lupe.*

### Neil's Diary, Nácori Chico, Sonora

Grennie has already noted that three Apaches have been killed, but there are no details so far. And now Gerardo is gone. All I know is that he was captured on October 15, 1927, and he would have been six years old, as Bill Curtis tells his story.

What Gerardo's life among the Apaches would have been like I have no real idea, since I hardly know what *their* life was like. He would certainly have been fluent in the Apache language, and he would have learned many basic skills from them. During his three years of captivity, the Apaches were probably very good to him.

Historically, captives taken by Apaches were adopted into the tribe, to compensate for infant mortality and for Apache children captured by the enemy. They were loved, but were not exempt from the rage of revenge. It sounds from my father's brief description as if Gerardo has died to avenge the killing, scalping, and beheading of these three Apaches.

This fragment tells me only that it hides a dreadful story. Newspaper articles repeat the belief that it was Lupe's mother who stabbed Maria Dolores Fimbres and thus earned this bestial end. In fact Lupe's mother was herself a kidnap victim; she was stolen in about 1900, along with her cousin, from Solomonville, Arizona, just south of the San Carlos Reservation, by a man described by Lupe as a great warrior who had once been a scout for the U.S. army.

Apache Juan, according to Lupe, was her brother-in-law, and was himself the son of a captive.[10] Juan is known to have had Mexican relatives—his father's cousins—named Figueroa, some of whom Rodolfo Rascón, a journalist we meet later, has interviewed. This family still lives about forty miles south of Nácori Chico, in the town of Sahuaripa, where Apache Juan's father, Elias, was born over one hundred and fifty years ago to a local Opata or perhaps Warihio Indian family. Both Opatas and Warihios lived in the valleys and foothills bordering the Sierra Madre. They and the Apaches were ancient enemies, and cases of such captive children would not have been uncommon.

Juan's father was captured by the Apaches as a child in 1844, and came to be known by the Mexicans as Apache Elias. He eventually married an Apache woman but maintained some contact with his birth family, paying occasional visits and bringing presents. The makeup of the Apache band to which he belonged was probably typical of the southernmost Ndéndaa'i Apache: a mix of people of a variety of origins, including Chiricahuas, local Indians, Western Apaches from San Carlos, and even Mexicans.

### Grenville's Diary, cont'd.

*Mr. Curtis thinks that these Apaches fled south from the reservation in Arizona sometime after Geronimo's removal in the '90s. The troops pursued them as far as the border, but were there stopped by the Mexican Government.[11] From time to time they used to go up to the reservation and steal a woman or two, but this they have not done for a good while. However, they incurred the bad feeling of the reservation Indians by doing this.*

*The last time the Sierra Madre Apache were in the U.S. was about 3 years ago when they rode up into the southwest corner of New Mexico, bringing two steers shod with rawhide which they rode. These steers they left there after raiding a ranch, and running off some horses.*

**Neil's Diary, Douglas, Arizona**

The southwest corner of New Mexico is known as the "Bootheel." It is a very sparsely populated, isolated nubbin of territory that juts into Mexico. It is today, as it has been for generations, occupied by a few immense cattle ranches in the broad, lush grassland valleys. Coming up from the south, like cresting waves, are the northern battlements of the Sierra Madre. For centuries, Apaches keeping to this high ground could move in and out of what is now the United States easily and without detection.

Bill has been telling Grennie a story that has, by now, been celebrated in folklore and written history for three quarters of a century. I first heard it in the B and P Palace Bar in Douglas in 1976 and knew right away that it was the same story my father had heard in the same town, maybe even in the same bar, forty-six years earlier.

A small band of perhaps a dozen Apaches crossed the border and entered the Animas Valley of New Mexico in the fall of 1924 (not 1927, as the diary states), though some writers place the event in September of 1923—right after the murder of Pedregón and Olivas.[12] Local ranchers began missing cattle and blamed each other until the haltered cattle mentioned by Bill Curtis were discovered. They had clearly been ridden or used as pack animals, and one of them had the Mexican brand of the Palomas Ranch. The Apaches' camp on Animas Mountain was soon discovered, but the band slipped away east into the Alamo Hueco Mountains, with twenty-eight head of stolen horses and mules. They were soon discovered again, and they vanished, leaving behind all the livestock, shod with rawhide; a quantity of hides; grass mats; bags of acorns; and thirteen handmade saddles.[13] In 1961 archaeologists discovered and described a long-abandoned Apache wickiup in fairly good condition but of undetermined age in the Alamo Hueco Mountains—a reminder that this was once all Apache country, and that well into the twentieth century the Apaches may still have known it better than anyone.[14]

It is virtually certain that the Apache band that slipped into the Bootheel was part of the same group that built and occupied the camps that Bill Curtis had discovered in 1926 just south of the border.

**Grenville's Diary, cont'd.**

*On asking about the possibility of seeing some of these Apache camps, etc., he [Bill Curtis] said to come along down to his ranch near Colonia*

*Oaxaca, that he was going on down for a month, and could leave me at his place to look around, as there was fine hunting and fishing, and one or two Apache camps fairly near. He said he was going on south to buy cattle, and would leave Douglas Wed., Nov. 19. This was fine so I arranged to be back by Tues. night, as had to go to Gallup.*

### Neil's Diary, Douglas, Arizona

After talking with Russell Taylor in the B and P Palace Bar, I go looking for a man he has told me about: one Ether Haynie, a man who knew Bill Curtis well. My father has told me hardly anything about Bill, and I want to hear more.

I try to imagine Curtis and my father together. My father was tall, slender, mild, and soft-spoken, all long arms and legs. From his pictures Curtis looks knotty, durable, dense, difficult to damage.

My father is going to spend two months with Bill but writes hardly a single descriptive word about him. I keep hoping for a reflected glimpse of my father in some unguarded, subjective moment of reflection on Bill. It doesn't happen, though, of course, the Curtis stories he records speak volumes about Bill. He has lived a remarkable life, Curtis, and must make an unforgettable, albeit private, impression on my father. My eyes bore into his pictures, hoping to discover something. He's short, he's bowlegged, he's built like a bull, and has a coarse-grained leathery face so closed against the elements that almost no expression escapes it.

I find Ether Haynie a few blocks away, sitting in a rusting lawn chair by an autobody shop. He is ancient and shrewd and considers me from behind his ample, furrowed face. Like Bill Curtis, he is another tough old Mormon from the Mexican colonies. He says he has bought and sold ranches, looked in vain for gold, and broken bread with Pancho Villa. He gravely informs me that he has never killed a man.

Bill Curtis, he says, was an old-time, dyed-in-the-wool cow man. His life revolved mostly around running livestock through the shattered rock of the Sierra Madre. No romance, it was dusty, gritty, dangerous, exhausting; only going broke was easy. Like everyone else, Curtis did a little prospecting too. Ether says he was maybe the strongest man he ever met.

Curtis was born near Salt Lake City, Utah, in 1882. When Bill was a boy, his parents, Horace and Martha Jane, and their very large family came to Mexico by wagon, horse, and foot. Bill grew up on a ranch in Colonia Morelos, one of the Sonoran Mormon colonies.

At the time my father meets him, Curtis has probably never set foot outside of the American Southwest and northern Mexico—geographically a large place, but a small world, in the sense that the lives of all its people are deeply interwoven through kinship, joint enterprise, acquaintance, and enmity. Small as it is, this world is most probably home to every conceivable facet of human nature, every strain of human behavior, and, in his lifetime, there isn't much of it that Curtis hasn't seen.

I wonder how Grennie strikes Bill Curtis. Although he has been living full time in the southwest for perhaps three years, my father can't have completely shed his patrician New England ways. He must still be something of a tenderfoot. It is hard to imagine two people with more different life experiences, but Grennie somehow convinces Curtis that he won't get in the way or get killed through foolishness, that he can ride, shoot, rough it, speak Spanish, and lend an able hand when needed.

Bill tells him all he knows about the Apaches, Fimbres, murder, kidnapping, gold mines, and life on the frontier. When my father just takes it all in—the naked truth along with the embellished—seemingly without comment, maybe Curtis sees something in this quiet stranger that appeals to him—sees a serious, self-possessed youth, ready to learn, someone to be trusted with knowledge.

# 6
# Double Revenge

**Nov. 18, 1930, Douglas, Arizona, Grenville's Diary**

*Got back from Gallup in time, and went up to Mr. Curtis' house in the evening. Found him home and he said he would start on Thurs. He gave me a picture of the party who killed the three Apaches this past April, clearly showing the booty taken, and the head of one of the women held in the hand of Fimbres. The booty consisted of a saddle, quirt [short riding crop], 3 pairs of moccasins, a rope or two, a cow hide shirt, and a few other odds and ends. The moccasins are typically Apache, but the woman's hair is done in braids, whereas these [Western] Apaches wear their hair long and loose.*[1]

*He also loaned me a magazine called* Strange True Stories *for June, 1929, in which had come out a story of Fimbres and these Sierra Madre Apache.*

**Neil's Diary, Douglas, Arizona**

Rumors have been rocking the border, but until this photograph appears, there is no real proof that Fimbres has killed any Apaches. This grim tableau makes the moment concrete. The photographer was José Noriega Calles, a military doctor. He has gathered all involved, and he's asked for booty as a centerpiece of the picture. He gets that and then some.

Is that a severed head that Fimbres holds? After all, triumphantly displaying your enemy's head is a rite as old as human conflict. Both Mexicans and Apaches have been known to do it. Mexicans today insist that what Fimbres is holding is only a scalp.

Bill Curtis says different, and if he's right, Fimbres, in a moment of restraint, perhaps, has turned the features of the severed head away from the camera. My eyes bore into the grain of the photo until it blurs; I try to estimate shadow, heft, bulk, but there's no way to be sure.

We talk with one man who personally knew Francisco Fimbres

and saw one scalp when Fimbres brought it to Douglas to prove what he had done. He only remembers that the scalp was full of fleas. A few days later we hear of another man who remembers seeing Apache Juan's head mounted on a stake in the plaza of Nácori Chico in 1930.

### Neil's Diary, Nácori Chico

Nácori Chico is the epicenter of the events of the final violent years of the tragedy of Francisco Fimbres and Apache Juan. Most of the Mexican families involved in the kidnapping and the manhunts have lived here for generations, and those events are seared into the collective memory of the place.

Like all the towns at the foot of the Sierra Madre, Nácori Chico has an immaculate, lovingly cared-for plaza and a handsome, blindingly white church established by Jesuits in the seventeenth century. An old saddlemaker in Tucson told me that in the '30s the town was still so isolated that it was said to have been a place where any outlaw could feel safe. Until 1940 the road from Nácori Chico to the next town was so poor that goods moved in and out mostly by mule train.

The school, facing the plaza, is where the "victory photograph" was taken. Where heavily armed men crowded around the pile of spoils and the trophy remains of three Apaches, boys now play soccer, and girls jump rope. The time when men from Nácori Chico mounted manhunts is sixty-five years in the past, but there is still a potential for violence in this town. The small prison in the town of Cumpas we passed through two days ago has inmates from Nácori Chico out of all proportion to its size.

Soon we are talking with an old-timer on a street corner. We're sitting on the sidewalk, creating an event. We are a crowd: Barney Burns; Nelda Villa; my friend, Don Metz; my son, Seth; and me. A pickup playing loud Tejano/mariachi music keeps driving past us. There are a couple of other old-timers on the opposite corner; I think maybe they're twins.

We're well into the interview when Don asks me what I think about offering the "twins" some tobacco. I say, "Sure." Don has brought some cigars. They politely accept, and pocket them while Don lights up. Soon a young guy sits down beside Don, and they fall into conversation. We are certainly the act to catch in Nácori Chico this day.

The pickup truck goes by again and this time stops, jammed at an angle in behind our van. Four guys get out, and one drifts toward us to hover over Barney. Don's still across the street. Seth is loose, taking stills. I'm leaning on the grill of a truck parked in front of the sidewalk interview.

Soon the other three guys from the pickup are there. A big guy with a beard leans over Barney, asking what he's doing. He's very drunk . . . leering at Nelda. She looks uneasy. His shirt is unbuttoned: slabs of rippling muscle. The other men are smaller. Barney seems unfazed.

This goes on for a while—the guys standing around talking rapidly to each other, their pickup radio blaring. Their faces are stunned drunk, with hard, vacant eyes, and they look dangerous, rabid.

They move away. Seth goes to the van to put away his camera, and when he's coming back, they crowd him, start talking to him in Spanish. He doesn't want to walk away from them, so he has to stop and try to talk. I keep an eye on him, but it looks okay.

Another guy who has been sitting with Don gets up and walks off.

Don comes over to me, leans on the truck and says, "That guy just walked off, that's a bad character. I mean real bad. Dangerous."

Nelda says, "Where's Seth."

"Over there," I say.

"Are they all around him," she says.

"Yes, but it's okay."

Don says, "It could be iffy."

I call to Seth to come over. He breaks away and walks toward me. I ask him if they were pushing their luck with him.

He says, "No, but I wasn't sure how to leave."

Don says, "They're just looking for an offense."

I'm very uneasy. It could get ugly for no reason. The four guys drift back, numb and reckless.

Barney pays them no attention. They don't get a rise out of any of us, and soon they're gone. Don was very worried. The bad character he mentioned tried to sell him dope, heroin, was testing and probing, sizing him up, looking him over too closely.

Don says, "He scared me." Don's not easy to scare.

The dust is settling now, but there is a layer of anxiety we haven't felt before. In the days to come we see the big guy twice more, once glaring from inside a corral, once from a doorway, glaring.

At different times we hear stories about the drug traffic and violence in the mountains and these little towns. The people who grow and run drugs through the Sierra Madre are so utterly ruthless and so infrequently challenged that a kind of reign of terror settles in certain places. We are careful to avoid the mountains in late fall when marijuana is harvested. We hear of brutal killings of people who "knew too much." Nelda tells me of a man who was "drug to death." I misunderstand and ask, "You mean given an overdose of drugs that killed him?" She says, "No. He was drug behind a pickup truck."

We have been hearing of a man named Rodolfo Rascón, a reporter for *El Imparcial,* the Hermosillo newspaper, who has researched and written about the Sierra Madre Apache story for twenty-five years. He lives in Nácori Chico, we discover, though he is here infrequently. During our sidewalk interview his name came up, and we now learn that he is at home. We were ready to go all the way to Hermosillo to see him, but instead we go to his house and find him there.

Rodolfo grew up in Bacerac, fifty miles to the north, but likes it here in Nácori Chico and is building a small house—a getaway. He spends most of his time on the road writing feature articles for *El Imparcial.* He is a compact man who wastes no motion. He uses his hands when he talks, not with Mediterranean overstatement, but with the economy and expressiveness of sign language. He keeps his gestures neatly framed in front of him, his fingers and hands making small, finely shaped movements.

There is much to tell, and he is very generous with his time. He talks with intensity. The story of the Sierra Madre Apaches and the Fimbres affair has gripped him as it has many others, but so many people have gotten it wrong, he wants to make sure we do not.

I show him the photocopy of the GG diary and he says, "Qué artista," as soon as he sees the drawings and the tiny, immaculate script. When he gets to the "victory" photograph he becomes animated. He knows the photo, but this is the best print of it he has seen. He names the people in the picture and then, to my amazement, points to the little boy whose name is Jesús Fuentes. He lives across the plaza as we speak, says Rodolfo.

Whenever I look at that picture, my eyes are drawn to the little barefoot boy, no more than three, leaning into the casual embrace of his hunkered father, Dolores Fuentes, the mayor of Nácori Chico. The men around him are armed to the teeth; Francisco, only a few feet away, is holding, perhaps, the severed head of one of the women. The child's expression is unreadable. I always wonder what effect it has on him to be part of this tableau, preserved forever in photographic time.

Jesús Fuentes himself appears as we talk in the plaza, but only briefly, and I give him a copy of the photograph. Then he disappears in the crowd that has materialized. His is a special status. He is the only one in that photograph who is still alive. It is an ambiguous distinction at best—in any case not one that he is eager to exploit in public. I do not mean that shame of any kind is attached, only that this may be a suddenly private rather than a public moment for him, and we will have to wait to be let in.

Soon we are sitting in the plaza with Rodolfo Rascón and two elderly gentlemen, Norberto Aguillar Ruiz and Estolano Madrid Fimbres—members of the Ruiz and Fimbres families and as knowledgeable as anyone, says Rodolfo, about how the Apaches were killed. The sequence of events has all the elements of classic tragedy: ancient hatred, a blood feud, kidnapping, murder, revenge, unbearable remorse, reversals of fortune, ruined lives.

We spend three days gathering the strands of the tale from a variety of people. Although the story of the killing of Maria, of the Apaches, and of Gerardo is no secret, these interviews have a confessional feel. A long time ago, a terrible thing happened here, and these old men engage the drama readily, as they would an old adversary, remembering the familiar details of the story, as if, through recitation, they might find redemption.

Fimbres's wife, Maria Dolores, was killed and their son Gerardo was captured in October 1927. By early 1930, they tell us, Fimbres has made many, some say nine, expeditions in search of Gerardo. Lupe has repeatedly warned him not to press the chase too closely but to let the Apache women—one her sister and one her mother—become so attached to Gerardo that they will not want to harm him. Fimbres has heard her advice, but he remains bent on escalating the pursuit on his own. At this time Gerardo is still alive, and as long as he is alive, Fimbres has a desperate hope.

The "international" punitive force is grounded in Douglas on April 5th. Within days Francisco Fimbres and a private posse of twelve men leave Nácori Chico on horseback, still hoping to find the Apaches, kill them, and recover Gerardo.

For two days they scour a new quarter of the Sierra Madre, following a new lead: they have word that a pack train has been ambushed between Nácori Chico and Casas Grandes. Forty miles northeast of the town, two and a half years of bad luck is reversed. They see smoke from a campfire and ride toward it. They crest a low rise, and, without warning, they come upon the Apaches. There are two women leading a burro. The Mexicans open fire, hitting one woman in the arm, nearly severing it. Cayetano Fimbres, Francisco's uncle, remembers her cry:

"Nakayé!"

It is the Apache word for "Mexicans."

She screams it three times. "Nakayé!" And another bullet kills her. The other woman tries to shoot back, but a cartridge is jammed in her rifle. She tries to free it with her knife. The tip of her knife breaks off in the breech of the gun, and she is shot dead.

During the attack the women call to Juan by name. He comes to their aid, but there is nothing he can do. Two are dead; others have escaped. Soon he is pinned down by gunfire, and for the next two hours more shots are exchanged. Cayetano Fimbres spots Juan hiding behind a tree and waits patiently for him to show himself. When he does, Cayetano shoots him, stunning him, then moves closer and shoots him again at point-blank range, killing him.

When the Mexicans examine the bodies, they find that Juan is wearing typical long-legged Chiricahua Apache moccasins and a leather skullcap without a brim or any other sort of embellishment.[2] Rafaela Ruiz said it was made of calfhide. This description suggests that it resembles a Chiricahua ceremonial skullcap used for protection in war.[3]

Otherwise, Apache Juan wears cloth garments. He and the women carry pouches containing leather dolls that are stuffed with grass. One of the women wears a heavy buckskin or soft cowhide dress. Two rifles are recovered: a 30-06 and an old 45-70.

We hear stories that one of the women was young and white; others say she had beautiful eyes, still others that she was pregnant. All we know is that Lupe later claims her as her sister.

The men that kill these three Apaches leave them there, without burying them—a fatal mistake. The posse has been proceeding under the assumption that if they attack the Apaches and wipe them out, Gerardo will be freed, and they will return in triumph with him to Nácori Chico. When they don't find Gerardo, they realize that, as far as his recovery is concerned, they hold even fewer cards than before. In fact, tasting a chance at vengeance too keenly, the men have done the very thing that Lupe has advised against.

It's completely understandable, though. Fimbres was whipsawed between two obsessions, his son's safety and his wife's unavenged death. Yet, in the end, it was inaction that must have been unthinkable.

A few days later two Mexican men, Ysidro Mora and Cirilo Perez, are riding near the scene of the battle, and their horses spook: the air carries the stench of death. They approach the killing ground to find the three Apache bodies carefully buried. They also find the lifeless body of young Gerardo dressed like an Apache: leather moccasins, a little knife, leather clothing. It is alleged in various reports that, in an orgy of Apache bestiality, Gerardo has been hung, crushed with stones, crucified, starved, mutilated, nearly beheaded, and then buried alive.

In October 1996, in Douglas, Pedro Urquijo tells us what is probably the truth. He knew Francisco Fimbres well, and Francisco told him how it happened.

He says, they stoned him. They tied him to a tree and stoned him to death. He was seven and a half years old and the women stoned him to death.

Fimbres is devastated—by all accounts a broken man from now on—but possessed more than ever by dreams of vengeance.

When the men of the posse tell Lupe about the Apaches they have killed, she keens with uncontrollable grief for several days. Mexicanized though she is, these are still her people. From their descriptions, she knows them—the older woman is her mother and the younger one her sister.

Endowed with an acuity the Mexicans don't have, Lupe could always sense the nearness of the Apaches, and, even though they frightened her, they were an unseen presence in her life. Like ghosts, they have been there watching her while she lived her new life, a chasm between them. For the Apaches blood kin is bedrock, but if Lupe is torn between her own people and the Mexicans with whom she has had to cast her lot, if she now loathes those who killed the last of her real family, there is not a sign of it in the record, though the stories of her private grief speak volumes.

I have to think that, in the interest of self-preservation, she must have written her people off long before — along with their way of life. She must now realize that, had she returned to it, the price of that way of life might well have been the same one just paid by her mother and sister and by Apache Juan.

1. Grenville Goodwin and other students
at Turkey Hill Pueblo near Flagstaff,
summer of 1929. John Hands is standing,
second from left. Courtesy Arizona
Historical Society. Negative #73858.

2. Left: The Apache captive, Lupe, captured between 1914 and 1917; about 1940. Courtesy Nelda Villa.

3. Above: Francisco Fimbres holding the scalps (or heads) of Apache Juan and two Apache women killed when these men attacked an Apache camp about twenty miles northeast of Nácori Chico in April 1930.

4. Top: Barney Burns and Norberto Aguillar Ruiz,
Nácori Chico, 1996. Photo by Seth Goodwin.

5. Below: Rodolfo Rascón, Estolano Madrid
Fimbres, Norberto Aguillar Ruiz, Nácori Chico,
1996. Photo by Seth Goodwin.

# Part Two

# 7
# Crossings

**Nov. 19, 1930, Douglas, Arizona, Grenville's Diary**

*Met Mr. Curtis at his place in the morning, afterwards going to Agua Prieta with him to get information on a passport for me. They referred us to the Mexican Consul in Douglas where I got a regular tourist card, good for six months.*

*The remainder of the day we spent in getting our outfit together, buying food, etc., in preparation for leaving tomorrow.*

**Nov. 20, 1930, Morelos, Sonora, Grenville's Diary**

*This morning was talking with a friend of Bill Curtis who said that the report of 5 Apaches being killed early last Spring by Moroni Fenn and party, was probably not true, as they were a windy bunch. He had talked with one of the party in a Douglas pool hall, some time after the fight was supposed to have taken place, and this man admitted he had not killed any Apaches, but that the others said they did.[1]*

*—The Kickapoos, some of them, were in town yesterday for their government money.[2]*

*—Met some Mexican friends of Bill Curtis in the harness shop, just come from Nácori Chico, who again verified the statement that Fimbres' boy had been killed.*

**Neil's Diary, Pomerene, Arizona**

Moroni Fenn was one of four brothers in a large Mormon clan, and Alvah, the youngest of the brothers, the only one still alive, is a content octogenarian paterfamilias.

Alvah and his wife, Carmen, and I are sitting on Alvah's patio next to a remarkable stone fountain he built some years ago. Proudly, he turns it on, and the water flows while we talk. They and the rest of the huge extended Fenn family live in this small Mormon town.

There are easily a couple of dozen houses, barns, sheds, and outbuildings observing a tidy and uniform setback from the main road. The farm machinery, welding outfits, disassembled bulldozers, and fat-tired bikes are behind, and beyond them the fertile, well-tended acres. Fine Mormon masonry runs by the square yard in walls, foundations, and chimneys. The front porches have collections of metates, manos, and an occasional fine stone ax—all gathered on the family's wide travels across the Southwestern and Mexican outback.

I ask Alvah about the old days and especially about his older brother Moroni. The Fenns were colorful characters who owned several ranches in Sonora and Chihuahua. Much has been made of their role in this story, but as my father learned in a Douglas pool hall, without a doubt the B and P Palace Bar, Moroni and his pals were a "windy bunch."

Alvah was Moroni's gentle younger brother, and he is playing down Moroni's reputation for violence: that is not supposed to be the Mormon way. But Alvah can't resist the memories of his legendary brother. Once, he says, during the Mexican Revolution in 1911 about twelve Mexicans had advanced threateningly on Moroni while he was living in Colonia Morelos: they wanted him to give up his guns. Moroni barricaded himself and his wife in their stone house; both were armed. He declared he would not let the Mexicans take his "artillery away from him." The Mexicans were impressed with Moroni's courage and finally left him alone.

Moroni knew Fimbres quite well, apparently, and of course had been much involved in the manhunt plans. Alvah says he knows that if Francisco Fimbres had realized what would have happened, he would not have hunted Apache Juan. If Fimbres hadn't done that he might have got his son Gerardo back. In retrospect it must have seemed obvious to him, and there was probably not a day of his life free of insupportable regret.

### Grenville's Diary, cont'd.

—*We got started for Colonia Oaxaca in the afternoon, but only got as far as the outskirts of Morelos, as we met two Mexicans in a car too drunk to drive. I drove their car for them as far as Morelos.*

—*This afternoon we came in sight of the first of the Apache country, the Sierra Espuela, whose highest peaks had some snow on them.*

### Neil's Diary, the Bavispe Valley, Sonora

We have just crossed the border. I am entering Mexico, just as my father did—also with companions I barely know. I am uneasy. It's 1976, my first trip to Mexico.

Barney Burns and Tom Naylor and Misse Smith are graduate students at the University of Arizona. A trusted mutual friend has brought us together. We met only days ago and spent hours poring over the diary and maps. My idea is to use my father's diary as a guide to find the Apache camp he went to in 1930. I have enlisted them as guides and traveling companions.

I have this faith that my father's diary will lead us to the Apache camps he so carefully described. I have no idea how difficult this is going to be. If I had known anything about the Sierra Madre, if I had ever even had a look at these labyrinths of volcanic rock, I might never have begun.

Barney and Tom are intimately familiar with the Sierra Madre just south of the border. Barney is an archaeologist and Tom an historian. Misse is a law student at once fiercely independent and inseparable from both Barney and Tom.

The two men have been collaborating on a history of Colonia Morelos, one of the two small Mormon towns settled in the 1890s in northern Sonora. They like nothing better than looking for the sort of hidden treasure contained in my father's diary.

They have known each other for years and in this setting function together as a sort of bipolar entity. Superficially, discourse is largely adversarial; it's built around argument—about referees' calls made at basketball games, about our current altitude, about Mormon history, about kippered herring versus Norwegian sardines. Underneath this sparring is an abiding mutual trust and affection.

They once ran the wild headwaters of the Bavispe River in inflatable kayaks on a more or less mutual dare. Both were nearly killed and had to walk for miles to the nearest ranch. Tom, a Texan from El Paso, is completely bilingual in English and Spanish. He seems more southern than southwestern; he is courtly, formal, reserved, a little testy. Barney has a big Celtic heart. He has energy and charisma. He's an optimist, but not a foolish one. He's an inveterate and inexhaustible talker and is always the last one to turn in at night, always ready to stay up while there is someone to talk with. He has a near-bottomless memory for bits and pieces of information, but Tom's memory, as is soon apparent, is truly bottomless.

We are in Barney's six-year-old, one hundred-thousand-mile-plus Chevy Blazer. It has a beefed up suspension, an auxiliary twenty-four gallon gas tank, fat desert tires, and an eight-track stereo system on which we listen mostly to opera. Right now, though, it's the *Carmina Burana,* whose crazed, earthy energy seems about right for this undertaking. Both Barney and Tom make a point of bringing special presents for friends: some honey for one, some fresh fruit for another, a pile of comic books for another, an assortment of clothes, a coffee pot, and a treasured can opener.

I don't know what to expect, but I loosen up as I come to understand what a gift I have been given. In just a few days I have gone from knowing that I could not possibly find the camps myself, to finding myself in the company of some of the very few, maybe even the only people with whom this enterprise might actually be possible.

We have copies of all my father's writings on the Sierra Madre Apache, and his photos, maps, and diagrams. They are all very complete and very detailed. We are going to follow his route exactly. I believe that if we do that unfailingly, he will lead us when we lose our way.

### Nov. 21, 1930, Colonia Oaxaca, Sonora, Grenville's Diary

*This morning got up early, having a look at Pitacachi Mountain, a sharp outset on the west side of the S. Espuela, just to the east of where we were, and which is visible for a long ways.*

*—Our host told us of the Apache camp which had been discovered near Colonia Oaxaca. The Apaches had a sentinel posted on a peak near the camp continually. From the sentinel post to the camp was stretched a long cord made of strips of rawhide tied together, which was in turn attached to an old-cow bell hung in a tree at the camp. By this telephone as it were, any danger could be signaled immediately to camp. He also said that the next morning after they had run onto this Apache camp, they had found the tracks of the Apaches, where they had stood in a circle through part of the night, with ropes from hand to hand by which they kept their stock from being run off, and ready for a get away.*

*—We stopped at Morelos, a Mormon Colony now only inhabited by Mexicans, built at the joining of the San Bernardino and Bavispe Rivers. Most of the houses are built of brick, and it must have been quite a settlement at one time. Now it has gone to pieces due to the revolution*

*in 1909. To the south of Morelos, and lying in the loop of the Bavispe*
*River, is Sierra el Tigre, a large mountain which runs a good many miles*
*to the south. It was in at the foot of this mountain somewhere a little*
*below the joining of the San Bernardino and Bavispe Rivers, that Gate-*
*wood finally made the treaty with Geronimo and his band in 1886.*

### Neil's Diary, Colonia Morelos, Sonora

The Bavispe River is broad and shallow here. It is 1988, twelve years
after my first visit with Barney and Tom, one hundred years after
Geronimo and Gatewood had their fateful parley. We are making a
documentary about Geronimo and the Apache Wars and are filming
the place as a way of setting the scene. My wife, Margot, is working
as sound recordist and associate producer. Doug Shaffer is cameraman, and Billy McCullough, our nephew, is assistant cameraman.
Historians Jay Van Orden and Becky Orozco complete the entou-
rage. A horseman crosses just downstream; two great blue herons
rise from the willows and glide low across the water, laboring for altitude, as if trying to reach for the canyon rim where Geronimo had
his last stronghold.

In late August 1886, after five months on the run in Mexico, Geronimo sent word to the U.S. army command in pursuit that he was
ready to surrender, and that a trusted officer should go to the Mexican town of Fronteras to await contact. Lieutenant Charles Gatewood and two Chiricahua Apache scouts, Kietah and Martine, made
the rendezvous and then were led to this spot by two Chiricahua
women. Geronimo eventually came down from the clifftop and
negotiated terms of surrender. The formal surrender of Geronimo,
Naiche, and thirty-three men, women, and children took place just
north of the border in Arizona at Skeleton Canyon on September 6,
1886, and twenty-five years of warfare was brought to an end.

### Grenville's Diary, cont'd.

*—We proceeded around the southeast corner of S. Espuela and up the*
*R. Bavispe to Colonia Oaxaca, another Mormon settlement of the same*
*type as Morelos, settled about 40 years ago, but now merely used as a*
*ranch headquarters by Liolito Gabilondo, a rich Mexican from El Paso,*
*Tex. The Sierra Chita Hueca lies to the southeast of us here, and can be*
*plainly seen. It is on this mountain that the closest camp of the Apaches*

*lies. Bill Curtis says that the Mexicans along the mountains are extremely afraid of the Apaches owing to the raids that took place in the old days.*

— *The west side of S. Madre is extremely rough and goes up steeply, but the east side rises more gradually, and in general the crest of the range lies to the east side.*

— *In talking with Bill Curtis it came out that he knew Hoffman from Columbus.*

## Neil's Diary, Columbus, New Mexico

If anything, Columbus appears to me even more exposed and vulnerable now than it must have been in 1916 when Pancho Villa and 360 irregulars briefly declared war on the United States, sweeping through the sleeping town, guns blazing. Initiated because the United States was taking sides against Villa in the Mexican Revolution, this attack on Columbus resulted in the death of 28 Americans and 1 Villista.

In an old building, needing paint, there is a museum dedicated to telling the story of the raid and of the punitive expedition. The Pancho Villa Museum is one of those regional museums made eloquent by its very artlessness. It is like the collective attics of all the people — never very many — of Columbus: fading, buckled photographs with typed captions paper the walls; rusty swords, revolvers, and cartridge casings are in glass cases, along with eyeglasses and belt buckles and postcards and ledger books. Items of daily life that bring the town and its moment of terrifying glory to life. There is a library of personal recollections and eyewitness accounts. Overnight, Columbus briefly became ground zero in the Mexican Revolution, and it must have been the most exciting place to be along the entire border.

Soon after the start of the Mexican Revolution in 1910, Mormons such as Bill and his family were run out of Chihuahua and Sonora, and they made huge temporary camps in Arizona and New Mexico close to the border. There was a big one at Hachita, New Mexico, not far from Columbus, and many Mormons were drawn from those camps to the military staging area at Columbus. Among them almost certainly was Bill Curtis.

I spend half a day going through the records in the museum, as I had spent half the day before in the records of the county seat in Deming, thirty miles north. Neither Curtis's nor Hoffman's name ever appears.

Whatever Hoffman was doing in Columbus, he was not the sheriff, nor, for that matter, any other official agent or officer of the state or federal government—any more than Bill was chief of scouts. My father's brief, matter-of-fact entry is all the more fascinating because it appears to be wrong. Either he simply misremembers what Bill told him (unlikely), or Bill or Hoffman were embellishing. As always, I suspect the whole truth would have been more interesting.

# 8
# Pulpit Rock

**Nov. 22, 1930, Colonia Oaxaca, Sonora, Grenville's Diary**
*Remained in Oaxaca this day, and had a chance to talk with a Mexican there who said that the Apaches were now in the S. Espuela, as their tracks had been seen going into that range.*

**Neil's Diary, the San Bernardino Valley, Sonora**
These few neutral words are all we hear when he records this news, but I am always wondering: what is he thinking, what is he not telling us? Does his imagination quicken at all? Maybe, but I'm only aware of the listener's silence, the watcher's stillness. His inscrutability is equal parts scientific dispassion and rustic understatement.

**Grenville's Diary, cont'd.**
*About the Fimbres boy his [the Mexican mentioned above] story varied. The Apaches had killed him at the graves of the dead Indians, scalped him, and then buried him in a shallow hole, leaving his legs sticking out.*

**Nov. 23, 1930, El Paso Púlpito, Sonora**
*This day we left for Bill's camp in Púlpito, Jose his man having come down yesterday with 2 horses and a mule.*
*—El Paso Púlpito is the big pass leading from Sonora to Chihuahua in this part, it being a gap between S. Chita Hueca and S. Espuela, and having a road over which it is possible to drive cars, though it is very rough. The telegraph from Morelos and the western points to Casas Grandes is carried across at this point also. Consequently it is an important position for troops to hold in time of war.[1] There is a pass north of here, at the upper end of the S. Espuela, and one south of here 20 miles, from Carretas to San Miguel. The pass south of here was opened up 3 years ago to travel by car, though it is rough. About the pass to the north, I do not know.[2]*
*—We got to camp in Púlpito about noon, passing the great rock on the*

way from which the pass takes its name. This camp lies about 12 miles east of Colonia Oaxaca; it is a two room adobe house, and makes good shelter. Art Schrader, a fellow who drifted down from Wyoming, stays here and takes care of things for Bill. There is also Cherraco, a boy who helps Art. Bill has a bunch of horses and a herd of goats and sheep here which is doing pretty well, although the coyotes receive their full share. Art had just shot a deer which we went to bring in, and which was very fat.

— The country right in the pass here is a mesquite to mescal type, with outcroppings and cliffs of dark igneous rock. This runs back to the high land where the character changes. Pulpit Creek which has its head in S. Espuela, runs by camp here and to the west where it joins R. Bavispe to north of Colonia Oaxaca. Along the creek bottom are many trees in stretches which form a cool woods, sycamore, hackberry, maple, walnut, willow, alder, ash, juerga, etc., all growing to large size. One mile above here on the creek are the Cuevas, a group of large caves which have served as shelter to travelers for many years. There had been a large vinateria in one in which mescal had been distilled, a part of the apparatus still being there. The men while staying here had fixed up one of the caves into a sort of house. The largest of the caves had several deep holes dug in the back where they say some rifles and ammunition were taken out which had been hidden there by troops during the revolution 2 years ago.

— The vegetation of the country here is about the same as that of southern Arizona, varying according to corresponding altitudes, with the difference that there is much more grass covering the hills down here. So far I have seen only two trees which are new to me, the Juerga, and a variety of ash. The animals of the country so far as can be found out are white tail deer, javelins, bobcat, panther, brown bear, black bear, silver tip (grizzly bear), wolf, coyote, fox, coon, ringtail, and other small animals. The fox squirrel is common here. Were talking of going to Apache camp on Chita Hueca, and will probably go while Bill is away up river buying cattle. It is about 15 miles from here.

— Bill says that the way these Apaches shoe their horses with rawhide is by putting the hide on while wet over the whole foot, and sewing it up the back of the foot. This leaves a track similar to the mark of the end of a post when stuck in the ground.

**Neil's Diary, El Paso Púlpito**

The San Bernardino Valley. This was one of two most heavily used Apache Gateways to Mexico. There are other broad north–south valleys to the east and west of us that were Apache routes as well. I'm traveling with Barney, Tom, and Misse. They've all been down this valley many times before.

The road winds across the San Bernardino Valley, which has deep, branching, well-watered canyons every few miles leading up into the Sierra Madre—points of entry for the Apaches to the stronghold where for hundreds of years no one dared follow.

I've never been in Mexico. As soon as we cross the border the land feels different, looks different—maybe because of the profound change in the way the presence of people affects the land. We're on one of the main roads south from Agua Prieta, the town right across the border from Douglas. The road is narrow, and we're off hard-top—won't see it again for days. There are several towns south of here, and heavy traffic moves on this road: many big trucks as well as the usual farm and ranch traffic. You can take a bus from here to Nácori Chico—a 170-mile, three-day trip, says Barney. In fact you have a choice: there are two competing bus lines for this route.

In the blazing midday light, the shadows retreat, pull in around stems and trunks. The mountains are distant, hazy, blue, two-dimensional jagged blades rising from the sea of creosote bush that carpets the valley floors with a vibrant, heavily saturated shade of tropical green. Everything else—the rocks, the grass, the weeds—are all parched and bleached of color.

Ahead is a valley opening deeper into Mexico, where the mountains will become starker; the valleys broader, hotter, dustier; the edges of everything in the landscape harder, sharper; the elements more savage.

The road makes hardly any impact on the land. In a contest between the elements and the things that people build here, the odds favor the elements even more than usual. We drive through stands of cholla cactus and thorny ocotillo that are thicker than any I have ever seen in Arizona. It's a volcanic landscape, and below the dark cliffs that contain the valley are acres of black basaltic debris. They are a constant reminder of the prolonged violence that brought

the land into being and of the elemental ferocity that has been dis-
mantling it ever since.

Instead of the gradual weathering process that shapes most land-
scapes, here it seems shaped by spontaneous explosion. The scattered rock has the look of shrapnel. There is no smooth rock; everything looks sharp and abrasive, as if shattered only yesterday.

In spite of the immense sycamores and cottonwoods in the river-
bottoms, in spite of the dense stands of cactus, yucca, mesquite,
ironwood, and other upper Sonoran flora, the overwhelming impression is one of raw, naked rock.

We arrive at Morelos and walk through the old Mormon town,
now entirely Mexican. Barney and Tom explain the history, the
houses, list the names of the Mormons who originally built and lived
in each one. In 1885 Mormons who believed in the practice of polyg-
amy, outlawed in the United States and officially rejected by the Mormon Church, established a colony called Colonia Diaz in Mexico,
near present-day Ascensión, Chihuahua. During the 1890s a series of
other colonies were established by hundreds of pioneering Mormons, who were welcomed by the Mexican government. In Sonora
there were Colonia Morelos and Oaxaca and in Chihuahua, Colonia
Juárez, Dublán, Chuhuichupa, Pacheco, and García.

The industrious, skillful Mormons lovingly made the doors of the
old Morelos mill with diagonal parquetry panels—now split and
splintered and orphaned. We cannot get in, but the Mexican woman
who now owns it shows up with a litter of shy, mischievous children.
They gape at us, bewildered, while Barney speaks with their mother.

During the revolution that began in 1908 and convulsed Mexico
for years, Mexican resentment of the Mormons gained momentum,
finally forcing them to abandon all the settlements they had built.
Within a few years many Mormons had reoccupied the Chihuahua
colonies, but now only Colonia Dublán and Colonia Juárez are still
occupied by Mormons. In Sonora only one family, the Langfords,
have returned. They have a large, self-sufficient farm, a colony really,
with dozens of towheaded kids, and they have spread along the fertile riverbottom between the villages of Bavispe and San Miguel.

Barney tells me about the Mexican raids on Morelos, and how
young Layne Lillywhite, only sixteen, saved his father's life in this very

mill. Some Mexican revolutionaries turned ugly and strapped his father to the mill machinery, started the waterwheel, and were about to watch him be crushed to death. Layne came in and with his bare hands pulled the belts off the racing drive shafts, stopping the machinery and so stunning the Mexicans with his courage that they could only gape, rooted to the spot as he released his father.

On the way out of town we stop at an extraordinary graveyard, a thick forest of white iron crosses with paper flowers and votive candles—so festive, so pretty, so—distracting in a way, that it can make you forget death, actually banish the thought of it for a moment. But only for a moment; the cemetery's brave gaiety in the end is only a reminder of the fragility of life—and of the fact that the celebration here is of the reign of death. The cemetery is full of children's graves. The great influenza epidemics of 1918 and 1919 decimated all these towns and devoured space in the cemeteries.

Colonia Oaxaca is still headquarters for the Gabilondo Ranch, as it was in 1930. The Langfords, when they came in the 1890s, built a house that is still there, though it is now occupied by a Mexican woman, a friend of Barney and Tom. She has a pet deer named Pámphile and is grinding corn in a hand-cranked device. Barney and Tom call her the hot comic-book lady, and have presents for her.

She's handsome, in her thirties, and has never been far from home, but she has heard the stories. When Barney tells her we are looking for some old Apache camps, she turns pale with real fear, and her hand flies to her throat. An intake of breath, almost a gasp. She says only, "Apaches," but the way she says it speaks volumes. For a moment she thinks we mean there are still Apaches in the Sierra Madre, and the thought of that is terrifying. We realize for the first time what a living thing the memory of Apaches can be in Mexico.

Like the landscape and the elements, this recall is different once across the border. Apaches mean something profoundly different for Mexicans than they do for Americans. Before Geronimo's surrender in 1886, Apaches had been part of the Spanish and Mexican experience for over two hundred and fifty years—of the American experience for less than fifty. As ferocious as the conflict was between the Americans and the Apaches, it pales in comparison with what generations of Mexicans lived through.

That we have touched this woman's raw nerve of Apache recall is a sudden insight that we carry with us as we turn into the Sierra Madre, finding our way to the enormous volcanic landmark called Pulpit Rock, the beginning of Pulpit Pass.

Stopping on a large expanse of smooth rock, we build two fires in the gathering dark: a bed of coals for cooking and a bonfire for light. We build it high, illuminating the darkness, holding back the night. We are not far from Bill Curtis's old camp and the caves and rocks my father pored over.

Opening his diary, I read aloud from it everything he has written up to this point, and we can all feel his presence.

# 9
# The Caves

**Nov. 24, 1930, El Paso Púlpito, Sonora, Grenville's Diary**

*This afternoon went up to look at cave on north side of pass, just opposite camp. It proved to run back about 100 feet from where it branched off, and went back yet further; it being too dark to see well did not go as far as the end. Two piles of rock were on the floor of the cave, each about 3 feet high by 4 feet wide, and one near the entrance, the other further back. The latter had been disturbed; and in it were the remains of some arrows. There were also several broken arrows on a ledge in the cave, feathers gone, but sinew still there. Took these arrows along with several pieces of corn cob, and a piece of pottery which had been used as a ladle. There were several petroglyphs on the west wall of the cave, done in black and red, which I am going to copy. From the cave it is possible to see far up and down the pass, and must have made an excellent look-out.*

**Neil's Diary, the Bavispe Valley**

My father was an obsessive collector. Growing up on Long Island, New York, he used to walk behind farmers' plows and pick up arrowheads from the turned earth. It was an almost magical adventure, and it determined the course of his life, leading first toward archaeology and then to ethnology and anthropology. He never stopped collecting fragments, such as the arrowheads and the bits of arrows in the Pulpit Pass caves.

He admired them intrinsically, but also knew, instinctively, that each one was part of an unseen larger picture. As he got older he collected everything from antique firearms to Indian artifacts of all kinds, medicinal plants, vocabulary words, photographs, snakeskins, birds' eggs and interesting bones—and it was all catalogued and cross-indexed, in neat notebooks that now fill a long bookshelf in our house. He would go to museums and make precise watercolor drawings of Indian clothing and artifacts—all kept in a meticulously documented notebook. My mother said he learned how to make arrowheads from flint and amazed her one day when he made her one from glass.

### Nov. 26, 1930, El Paso Púlpito, Sonora, Grenville's Diary

*This day went south towards S. Chita Hueca, as far as foot of the first ridge, having pine. There was a lot of white oak growing up there. Found 2 small caves that had been camped in at the top of a ridge, and found a small, sandstone polisher in one. From the first timbered slope of S. Chita Hueca to that of S. Espuela, must be about 15 miles.*

*—Bill says the Apaches when crossing this gap probably keep to the height of land to the east of here, just this side of Las Varas.*

### Nov. 29, 1930, El Paso Púlpito, Sonora

*Rained all day. They say that from Nov. to Feb. a rainy spell of 5 days to 2 weeks is not uncommon.*

*—This afternoon went up to the Cuevas and found several petroglyphs, now almost obliterated by smoke from campfires.* [1]

## 10
# Apaches and the Bavispe Valley

**Nov. 30, 1930, Colonia Oaxaca, Sonora, Grenville's Diary**

*Today Bill started on his trip up the Bavispe R. and I went along with him. Most of the morning was spent in catching up our horses and packing, but we finally got started and made Colonia Oaxaca this night.*

**Dec. 1, 1930, San Miguel, Sonora**

*Was talking with Reyes,[1] ranch foreman for Gabilondo at Colonia Oaxaca, this morning, and he said that when they raided the Apache camp on Chita Hueca, they found where a small space had been planted in corn, melons, and squash.[2] He also said they had baskets and spoons of wood, and that he found 3 arrows which had tips of a hard, red wood.*

*—As the river was up we had to take the trail around by the foot of S. Chita Hueca, and Rancho del Alisos. We met an old Kickapoo and his wife on their way to Douglas for their pension money. The old man was tall of stature, and it was easy to see he was no Mexican Indian. The Kickapoo settlement lies about six miles above Bacerac, on the R. Bavispe.*

*—We crossed the R. Bavispe about 3 miles below San Miguel, and here the water only came up to the horses' bellies, but all the same the current was very swift.*

*—San Miguel is a pretty little town of about 2000 people which lies on the west bank of the R. Bavispe. The southern spur of the S. Chita Hueca, on which there are some silver and lead deposits, ends across the river and a little to the north-east of here. After riding through the plaza of the town, where stands an interesting old church, we came to the Gomez house, where Bill had friends, and where we stopped for the night. They certainly were good to us and the meal we had this evening was fit for a king. This Mexican food certainly is good; corn tortillas, beans and chili, etc. The moon is out these nights and it gives enough light to look around in. There was a baile in one of the houses, the dance music furnished by a small organ. The room was small, the floor was*

*rough, but the dancers managed all right, using the regular step one sees at the bailes in New Mexico. Later on, we called on a friend of Bill's, Enriquez who spoke very good English. He had some ore samples of gold and silver which he wants Bill to take out and have assayed.*

*— The pass through which the road goes to Carretas and Chihuahua lies opposite this town, to the east, across river. Carretas, the first ranch on the way, lies 15 miles to the east of here, just in Chihuahua.*[3]

*— Most of the doors and shutters in this town are the old fashioned kind with panels, the same as those in New Mexico. They make these boards in a saw pit, with a whip-saw, and up till three years ago they were still sawing all their lumber in this way.*

*— Several years ago the people of Bavispe had a quarrel with the people of this town, and drove the entire population away, the latter having to take refuge over in Chihuahua at Carretas till the quarrel was over. This morning an old woman came in whom they said was 100 years of age. She remembered a long time back, and said that the house itself where we stayed was 117 years old.*

## Neil's Diary, the Bavispe Valley

The Mexican Revolution was the first of the great revolutions of the twentieth century, and some say it really began with the violent 1906 strike at the Cananea Copper mine, only fifty miles northwest of Bavispe. Many of the revolutionary leaders hailed from the states of Sonora, Chihuahua, and Coahuila: Venustiana Carranza, Álvaro Obregón, General Miguel Samaniego, Pancho Villa, Francisco Madero. The earliest uprisings and battles took place in 1909 and 1910 in the north, in Chihuahua and Coahuila; they were followed by a 1911 uprising in Baja, California, and by the capture of Ciudad Juárez by Madero forces.[4]

Within a few years the Revolution became so factionalized that it degenerated for long periods of time into civil war, leaving the country with neither unified leadership nor even a functioning government at times until well into the 1920s.

Law and order suffered sporadic breakdown. In Sonora, Yaqui Indians, long brutally oppressed by the Mexican government, rose in a series of revolts. We have met people who remember the day three hundred Yaquis sacked the village of Bacadéhuachi in 1918, stealing livestock and ransacking houses, and killing one man.

When armed bands of roving partisan revolutionaries were not fighting with each other, they were frequently looting Mormon villages in both Sonora and Chihuahua, living off the land and making off with whatever crops and livestock they could. The Bavispe Valley was not spared. Not only was the downstream Mormon town of Morelos raided,[5] the two ancient Mexican villages of San Miguel and Bavispe were at each other's throats, as Grennie heard when he was in San Miguel.

The two towns supported different factions of the Mexican Revolution. The people of San Miguel were Villistas, siding with Pancho Villa, and those of Bavispe were Carranza supporters. In 1910 two wagonloads of people from San Miguel were attacked and killed by Bavispe people. The hostilities between the two towns did not abate until 1917, at which point the people of San Miguel felt it safe to return to their homes.[6]

### Dec. 2, 1930, Bavispe, Sonora, Grenville's Diary

*We left for Bavispe, and arrived there, after traveling 3 miles up the river. This town, much like San Miguel, but somewhat older, stands across the river from the northern end of S. Durarno. There is a large old church here which is now in ruins due to the earthquake of 1887, only one wing being used as a chapel. The fault line of this earthquake runs clear from above Colonia Morelos to below Bacerac, and may be seen to this day in certain places. When it took place the people of Bacerac crowded into the church for refuge. The heavy dome and roof fell on them, killing many. Most of the houses were shaken down, so that the town was in ruins. A gate has been put up to keep the cows, etc. out of the church, and the old bells are now hung on a wooden frame, beside the church. These bells, like those of the church in San Miguel, are old. Two of them bear the date 1733, the third has the inscription San Francisco, Año de 1733, and the fourth San Gabriel Año 1707. The population of Bavispe is about 1500, and this town is the leading one of the district, corresponding to a county seat.*

*—We stopped at a grist mill about 1 mile south of town, run by an American named Chy, a friend of Bill's.[7]*

*—A great many of the poorer people wear tejiras which they make themselves. These have rawhide soles like moccasins, and uppers like a shoe.[8]*

## Neil's Diary, Bavispe

It's Sunday, and there is a baseball game going on just outside town—only old men and young boys are playing. The infield is rocks and dust. Teenagers are dressed in Sunday best and they are strolling in the plaza, at once brazen and formal. Two little girls in pink satin and frothy lace hurry, arm in arm, whispering desperate secrets to each other.

This is the oldest of the Bavispe River Valley villages. It is built around a plaza with an immaculate white bandstand, crisp and confectionary, under big shade trees. The plaza is the brilliant green core of an otherwise white-to-adobe-colored town. Centered on the west side of the square a church is the village showpiece.

The church is blinding: whiter than any other white. White not just on the surface, but white through and through—so white it might have been carved from a single block of solid chalk. It is a miniature in gothic style—its lean profile out of place among the town's blunt geometry.

The people of these Sonoran towns have an unexpected polyethnic look. Not only are there Opata, Yaqui, Lower Pima, Mayo, Tarahumara, and even Apache faces, but we also see an occasional girl with long blond hair, or redheaded freckled-faced boys on bikes, Dubliners for sure, or others with brown hair and pale faces, and an unmistakably Chinese face or two. Sonora is like that. Mining and political upheavals have brought in many American and European laborers, engineers, soldiers, and entrepreneurs. The coastal towns of the Gulf of California, like the rest of the North American West Coast, have always been ports of entry for immigrants, many from Asia.

The Spanish came to this valley over three hundred years ago. Church records say that a Franciscan missionary named Father Mancos baptized thirty-four Opata Indians in Bavispe in 1610, then went upstream to Bacerac, where he did the same thing for forty-five more. The Opatas and the Mayos, just to the south, seemed to have made the Spanish welcome. Perhaps it was because of certain cultural similarities between the Spanish and these sedentary, agricultural Indians, perhaps because they eventually were united against a common enemy, the Apache. In any case, by 1678 there was a very substantial church structure in Bavispe, as well as in the towns of Bacerac, Huachinera, Bacadéhuachi, and Nácori Chico to the south.[9]

As the northern frontier of New Spain became settled, Apache raiding increased throughout the seventeenth and eighteenth centuries until there was a no-man's land dominated by Apaches all the way from the Zuni pueblo in present-day Arizona south to Sahuaripa in Sonora, a distance of well over four hundred miles.[10]

In the eighteenth century a line of presidios was built along the northern frontier, stretching from the Rio Grande almost to the Gulf of California, but it could neither hold back Apache raids nor provide enough security to stem the flight of Spanish settlers back to the south, away from the frontier. Except for constant raiding, the Spanish had no contact with the Apaches and in the eighteenth century hardly even knew who they were. All they knew was that they appeared to be coming down the Bavispe and Moctezuma Rivers from somewhere far to the north. The northernmost outpost, Santa Fe, became utterly isolated from the rest of New Spain by an Apache corridor stretching across the states of Sonora and Chihuahua. The Spanish could neither subdue the Apache nor secure the frontier.

By the end of the eighteenth century the colonization of much of northern Mexico had been at a standstill for nearly a hundred years. In 1786 Bernardo de Galvez, the viceroy of New Spain, concluded that the only policy that would produce permanent results would be one of extermination. However, without the means to accomplish that, he decided to pursue a peace policy as cynical as it was effective. He would try to destroy Apache social organization. The policy was to induce the Apaches to trade at frontier towns, and in that way to make them dependent on trade goods, food handouts, and cheap, abundant liquor.[11]

It worked—at least as far as the Spanish were concerned. Peace reigned until Mexican independence from Spain in 1821. The new government of Mexico was strapped and did not have the money to support what had come to be called the "establishments of peace." Apache raiding soon resumed, and by midcentury it had become even more widespread than it had been in the 1770s.[12]

Mexico elected to reconsider an extermination policy. Bounty hunters were invited to ply their grisly trade in Mexico in the 1830s. One of the most infamous was an immigrant Irishman named James Kirker.[13] He was attracted by the good money to be had from killing Apaches and presenting their scalps to the federal representative:

$100 for every man, $50 for every woman, and $25 for every child. The Mexican government finally repealed this practice when it became clear that not all the scalps being brought in for redemption at frontier presidios came from slaughtered Apaches.[14]

Apache raiding intensified, and villages and ranches in the north were abandoned, as they had been a hundred years earlier. Indeed, Nácori Chico was abandoned twice during the nineteenth century because of Apache attacks. The people moved to nearby Bacadéhuachi until they gathered the numbers and the resolve to move back.

Mochopa, Serva, and Satachi, all south of Nácori Chico, were one by one totally destroyed and abandoned. Mochopa's story is typical. The townspeople, long accustomed to Apache attack, had survived for years by rushing into a massive stone-walled corral when Apaches appeared and fighting them off from there. But, attacking on Easter day, 1839, the Apaches caught all the people of Mochopa in their church. The Apaches barricaded the doors from the outside and torched the building.[15] All inside perished, and they were buried within the ruined walls of the church. Today the graves are marked by wooden crosses and big round river stones in which names and crosses are deeply incised.

Within less than ten years of the destruction of Mochopa, the Mexican-American War brought the vital interests of the United States into the heart of Apacheria, and it was only a matter of time before the U.S. army would be at war with the Apaches. Like all Native tribes, the Apaches considered themselves a sovereign nation, under the control of neither Mexico nor the United States, and raiding continued unabated.

American soldiers pursuing Apaches in the 1880s thought it a wonder that anyone at all remained in this part of Sonora, the towns were so small, so isolated, and so vulnerable.[16] But the people of the Bavispe Valley have held tenaciously onto their villages because of the river and its fertile flood plain.

**Dec. 3, 1930, Bacerac, Sonora, Grenville's Diary**
*We left Chy's mill, and came up the river about 12 miles to Bacerac, riding through La Galera, a settlement consisting of about 8 houses, on the way. Bacerac has a large old church which also suffered from the quake of 1887, but which still retains the major portion of its roof, however not*

*its belfry. The bells, 4 of them, are set up on a frame outside. They all date from 1707, 3 of them being dedicated to San Josephe, and 1 to San Ignacio. This church, like the one in Bavispe, is built of brick. In going around the back part of it, I found a section which was roofless, and back of this a small room in which were stored 2 bells, and several of the old, carved wooden Santos and Bultos, the latter almost life size. These original ornaments of the church had been thrown in here, and replaced by cheap, plaster ones.*

*—The place we stopped here was at the house of Charlie Lynd, a Swedish American, who had followed the mining down into Mexico, and finally ended up by marrying a Mexican woman, native to Bacerac. Many of the houses of this town have little patios, planted in flowers, some of them even having orange trees growing.*

*—This night they held a mass in the old church which we listened to. Later on Mrs. Lynd talked with us for a while. She says she can remember her sisters telling her of the coming of U.S. troops with Apache scouts in pursuit of the Chiricahuas. At that time her family lived on a farm on the other side of the river from town. It was a bright moonlit night, and her father heard a big body of horsemen ride in and camp close to an acequia on their farm. He could not figure out who these people could be, as they talked in both English and Indian. But finally one of this party who spoke Spanish came to the door and told them this was an American party in pursuit of Geronimo. The next day some of the Apache scouts got drunk, and when the troops left, they had to catch these and tie them on their horses and drive them along. However one scout refused to be caught, the American chasing him through the stream at foot of the town, and finally capturing him but not till most of his clothes were torn off.*[17]

## Neil's Diary, Bavispe

The U.S. army began its twenty-five-year campaign against the Apaches in 1861, but it wasn't until 1883 that General George Crook sought and received permission from the Mexican government to pursue Apaches across the international boundary. This, in effect, would be a tolerated armed invasion of Mexican soil, but the situation had become desperate, and the two countries had decided to cooperate in subduing the Apaches. In spite of the years that they had spent as adversaries, there was much mutual respect between Crook and the Apaches. The general knew enough about the terrain in which Apaches lived and fought to understand that his soldiers were no match for these master guerrilla warriors. Crook realized that he would have to fight fire with fire—Apache with Apache.

Geronimo was a Chiricahua Apache, a group distinct from the Western Apaches. Though the two tribes shared a closely related language and culture, they were traditional rivals, so when Crook asked the Western Apaches for help, they readily enlisted as scouts. In May of 1883 Crook, a handful of officers and enlisted men, and two hundred Western Apache scouts tracked Geronimo and some three hundred Chiricahuas to the heart of their Sierra Madre stronghold, southeast of the village of Bavispe. The U.S. army and its Apache scouts traveled down the Bavispe River Valley and through Bavispe and Bacerac, where they made an unforgettable impression.[18]

## Grenville's Diary, cont'd.

*—The Padres of the Bacerac church here were supposed to have worked a mine called Tiopa, which was very rich. This mine, they say, lay in the Sierra Madre to the east of here. The miners even had a small town from which it took them about 1 days ride to reach Bacerac. They used to come in once in a while to get provisions, and have their children baptized, etc. But now, all traces of the mine and settlement are gone, and no one seems to know where the old location was, although it has been the style among the natives here to search for it, Bill says there are 3 trails, in some places having deep dugways, showing much former travel, which lead up into the mountains to the east, but which apparently go no place as they just fade out on the top of the mountain.*

## Neil's Diary, Pomerene, Arizona

Alvah Fenn, the gentle Mormon patriarch who grew up in Mexico, and whom I have now visited a couple of times, is telling me of his personal views on the location of the lost Tayopa mine and why no one has ever found it. He has looked for it himself and, though he is well into his eighties, is not done with it. This fabulously rich silver mine is one of the legendary buried treasures of northern Mexico. Everyone has heard of it, and no one agrees about it. It's not certain that the padres of the Bacerac church worked it. All that is known is that the mine is somewhere in the Sierra Madre, well to the south and east of Bacerac.[19]

### Grenville's Diary, cont'd.

—*The distance from here to Casas Grandes, Chihuahua is about 120 miles, by trail, straight over the Sierra Madre.*

—*This afternoon I saw two Kickapoos, a man and his wife, trading in a store here. They spoke Spanish fairly well, but not fluently.*

### Dec. 4, 1930, Bacerac, Sonora

*This morning we rode up the river to the Kickapoo settlement, but due to missing the trail did not get back to Bacerac till mid-afternoon. While up the river we stopped at the ranch of an American named John Swanson. He had married a Mexican woman, and made a nice little place for himself.*

*From near this place we were able to see the roofs of houses in Huachinera, about 5 miles distant. This town is the last settlement in the valley, the river swinging east into the mountains, and the valley coming to an end, somewhat to the south. From Huachinera, the only way out to the south is by trail, over the mountains to Oputo, a distance of about 12 leagues. From Huachinera to the Rio Aros it would be about 20 leagues. From Huachinera to Bacerac is 12 miles.*

### Neil's Diary, Bacerac

We are never out of sight of circling vultures. You never see this many in Arizona. Instead of omens of death, I decide these birds are our advance units, our companions of the road. I remember having bird experiences—strange, solitary encounters with birds in which the birds were creatures somehow not of this earth, but from some other place of being briefly intersecting mine. They were not ambiguous, these events. Each time, I experienced uplift and reassurance, unsought, but welcome. These vultures, cast against type, may somehow be watching over us.

Barney and Nelda and I are between Bacerac and Huachinera, momentarily lost, just as my father was sixty-six years ago. We're looking for the Kickapoo village just as he was, and we're wondering where the old John Swanson place is, knowing it must be close by. We turn down one or two dirt roads lined with thick brush, then emerge from the scrub by a white adobe house. Barney talks to a lady in the house. We have blundered into the old Swanson place, now owned by Charlie, Johnny's son. He is away in Agua Prieta and comes down every two weeks or so to look after things.

Behind a fence, facing the adobe, there is an imposing stone house done in a more or less southern California idiom—Charlie's house when he's here. There are well-tended fields spilling away to a wall of cottonwoods by the river. Swanson, hardly more than a footnote in the diary, now occupies more space in my mind, assumes the shape of a link to the past.

The original house is not far away. It is a handsome old adobe building, with an immense palm tree crowding the front door. It's abandoned, boarded up, taken over by farm animals and swarms of wasps that have built paper nests as big as basketballs in the rooms. There are arches in the exterior walls over what must have been outdoor fireplaces or ovens.

I reach only a few specific spots where I can say with assurance that my father had been, and this house was one I never expected to find. As always, in places he has been, there is a faint but detectable resonance ringing across those years from the time when he once displaced the air in these very rooms.

This feeling takes me quite by surprise, and it's not always an altogether pleasant one. I am aware of a faint unease, though this is just the sort of thing I have come for. I have come looking for my father's footsteps, believing they may lead me to him, or at least close to him. The decay and ruin at this deserted house make it nearly impossible to imagine him here. It reminds me too much of death, of a grave perhaps, of an irretrievable past, this old Swanson place.

Barney and I take pictures of the place. I try to imagine it in use, but it won't come to life. I can't see the hitching post, the gardens, animal pens, fences. I can't see how the huge palm tree fits in, or where furniture used to go, where the laundry was hung, the drying chilies, or where the dogs would sleep. I can't see my father. The place is a shell. It's mute. Grennie was someone who recorded the physical landscape in minute, satisfying detail, but I am missing the people he meets. He seems rarely to have been tempted to venture a subjective impression of someone. If he had, these now empty places might have more life.

### Grenville's Diary, cont'd.

*— To the east of Huachinera lies the Sierra de Huachinera, a big black mountain which may be seen a long ways.*

*— In several of the arroyos down which we rode were the remains of trincheras, backed up by stone walls from 2 to 5 feet high, these walls extending across the arroyo for a distance of from 20 to 40 feet, and in one place extending at intervals from 16 to 40 feet for fully a quarter of a mile. This country must have been heavily populated by Indians at one time. Bill says that in the mountains to the east, some of these trincheras run clear to the top. The Mexicans attribute them to the* antiguas *which is about all they know of them.*[20]

### Neil's Diary, the Bavispe Valley

My mother said that when she and Grennie went for long drives across Arizona and New Mexico he could identify a smooth, distant mound as a pueblo site the way a copyeditor can spot a run-on sentence. In this way, traveling with my father must have been like traveling with Barney. Barney is a trained archaeologist, and he sees signs of prehistoric habitation everywhere. It is well known that there are many large unexcavated village sites throughout the Bavispe River Valley and the Sierra Madre. He knows many of them already and keeps up a running commentary, and as he does so I realize I can't imagine doing this with anyone else. I learn that a *trinchera* is a level terrace made by building a masonry wall across an arroyo backfilled with earth. The level surface was probably used for small garden plots, though they may have been defensive as well. Some archaeologists classify the "Trinchera Tradition" as a general northern Mexican tradition, possibly contemporaneous with Casas Grandes of the 1300s. The Casas Grandes culture, with its center at Paquimé, was the dominant culture of the region until 1340. Satellite communities might have existed in the Bavispe River Valley and, if not of the Casas Grandes themselves, these would have fallen under its influence.

**Grenville's Diary, cont'd.**

— *The Kickapoo settlement lies on a bend of the R. Bavispe, and about 6 miles from Bacerac. They call it Tamichopa, and the people living there must represent about 10 families. These Kickapoos came over from Coahuila in about 1908, looking for a suitable place they could buy and live on. They bought the Zozaya ranch, and so settled here. They live pretty well as they draw money from the U.S. government, for which they go to Douglas, being essentially U.S. Indians. There were several large corn fields along the river bottom, and the place looked well. They are left alone by the Mexicans, who are afraid to steal from them. During the revolution in Villa's time, some of the horses, which by the way are usually good, were run off by Mexicans, but were quickly returned when the Indians started to get ready for action. A great deal of time they spend in the mountains, hunting. They make much deer jerky and buckskin which they sell in Douglas. Their houses are the old style, reed mats laid on a pole frame, and also jacales of Mexican type. Each family has its group of houses surrounded by a circular fence. The men wear regular overalls, shirts, etc., but still use the moccasin, the style being the old eastern kind, but with a rawhide extra sole sewed on the bottom. The hair is bobbed just below the ear, with one thin braided strand hanging in back to their shoulders. The women wear the old style gingham dress, and some had on silver ornaments of their own manufacture. They wear moccasins of the old style, eastern woman type. The hair is done in two long braids. I saw one old saddle of theirs which was the plains Indian type, with high horn and cantle. They were touchy about pictures, and must be in fairly close contact with the U.S. Indian Bureau. There is a Chinaman living with them, and also a Mexican boy who married one of their girls at the Bacerac Church.*[21]

**Neil's Diary, Bacerac**

After leaving Swanson's, we find Tamichopa, the Kickapoo Village. It now is remarkably squalid: tarpaper shacks and hovels squat in the dust. Chickens and thin dogs dodge in the weeds, chased by barefoot children. A few burros, goats, calves, and mules run loose in the frayed underbrush. We pass a one-room schoolhouse with no glass in the windows and come to the middle of things. There is a crowd gathered under a big mesquite tree next to a building that might be a community center, maybe a store. Beyond it, and beyond some more mesquites, a small roundup is in progress. There are cowboys gathered around a corral, the milling, bawling cattle inside, veiled in dust.

Barney talks to the group for a few minutes, then reports to us as we drive away that there are hardly any full-blood Kickapoos anymore, they have almost all intermarried with Mexicans, and few even speak the language today. Many have left this settlement for the larger one in the state of Coahuila, from which they originally moved.

As strange as it may seem, a number of tribes from the United States sought land in Mexico as a way of gaining autonomy and stability that may have appeared impossible otherwise. In 1852 a band of Kickapoos with a few Potawatomis went to Texas from homelands in Wisconsin, and from there to Mexico. In 1863, and later, more Kickapoos joined them. In 1905 the Kickapoos in Mexico were given a village site in the Santa Rosa Mountains of eastern Coahuila. At about the same time, a group of two hundred broke away and moved from Coahuila to Huachinera, Sonora, and were soon joined by a group from Oklahoma. If any of these people were heirs of Kickapoos who had once owned land in Oklahoma, the money they were collecting might have been due them from land-allotment rental or from Oklahoma oil leases.

### Grenville's Diary, cont'd.

*—On getting back to Bacerac found Dr. Spencer at the Lynds. He is an American doctor who is practicing in the valley here.[22] He had been off in the mountains and had only just got back, having been sent for to fix a boy up who had a broken leg.*

### Neil's Diary, Bacerac

People remember the Lynds in Bacerac. Josefina Chua, who owns and operates the hotel and restaurant where we're staying, says that Mrs. Lynd was Rita Cordoba. Josefina and Barney have become fast friends. He has met his match in rhetoric and theatrical style, which doesn't often happen. They refer to each other now as "la Famosa Josefina" and "Bernabé, el Oso." She has an expressive, rubbery face and is renowned for her cooking, her affection, and her good nature. Friends drop in for a minute and stay for hours. No one likes to leave Josefina's.

We arrive in the dark after a long day, and she wants us to meet an old friend of hers, here for one of those short visits that lasts all day. It's Charlie, old John Swanson's son. Charles Walter Swanson. After the events of this day, I can only think that this was meant to be.

Charlie has lived all his life in Mexico and is married to a handsome Mexican woman who stays in the kitchen talking with Josefina. Later she says Charlie hasn't spoken English since his father died many years ago, and it does her heart good to see him do so again and to talk about the old days.

Charlie's English is perfectly fluent, but moderately accented. He has a slightly mischievous look, pale skin, a lot of reddish hair, and a streak of wry Irish wit, although his father, John, was a Swede from Minneapolis. John Swanson came down at the age of nineteen, before the Mexican Revolution, lured, like so many Americans, by mining.

Mining is a weakness, nearly an addiction, Charlie thinks; he believes he has prospered by staying away from it. Charlie is a businessman and a rancher and serves on the board of an Agua Prieta bank. He is seventy-two years old and would have been six when my father visited his home in 1930. He doesn't remember my father, though he almost certainly saw him.

All the life missing from the old Swanson adobe I find in Charlie. As he talks, his ties to people my father met, to people I have met over the years, broaden into a fabric of connective tissue. To begin with, Charles Lynd, my father's host for several days in Bacerac, was Charlie Swanson's godfather and namesake. There was an American cattleman named Stewart Hunt, whom my father was to meet on a subsequent trip, who was an inseparable friend of John Swanson and a second father to Charlie. He says that in his father's day the Apaches used to steal a few of their horses. Then, remembering, dryly: the Apaches took the horses and the Mexicans took the corn.

Charlie spent his childhood here on the Bavispe River. His nearest neighbors were the Kickapoos; their children were his playmates. He hasn't uttered their names in fifty years. He starts to name them. Slowly, as if he's feeling for them below the surface, not sure the names will rise of their own accord. He and Barney and Nelda and I are sitting around Josefina's long dining table in the dim light of one bulb, and Charlie says,

Ma-te-pu-ya.

His eyes are half closed, and he's looking at the dim wall at the end of the room. I can imagine that the faces are floating at him from the half light, and as each one appears he names him or her. He pronounces the names for us, slowly, savoring the sounds he has neither heard nor uttered since childhood. I write down the names, just as he sounds them out.

The father was Matepuya.
The mother Tepaia.
The children were
Pespichi
Ecochi
Namasica
Quequechi
Tuetaque
Tamuqua
Chesoko.

Charlie drifts back; his eyes focus on us and the pace of his storytelling picks up. Matepuya was a big fat man with pigtails, and he always wore bib overalls. As Grennie observed, Charlie also recalls that the Kickapoos always had excellent horses. He remembers the grass houses they used to build, but he says that there was a fire that consumed Matepuya's grass house. His wife died in the fire, and after that they did not build those houses anymore.

My father says there was a Chinese man living with the Kickapoos, and Charlie expands on that: there were some Chinese who raised opium poppies on leased Kickapoo land, but when Mexican officials found out about it, they burned those fields.

Charlie says he was afraid of Matepuya and, slowing down again, drifting back, remembering, wondering why . . . says that having heard Satan was a man to reckon with, he cast Matepuya in his imagination as the Devil himself. Charlie is smiling his inward Irish smile, and he looks at us, amused by this unbidden memory.

### Dec. 5, 1930, Bavispe, Sonora, Grenville's Diary

*This morning the high mountains had some snow on them, and the valley was foggy. We left Bacerac and came to Chy's mill here.*

*—The Apache camp on S. Chita Hueca has been entirely burned, corral and all, by the people of Col. Juárez, who did not want the Apaches to come back in that district.* [23]

*However, he said 5 of them had been back some time ago, as their tracks had been found. The doctor, who came on here this afternoon, says that where he was camped in the mountains, the Apaches had been just lately. It seems to be in fashion down here to say that you ran onto the Apache camp so soon after they had left that the ashes of their fires were still hot. The only things of the Apaches that doc. had seen were 2 or 3 tanned cowhides and a blanket woven of rags which were taken from some one of their camps. He most kindly gave me his address and told me to keep in touch with him, that if he could do anything for me to let him know.*

### Dec. 6 to Dec. 12, 1930, Bavispe, Sonora

*We waited over here at Chy's mill in order to give the people a chance to start selling cattle.*

*—I climbed up to the foot of S. el Tigre, and was able to look over S. Durarno and see that the Sierra Madre at this part seems to form a continual chain from where it rises just south of Carretas till as far as I could see to the south.*

*—Got a few things straightened up on my map, with the help of Bill who showed me a good many errors. Bill says the Canyon of the Caves is an invention of Moroni Fenn's. Also that the Fimbres Apache Expedition was really for the purpose of taking men down in this country to hunt and prospect. As for the Apaches, he does not believe any were killed last March by Moroni Fenn and says the only way they will ever catch them is to run them with dogs, as it is impossible to track them. The big ranches, who have suffered most from their depredations, will not put up any money to hunt them.*

### Neil's Diary, El Paso, Texas

That's how Aïda Desouches Gabilondo remembers it too. Now over seventy years old, elegant, cosmopolitan, with a raucous, bawdy sense of humor, she's the daughter of Liolito Gabilondo, whose Sonora headquarters at Colonia Oaxaca my father has already visited. Gabilondo is one of the big ranchers just across the mountains in Chihuahua. Many of them were owned and operated by Americans or Europeans and were often corporate enterprises, especially before the Mexican Revolution. The Gabilondos are an old Sonora and Chihuahua family, and have ranched in the area for well over a century. Like many of the northern ranching families, they always had a pied-à-terre in El Paso, and now Aïda lives there full time.

She remembers that there was an Indian camp in the mountains above the ranch, and that her father tolerated the loss of a few cows every year. "They never bothered anyone—why not let them have a few?" In Nácori Chico, the ranches were very much smaller, and the loss of even small quantities of livestock and crops was a serious economic matter that did not go unanswered. Because of this and perhaps because of old, deep-seated resentments in Sonora, the conflict escalated sharply to all-out violence in Nácori Chico. This was the chance to settle an old score with the odds reversed and the mission of extermination at last within reach.

### Grenville's Diary, cont'd.

*That the Apaches have rifles is certain, as Bill says he found a reloading outfit for a 44 cal. rifle in one of the S. Espuela camps as well as an empty powder horn, some lead, and some empty 45–70 revolver cartridges.*

*—Last evening we had an interesting talk with an old Opata Indian who works here.[24] He was born in Huachinera over 70 years ago, and remembers much that happened in the old days, knowing by name Geronimo, Juh, Cochise, Mangas Coloradas, and Victorio. He wanted to know if the latter was still alive as there was an old man, a friend of his, who had fought against Victorio in Chihuahua. Of the Geronimo campaigns, he remembered the coming of the troops, and the killing of an American Captain by the hostiles down below here. He saw them bringing him back to the U.S. in a coffin by mule.*

*(This was Captain Crawford, in command of a U.S. scouting party, after the hostiles, who was shot somewhere to the east of Nacori, Jan., 1886, when his party met a body of irregular Mexican troops under command of a Major Correador. Captain Crawford was buried at Nacori, and two months later taken up, and brought to the U.S.).[25]*

*The U.S. troops, according to him, went as far south as Nacori, and a little beyond. In Bacerac there are 2 women, now living, and married to Mexicans, who are Apaches, taken when mere girls from the Apaches during the old wars. One is Cruz Valencia at Bacerac, and the other is Maria Samaniego at Huachinera.*

### Neil's Diary, Huachinera, Sonora

Everyone knows everyone else in the villages of the Bavispe River Valley, and we have learned that sooner or later a detail like this in my father's diary can be coaxed into a human drama if only we can find where it's hiding.

Entirely by accident we discover a member of the Samaniego family: Doña Natalia Samaniego Bruda de Davila, one of the oldest people in the village of Huachinera. Her bright and businesslike granddaughter, Angelica, lives next door and looks after her. We find this again and again—frail old ladies who are treasured by their families and seem always to be blessed with granddaughters who stay close at hand to keep them company and help out around the house.

Natalia is ninety-one, a pale, luminous, ethereal presence in the dim kitchen. She remembers that there was an Apache captive named Maria, and that Antonia Samaniego, her paternal great-grandmother, bought Maria for five pesos in Bavispe when Maria was three years old. Boys could be bought for ten pesos, but no boys were available, so Antonia Samaniego bought Maria.

Apache children captured after battles were bought and sold as slaves—standard Mexican practice in the nineteenth century when Maria was acquired. The Mexicans appear to have been thorough in documenting these captives, though I would have thought they'd have preferred that such captives simply disappear without a trace. One list of captive Apaches, dated June 12, 1885, gives name, age, gender, place and date of capture, as well as the name and location of the family to whom the captive was sent.[26] The list states that following the Battle of Alisos Canyon, in 1882, a ten-year-old girl—certainly the same girl my father speaks of—was taken in by the Juan Jose Samaniego family of Bavispe and given the name of Maria.

Natalia Samaniego remembers only that Maria eventually married, and that she may have continued to live in Huachinera. She remembers another name, Lola, the name of a woman who also lives in the village who may know more; then her memory blurs.

### Neil's Diary, Huachinera

Six months later we are back, and we have found Lola of Huachinera to hear the story of Maria Samaniego, the Apache captive.

It's a quiet Sunday morning—a good time to visit because people are usually home. We sit in the dappled light in front of her house. Lola's dogs are collapsed in the dust in the middle of the lane. Lola speaks in a gentle, almost reverent voice that drops to a whisper at sentence end. She chain-smokes, makes sarcastic political jokes, and says that because of robbers, she always keeps a machete and a loaded pistol in the house. She says she is only following the example of her intrepid grandmother who had encountered intruding thieves on two occasions. Her grandmother lopped off the hand of one with her machete, and the other she shot dead.

Although the record indicates that Maria Samaniego was caught during the 1882 Battle of Alisos Canyon, Lola has a version of her capture that has altered the actual events of that ferocious massacre beyond all recognition. She says the Apache girl was caught in the 1880s or 1890s on one of those rare occasions when a group of Mexican villagers ventured into the foothills of the Sierra.

At a place she called the Sierra de los Alisos, in the mountains just to the east of Huachinera, there was a small encampment of Apaches. Lola says they were "tired Indians." Some Mexican cowboys looking for cattle came upon this camp suddenly. There was no fight, and no one was hurt, but the Apaches, taken by surprise, were terrified and fled, leaving three children behind. There were two girls dressed only in gee-strings and a boy with no clothes at all.

One little girl, about three years old, was raised by a family in Huachinera and was named Loreta Cortes. A little boy of seven years was taken by a family in Bavispe, and they called him "Tutuaca." The other girl became Maria Samaniego.

Lola points to a pile of adobe across the road from her house. That's where Maria lived, she says. Fragments of Maria's life drift in and out of our conversation with Lola, never quite coalescing into a whole. When she was a little girl, Lola knew Maria well, and her description is an odd mixture of the mundane and the poignant.

She was, Lola begins, not skinny. Not fat either.

She wore her hair in one long braid, had high cheekbones, was tall and, when she walked, her gait was different, not like a Mexican's. Maria, of course, knew what she was, but the Samaniego family never reminded her about her people, nor did she ever speak of it herself, though it was clearly common knowledge in the villages of the valley. Lola says Maria always averted her eyes when she spoke to people, as if she were ashamed. In fact this behavior is no more than proper Apache etiquette, and must have been ingrained in Maria at a very young age.[27] Among the people of these villages, bitter memories of the years of warfare would have been part of every day life and conversation. Maria would have heard it all, and it would have reinforced her natural reserve.

Eventually Maria married a Mexican, Antonio Bácame, and they had four children, all of whom have since died, some in childhood. There was, Lola remembers, a Chinese doctor who used to come over the mountains from Casas Grandes in Chihuahua. He looked after Maria from time to time and declared that her children were sickly because Mexican and Apache blood did not mix well.

Lola remembers that the other Apache captive, Loreto Cortes, never married, worked as a cook or housekeeper in various ranches, and was not "friendly." The boy, Tutuaca, was raised by a family in Bavispe. All Lola could tell us about him was that he never married and that he was killed by lightning while working in a field.

These stories are like bolts of cloth, caught for years in the thorn thickets of Sonora, reduced to ragged shreds by time and the wind. Like the people we talk to, those captured Apaches were once vivid and possessed of presence, force, passion, but they are now only vague memories. It keeps running through my mind that the boy was bought for ten pesos and the two little girls for five apiece. It was standard practice.

### Grenville's Diary, cont'd.

*He (the old Opata Indian) remembers a big fight between Apaches and Mexican troops which took place in Arroyo de los Alisos, on the east side of S. Chita Hueca, near Carretas Ranch, which lasted 2 days, a good many Mexican and Apaches being killed. There were about 300 Apaches in this fight. The reason for this battle coming off as it did was that there was an Apache in Bavispe at this time, friendly to the Mexican, who had told them the place to be in order to catch the Indians. Both sides had percussion locks and cartridge rifles, as well as one or two flint locks still in use.*

### Neil's Diary, Bavispe

Barney and Nelda and I have made some new friends: Francisco Zozaya and his wife. Francisco is known locally as an amateur historian, and people say we should talk to him. He is a born storyteller and has spent a lifetime gathering and remembering the oral history of the town.

Because, in 1930, my father is talking with people who might well have been alive in the 1880s, I am not at all surprised that he hears of a turncoat Apache ready to help the Mexicans. But it is astounding when, some sixty years later, we hear the same story from Francisco Zozaya, in even greater detail than Grennie did. Francisco knows all about the "friendly Apache" who told the Mexicans when the rest of the Chiricahuas would be passing through on their way south into the Sierra Madre. This was an Apache known as El Gato Negro who served as a scout to the Mexican military. He settled in Bavispe, and there were, until 1950, descendants of El Gato Negro, named Arista, still living in Bavispe.[28]

As a result of this tip-off, on April 27, 1882, Colonel Lorenzo García of the Sixth Mexican Infantry ambushed a large group of Warm Springs Apaches under Chief Loco that had recently fled San Carlos. According to the Mexicans' careful body count, seventy-eight Apaches, most of them women and children, were killed. At least thirty-six were captured and sold into servitude in Sonora, one of them Maria Samaniego.

### Grenville's Diary, cont'd.

*Janos was the place where the treaties were signed with the Apaches, who when traveling down always stayed to that side of the mountains, the east.[29]*

*This Opata says that most of his tribe are dead, and that the language is not spoken any more, just a few still retaining some of the words. The ollas used in this locality now are made by the descendants of the Opatas here in the valley.*

*—Formerly Bavispe was a presidio and had a sentinel house on the top of the hill there, to guard against Apache raids.*

*—There is a ruin on the mesa just south of Bavispe which I looked over. The pottery as far as I can tell is the Casas Grandes type.*

*—Miguel Torazon, a man from whom Bill is buying cattle, says that there were no Americans in the party which killed the 3 Apaches last April. There was one man in the party from Huachinera who brought back 2 tanned cowhide blankets which they took from the Apaches. They also took a deck of horse hide playing cards, and a doll about 16 in. high, dressed as a man with knife in belt, and a feather headdress on of some sort.*

### Neil's Diary, Bavispe

Francisco Zozaya is less well informed about Apache Juan and the Fimbres attack than those in Nácori Chico, but he is an authority on the Bavispe locale. He knew Agustin González, one of the men who discovered the Apache camp in the Chita Hueca Mountains to the east in 1929, and it was from hearing the old man tell stories that Francisco's passion for history grew. He feels it is fundamentally important in a way I didn't quite understand at first, but he practices it as an art form, and it is through the recitation of his knowledge of history that he expresses himself. This is never more vivid than when he draws his maps and illustrations. He creates diagrams of old Apache campaigns of the nineteenth century and portraits of the characters in his stories. They are lovingly done with graphic and narrative power. He has them waiting for us when we return to see him months later. He sends them to me in the mail. It is as if he understands that the language barrier that separates us can be surmounted with his eloquent pictures.

Francisco's pictures contain material we have seen nowhere else: the locations of Apache campsites, migration routes used by Apaches in and out of Mexico, the Apache names of Apaches whom I have always known by the names in American history books. Francisco has a few books in his house, but the breadth of his knowledge goes beyond books. He is telling us the oral history and folklore version of events that we have only read about.

We have been deep in discussion for an hour or so and have been talking about my father and the people he met while he was here in this very town in 1930. Francisco says, "You know your papa was maybe in this very room. This was the house of Miguel Torazon's mother." We open the diary and look at my father's photographs of the village, taken from the hill above. "There's my house," says Francisco. "There's Doctor Spencer's," adding, "He delivered me and most of the other children in town then. He was the only doctor in town."

He turns another page and looks at a picture of an unidentified man in front of the Bavispe church, and says,

"Where did you get that picture? I have the same picture. That's my papa."

"My father took that picture," I say. "If that's your father, then they knew each other, and my father sent it to your father."

My father hardly ever did anything without some reason. He not only took this picture, and sent a copy of it to Francisco Zozaya's father, Jesús, he also pasted it into his diary. Jesús knew Bill Curtis well; Francisco heard his father speak of Bill often, but never heard his father speak of mine. We are both intrigued, puzzled, and his interest in my quest deepens.

As forthcoming as he has already been with his understanding of the Sierra Madre Apaches, this unexpected personal link has created common ground that I never expected to find.

## 11

# Enemy People

**Dec. 13, 1930, El Paso Púlpito, Sonora, Grenville's Diary**

*Today Bill went to see cattle at Miguel Torazon's ranch, near Dos Cabezas. I rode back here to the camp, coming across the big mesa at the foot of Chita Hueca, east of Colonia Oaxaca, and not getting in till after dark. It's 26 miles from Bavispe to Colonia Oaxaca, and must be about the same from Bavispe to Púlpito.*

**Dec. 15, 1930, El Paso Púlpito, Sonora**

*Today Art and I rode from here to Liolito Gabilondo's ranch at Las Varas, just across in Chihuahua, and at the head of Paso Púlpito. About 4 miles up from camp, Púlpito Creek swings over to the north and runs back into S. Espuela. We had a good view of the S. Espuela. They were rough looking and appeared to be an oak country, except along the high ridges where it looked as though pine grew. The head of the pass is a white oak country, with big, open, grassy flats. There was one ruin of the regular type here on the flat. Gabilondo comes in by car from Hachita to his ranch.[1] He says it is 260 miles by car to El Paso, 40 miles to Janos, and 75 miles to Casas Grandes.*

*About the Apache camp on Chita Hueca, he says his foreman Reyes and another man were the first to see it, finding a cave with some tanned cowhides in it, and later seeing the brush fence of their corral, which he said was quite large. The camp consisted of seven brush houses, the big corral, and a smaller one, and a little reservoir to catch rainwater in. Here they found tanned hides, some baskets, a part of a forge stolen from Gabilondo, some blocks of American cattle salt. Gabilondo says that the Apache had stolen 4 sets of harness from him, of which they found 2 in the camp, but not the collars. They had fastened 2 of the tugs together and made one long one out of them. They found the harness and part of one set of harness on an ox in a pasture near camp, the Apaches having neglected to remove them. He said he thought they had probably hauled brush or wood with the harness. In his opinion those Indians are mixed with Mexicans.*

**Neil's Diary, Bavispe**

Francisco Zozaya says that the old cowboy, Agustin González, knew for a fact that there were whites mixed in with the Apaches in that camp. He had seen them himself: a young Anglo man and woman, probably Americans. He described them as wearing leather and as being well armed. He believes they were either buying or trading with the Apaches for the tanned hides of the livestock they stole from the big ranches.

Francisco goes on to say that the young man was killed by the Apaches because he told the foreman at the Gabilondo Ranch what the Apaches were doing. The fate of the young woman was unknown. Although this intriguing fragment suggests that the Apaches may have been stealing cattle in Mexico and moving them across the border, I am skeptical about the details of this story.

We frequently hear about secretive, solitary people who were thought to run with the Apaches. Francisco continues, settling into the beginning of an epic story about a man named Bil Bao, who may have been Swiss, maybe Irish — that's all we hear until later — and who lived in the Sierra Tasahuinora, east of Bavispe, with a pack of dogs. Living in a remote box canyon, where he built a tree house in an immense cottonwood, he did some small-scale farming and probably some hunting and prospecting. Living like that, he would have had the opportunity to make contact with Apaches. In fact, Francisco continues, he could not have lived there without the consent and cooperation of the Apaches. The Tasahuinora was a vast wilderness and a known Apache refuge. No one in his right mind would be there without the friendship of the Apaches. More to the point, one would only go there to seek out the friendship of the Apaches.

Whites who run with the Apaches. The mythical renegade who once was one of "us" and now is one of "them." Mexicans feel a shudder of loathing and fascination at this act of betrayal and metamorphosis. The possibility that there may well be such people makes the stories we hear about them correspondingly compelling. Lupe herself said that there was a redheaded white man in her own band before capture.[2] Many times we have heard old cowboys say that pinecone hairbrushes with red hair in them had been found in Apache camps.

### Neil's Diary, Nácori Chico

"When they killed Apache Juan in 1930," says Rafaela Ruiz, "there were two women. One of them was 'American.' She was very beautiful, and they say she had blue eyes. They used to say she was the daughter of an American, Señor Thomas. The one who lived up near La Hosita. It's near Nácori, up there by Rancho Corral de Piedra. Señor Thomas was a miner and he got his supplies from the U.S. The Apaches used to pay him with stolen goods."

Rafaela goes on, repeating her favorite particular: "Others say she was a white captive who chose to stay with the Apache. A lot of people remember she was beautiful, with big beautiful eyes."

The girl's beauty is a striking detail, intriguing in its contrast with the stereotypical Apache bloodlust. Is it remotely possible that time and folklore has softened some Mexicans' collective memory of Apaches, transforming at least one of them into an exotic Rima-like creature? Or perhaps her appeal is as a corrupted beauty, a truly fallen angel. This mystery woman may not be real, but she has become part of the story.

I find that there is even an element of my father in this kind of figure—a white man who ran with the Apaches. He is the other side of the coin of the outlaw renegade; he is a man of peace who moved in both worlds and who underwent a kind of metamorphosis among the Apaches at San Carlos and Fort Apache. They remember him as someone who liked to sit and talk with the elders in their own language. They remember him as someone who respected them as he respected himself, who approached them as an equal, and who, in spite of himself, was irreversibly entering their world.

### Dec. 16, 1930, El Paso Púlpito, Sonora, Grenville's Diary

*Went up to caves on the creek and took down pictures there. One of them looked a lot like Apache or Navajo work. Tried to rob a couple of bee caves but they didn't have any honey.*

### Neil's Diary, Mescalero, New Mexico

The grandfather of Berle Kanseah, my Chiricahua friend, was one of Geronimo's youngest warriors. He ran with Geronimo during the terrible summer of 1886 and, with Geronimo, surrendered and was sent to Florida. Berle acquired much of his profound knowledge of the culture from his grandfather, Jasper.

I am visiting with Berle and show him the drawings my father made. He looks at the more figurative and sophisticated designs and says they look interesting, but are definitely not of Apache origin, though the simple geometric designs on page 40 of the diary (circles and wavy lines) might well be. They bear a strong resemblance to known Apache rock art on cave walls in the Dragoon Mountains of Arizona. On the corner of page 144 there is a complex abstract geometric figure sketched in pencil. Berle immediately identifies it as Apache work.

### Dec. 19, 1930; El Paso Púlpito, Sonora, Grenville's Diary

*Today Art and I went hunting to south of camp and I killed my first deer, a white-tailed buck. Brought him back to camp in the evening.*

### Dec. 21, 1930, El Paso Púlpito, Sonora

*Five of Miguel Torazon's men came in with some of Bill's cattle this evening. One was a Yaqui who appeared to be of typical Mexican Indian type, with light beard and mustache. Found a good stone ax right at the corner of the goat corral today.*

### Dec. 22, 1930, El Paso Púlpito, Sonora

*Torazon's men went today, and we moved the cattle into a good grassy place, up the creek. In afternoon Art and I explored all of cave opposite camp, and found it to go far back, about 400 feet in one place. Found a pocket in rear of cave which had a good many sticks in it, and among them 3 spears or darts, made the same time as the arrows of cave, except for no feathers. The arrows found in the cave are of 3 types. The first is one of cane with a hard wood fore point, the same as an Apache arrow, except that the feathering extends slightly farther. The second is similar to the first, except for it being smaller all the way around, with short feathering, and bands of color in red and black, painted on shaft where feathering is. The third type has a wooden shaft which seems to be of willow, and is pointed with a hard wood tip, in other respects being similar to the first type in measurements, etc. Only one foreshaft which had a stone point in it was found.*

*—Ramon Vegas says that he thinks the Apaches which were camped on S. Chita Hueca had some Americans with them, or possibly Mexicans, as he was told that some hair of a light color, human, had been found in the camp, as well as some El Toro cigarette packages and a cigar. He thinks they must trade at some place for ammunition, etc. That their camp was well hidden is shown by the fact that Ramon and Reyes rode over Chita Hueca several times when the Apaches were there and never saw sign of them.*

## Neil's Diary, Bavispe

That the Apaches maintain contact with the "civilized world" and are at the same time masters of concealment is a favorite paradox in Mexican folklore describing Apache sleight of hand.

*Concealment:* Francisco Zozaya says that when the camp on the Chita Hueca was discovered the Mexicans tried to follow the Apaches, but the Apaches hid along the trail. The Mexicans rode right past their hiding place. They discovered this later as they backtracked and found the place where a large group of Apaches had hidden in the bushes and behind rocks along the trail. Men, women, children, even babies had not made a sound or otherwise betrayed their presence. Then the Apache disappearing act: they had scattered like quail and vanished into the Tasahuinora.

Over the years the Mexicans became used to what amounts to Apache invisibility. Rarely could they find Apaches when they wanted to, and they knew the Apaches could watch them from hiding whenever they chose. If someone said that a group of mounted Mexicans passed within a few feet of a band of concealed Apaches without ever seeing them, no one in the Bavispe Valley would doubt it.

In the old days, Apaches had Power. Melferd Yuzos, a remarkable Chiricahua holy man, described it to me like this: "Whatever was around them, they had the power to turn to that. They could turn to rock, and the soldiers would walk right by them and never see them." Apache children were taught from a young age how to hide. If there was danger they would be told to go to a certain place and hide, to become the rock, become the tree, remaining utterly motionless until someone came for them.

*Contact:* A rancher named Valenzuela from Nácori Chico sustained so many losses for which Apaches were responsible that he eventually had to abandon his ranch, but before he did, this is what happened to him.

Out looking for strays one day, Valenzuela comes upon an Apache asleep under a pine tree and decides it's a good chance to kill a thieving Indian. He will do it with a big rock. Hefting a boulder over his head, he soundlessly approaches the sleeping man. Valenzuela hears a rustle behind him. Turning, off balance with the rock still held high, he finds himself covered by three Apaches with rifles. He lowers the stone, drops it, and quickly shapes a cross in the air before him, his last act, for sure. But—awaking, the resting Apache speaks to Valenzuela in Spanish, first saying that he is Juan, the chief. They talk. Valenzuela asks where he has learned Spanish. The Apache only says that at times he puts on conventional clothes and comes down out of the Sierra to walk the streets of Nacozari, Agua Prieta, and Douglas unrecognized. Much to Valenzuela's astonishment, Juan lets him go.[3]

This could be true. Apaches may have been dressing like whites and mingling with them for generations, and according to one account (see chapter 4, above), the renegade Natcułba•ye did it in the 1890s. It would have been easy for Juan to do so as well. He was bold and reckless and would have known that an Indian face would go unnoticed in the streets of most Mexican towns. But of course, it is also possible that the man who had the brass to dare the Mexicans to come out and fight by night—"Yo soy Indio Juan"—might also have had the wit to want some fun with Valenzuela: first he spares his life, then pulls his leg with a bit of bravado.

### Dec. 23, 1930, El Paso Púlpito, Sonora, Grenville's Diary

*Today Art and I set out for the Chita Hueca peak, south of camp. Were gone all day, till 8 this evening. Went up by ridge east of big mesa. It was an oak country till we got clear up on the high part where it turned to manzanita, pinon, and cypress. The country was very rough and brushy, on the north slopes the ground being frozen hard. In sheltered north slopes some pines grew to fair size, as they also did on the crest of the mountain at this part. From here we could see the plains of Chihuahua bordering the Sierra Madres and stretching far to the east. The Sierra Medio lay out in this plain, to the northeast, a distance of about 10 miles. This range is near 25 miles long, running north and south. The crest of the S. Espuela was visible in the northeast section of that range, as was also Hatchet Mountain, far to the northeast, in the U.S. All the country west of the Sierra Madres appeared rough and broken by mountain ranges running north and south. We came back by the canyon between the two peaks. This was quite brushy and had a good many large cypress in it. The manzanita grew large here, and had red berries on them which were good eating. Saw quite a few bear sign in this canyon. On return we found Bill in camp, and we leave for Douglas and the States tomorrow.*

## Dec. 24, 1930, Douglas, Arizona

*Left the camp in El Paso Púlpito, and took car on to Douglas, getting in there about 11 P.M. Bill says the Chihuahua plains border the S. Madres on the east for a long way south. He's going to go down into Nácori Chico about the middle of Jan., and says I can go with him if I want. There is a good chance to pick up some of the things taken from the 3 Apaches killed near there last April.*

*— This ends the first trip to Mexico.*

## Neil's Diary, Douglas, Arizona

Grennie never hints, on paper, at his personal reaction to the adventure he is beginning, but still I often wonder if he is a closet romantic. He was at this point perhaps more archaeologist than anthropologist. As rigorous a science as archaeology is, it is also a dreamer's game. It has a certain romance, a certain mystery, and it would appeal to the imagination of someone like Grennie, for whom the past has a tangible reality: there is always the chance of finding "buried treasure," and Grennie knows he has found the scent of ethnographic buried treasure — in the form of artifacts and oral history in Nácori Chico and elsewhere. Just as important as knowing there is treasure to be found is his guide and priceless ally and mentor, Bill Curtis. As long as he is with Bill, he has a ticket to Nácori Chico, and with it some of the secrets of the Sierra Madre Apache. Bill is trusted, and if Grennie tags along no questions will be asked. There is no telling how an overinquisitive, unaccompanied outsider would be received in the tight little world at the end of the line in Ná-cori Chico.

Through Bill, the fates of Francisco, Gerardo, and Maria Dolores Fimbres, of Apache Juan and of Lupe, have become known to my father, and his exploratory search has led me to the rest of the story. More like an epic, it is a blend of history and mythology about the region, the ways of the Sierra Madre Apaches, and the American and Mexican outcasts who may be trafficking with them.

Most intriguing, Grennie has every reason to believe that there are still Apaches in the mountains—in the Nácori Chico area and to the north, near the border. Their tracks have been spotted by cowboys, but, perhaps not surprisingly, given the Apache gift for invisibility, there has been no contact for eight months since the Mexicans killed Apache Juan in March 1930. No one seems to know how many groups there are, how they are distributed, how they move through the Sierra Madre, and whether or not they have any contact with reservation Apaches. At this point, neither do I.

6. Pulpit Rock, October 1996.

7. Above: Petroglyphs in the caves in El Paso Púlpito.

8. Left: Grenville Goodwin and his first deer, El Paso Púlpito, 1930.

9. Top right: The church at Bacerac, 1930.

10. Bottom right: The church at Bacerac, 1996. Photo by Seth Goodwin.

11. Top: Nelda, Lola Barela,
and Barney, Huachinera, 1996.

12. Below: Bavispe, 1996.

# Part Three

# 12
# Taking Stock

**Jan. 18, 1931, Douglas, Arizona, Grenville's Diary**
*Came back and looked up Bill. He's not going down to Nácori Chico af-*
*ter all, so I guess I'll go up onto the Fort Apache reservation for a time.*

**Neil's Diary, Tucson, Arizona**
Grennie is a sophomore at the University of Arizona, and he has registered for four courses in the second semester: Descriptive Astron-
omy, Botany, Latin American Republics, and Ethnology. He wants to
know more about the stars, the plants, Mexico, and the craft he will
be practicing for the foreseeable future. It is an interesting mix for a
course of study, but it pales in comparison with the experience he
has just had in the Sierra Madre. Given the chance, he is perfectly
willing to skip school and go right back to Mexico with Bill. Perhaps
he intended to skip school anyway, because, even though the Mexico trip is off, Grennie slips off to Fort Apache, certain there is more
to be learned there than at the University of Arizona.

But how he must have wished that Bill was going to Nácori Chico.
Grennie would have met the people in the photograph — Francisco
and Cayetano Fimbres, Felipe Grajeda, Dolores Fuentes.

Perhaps most important of all, my father might have met Lupe.
Imagine what he could have learned from her. He was just beginning
to understand the Apache language, and he would have been able to
study her dialect, compare her speech with what he had learned from
the Apaches in Arizona. He might have been able to identify it as either Western Apache or Chiricahua.

Probably about thirty years old, she was not yet refusing to talk
about her life as an Apache and would certainly have talked with my
father, as she did in 1938 to another anthropologist, Helge Ingstad. He
managed to conduct the only recorded interview with Lupe about
her life before capture.

I inquired as to whether her people had any connection with the Apaches
on the San Carlos Reservation, but she avoided this question. She is bitter
about San Carlos.

Her father was a scout for the American soldiers in San Carlos, but was arrested and then killed two men. She went on to say that he fled to the Sierra Madre and that he and her mother were killed by Mexicans and that she was taken captive. Her father was quite a warrior she added.

## Neil's Diary, Tucson

Lupe had told others that her mother was a Western Apache kidnapped from Solomonville, Arizona, and this intriguing reference implies that Lupe's father could well be Western Apache. An article in the *Douglas Daily Dispatch* of Feb. 1, 1929, quotes Moroni Fenn's assertion that she told him that her father was the Apache Kid. To be sure, Lupe's account of the circumstances of her father's escape bears a vague resemblance to that of the Apache Kid, not to mention numerous other Apaches in trouble with the reservation authorities.[1] Whether her father was the Apache Kid or not is of far less interest than Lupe's apparent knowledge of San Carlos—presumably through her mother and father or other members of her group. She might have been able to remember the names of people who moved back and forth, the Apache names of her parents and other people in her own band, and, most important, their clan affiliations. The Chiricahuas do not have clans, but the Western Apaches do; and if Lupe's people had clans, this information would have been key to Grennie's understanding of the Sierra Madre Apache and where they came from.

Ingstad's interview continues:

She said she lived with ten to fifteen other people, mostly women. She said they often sewed rawhide around their horses hooves, leaving the confusing tracks so often mentioned by Mexicans.

They sang and told stories, although they kept fairly quiet so as not to be discovered.

Mexicans say that they would tie branches or grasses to their feet to obliterate foot prints as they walked. A wounded and bleeding Apache would pick up any blood-soaked dust and throw it away to make his trail harder to follow.

A white man—an old fellow with red hair—lived with them for a while, but eventually disappeared.

In regard to how many Apaches there were in the Sierra Madre when she lived there she couldn't really say, because they all stayed pretty much in small bands that had little contact with each other. Sometimes a man would go in search of animals for food and never return. They never felt safe.

They had a couple of guns, but very little ammunition. They lived mostly on deer meat, mescal, roots and berries. They made fires by rubbing sticks together.

They lived entirely off of what could be found in the mountains, and had to make everything by hand, and they owned almost nothing. They wore clothes made of deer, and sometimes cow leather. They wore moccasins that went high up the ankle. Sometimes women wore skirts, but often pants.[2]

## Neil's Diary, Tucson

From neither of these descriptions, nor from the descriptions of recovered artifacts, would Grennie have been able to know conclusively whether these people were Chiricahua or Western Apache. What he might have found instead, especially after talking with Lupe, was a blend of the two cultures, as she remembered it from her girlhood before capture, about fifteen years earlier.

Although the most recognizably Chiricahua items in the "victory photograph" are the long moccasins with the upturned toes, as described by Lupe to Ingstad, these were not worn only by Chiricahuas, as many nineteenth-century photographs of Western Apaches reveal. She apparently did not say anything to Ingstad about the dolls so frequently found by Mexicans. From their descriptions, the dolls found in Apache Juan's pouch closely resemble known Chiricahua dolls as well as Western Apache dolls. They were made of buckskin, were stuffed with grass, and had no features.[3]

Not surprisingly, captured Apache toys are remembered by many people. Beula MacNeil, now in her vigorous eighties, is the daughter of Joe Fenn, Moroni Fenn's brother. She tells us that she grew up with a pair of Apache dolls her father and uncle Moroni carried away after jumping an Apache camp before she was born. They were her mother's treasured possessions and the children could not play with them —they were only allowed to look. They were a man and a woman, about a foot high, dressed in dark clothes, she remembers. The man had on high moccasins with little bells down the side.

Others that we speak with remember toy horses, toy saddles, clay whistles, and clay rattles—symbols of play and sanctuary—eloquent in their contrast with what appear to have been the stark realities of life for the Sierra Madre Apache, and in contrast with the inhuman stereotype promulgated in the press of the day.

A mental inventory of the descriptions of campsites and artifacts tells me much about the Apaches. But both these details and the details of the escalating violence make me wonder how the Apaches must have seen the fast-changing world around them.

A glance at the chronology in appendix 1 shows a series of events that mark contact between the Apaches and recorded history. Following Geronimo's surrender in 1886 there is frequent contact and occasional violence, and it all culminates on October 15, 1927, as Maria Dolores is killed and Gerardo abducted, setting the stage for the seemingly inevitable outcome: a fight to the death. And if the outcome was inevitable, how did it all begin, that is, begin again, following Geronimo's surrender, the watershed event that was supposed to have brought hostilities to an end?

At its most fundamental level, the conflict between settlers and Apaches had always been largely about land, about territory. Even before the end of the Apache Wars, a noose was being slowly tightened around the Apache heartland in the Sierra Madre.

All along the eastern flank of Apache country there were immense ranches, many established in the late nineteenth century, some much earlier. During the 1890s the Mormons began to settle in the Sierra, and by the end of that decade copper mines were being developed at Cananea and Nacozari, just to the west of the Bavispe River Valley. Colonel William Greene of the Cananea Copper Company had acquired the logging rights to millions of Sierra Madre acres: the entire range from the Carretas Pass nearly to the Barranca del Cobre — all Apache country. William Randolph Hearst's father, U.S. Senator George Hearst, had had, since 1882, an immense hacienda in the Baviacora Valley, south of Greene's logging empire. Lord Delaval Beresford, a colorful, ne'er-do-well Anglo-Irish remittance man, had the historic San Pedro Ojitos ranch, located where the Carretas Plains meet the Sierra Madre.[4]

Fear of the Apaches ran so deep among most Mexican small holders that it was not until after the turn of the century that they began to settle in the mountains. The villages of Altamirano and Los Pozos were settled in 1908 by Mexican homesteaders in the heart of the Sierra Madre in Chihuahua, just south of the Carretas Plains. From the Sonora side, families began moving into the mountains from the villages of the Bavispe Valley. By 1910 there was a mine at Piños Altos, and there were small ranches at Tres Rios, Mesa Tres Rios, and south of Nácori Chico on the Bonito River. For the first time, families of farmers and ranchers were moving into the mountain heartland, and they were staying. There were more and more of them, fewer and fewer Apaches.

Events in the mountains of Sonora and Chihuahua were taking place against an historical backdrop of the greatest turbulence. Between 1910 and 1920, Mexico was in a state of political chaos. At times there was virtually no government, and it is conceivable that the Apaches saw and took advantage of this situation. At the same time the widespread revolutionary violence might have made it convenient to blame certain acts on the Apaches.

Sometime after 1915, approximately when Lupe was captured, the pattern of increasing contact with the Mexicans must have made the Apaches realize that territory was being irretrievably lost, that they were trapped, and that it would be only a matter of time before they would be safe nowhere in their homeland.

In 1920, perhaps precipitated by a combination of all these factors, the violence seemed to escalate. As the decade advanced, there were, almost every year, killings, kidnappings, stolen livestock, and ambushes, as well as the usual mischief. Increased settlement and a general atmosphere of violence and lawlessness meant that, as contact between the Apaches and the Mexicans became more common, it was bound to cause friction anew. Now, however, for perhaps the first time, the Mexicans had the upper hand.

# 13
# The San Carlos Connection

**May 26, 1931, Tucson, Arizona, Grenville's Diary**

*This afternoon read Lumholtz's book,* Unknown Mexico *in which he gives the account of a trip he made in 1891–1892, from the region of Nacori, south along the Sierra Madre to its lower part in southern Mexico. He states in this book that at this time it was still dangerous for small parties to cross the mountains into Chihuahua, due to the presence of dissatisfied Apaches from San Carlos, who were then in the Sierra Madre. In the region of the head of the Rio Bavispe, Pacheco, and Chuhuichupa, his party ran across yuccas with their leaves tied in a certain way, and rocks piled one on top of the other, both left as signs by the Apaches. A Mexican officer visited their camp in pursuit of a band of Apaches, from whom he had taken their horses.*[1]

*—Have been saving all clippings from the Douglas Dispatch, of which up to date there are several.*

**Neil's Diary, Tucson, Arizona**

His mind buzzing with what he heard in Mexico during the fall, my father finishes out the school year. The only class in which he's not barely passing is Ethnology, in which he predictably excels. He then moves up to the San Carlos Reservation for the summer for an intensive study of the Apache language. He is learning to speak Apache by ear, and as he does so he compiles a grammar and a dictionary. At summer's end he has gathered hundreds of pages on Apache linguistic construction and vocabulary.

By now my father counts some very close friends among the Apaches he has met, and he goes out for several weeks in the summer of 1931 with two Apache cowboys who are looking after the tribe's herd of cattle. He makes a ground rule: only Apache is to be spoken. He believes that the language is the key to the culture and to mutual trust.

**Aug. 1931, San Carlos Res., Arizona, Grenville's Diary**

*This summer, while out with two Apache Indians, from Bylas, I heard several stories concerning the Apache Indians who still remain wild in the Sierra Madre of Mexico. They are as follows.*

*—About 1895 the Apache Kid appeared on the San Carlos Res., and Fort Apache Res., with four Chiricahua men who had come up with him from Old Mexico to steal Indian girls and women, which they wanted to take back with them to Mexico. They succeeded in stealing a girl of the* tá(ha)gaidń *clan,[2] from Fort Apache. This girl was then some eighteen years of age. From Fort Apache, the raiders then proceeded to the San Carlos Riv., near Rice. Here they ran onto a Tonto Apache and his wife out working in the brush. The Kid killed the Tonto, and took his wife, who he gave to his Chiricahua companions, while he went off to see if there were more women about. As soon as he went, the four Chiricahuas, who apparently did not approve of the killing, told the woman to hide from that crazy one (the Kid), so he could not steal her. She did so, concealing herself in a pile of grass close by. Just then the Kid came back, and asked where the woman Tonto was. The Chiricahuas said she had run away. The Kid soon found her in the grass and pulled her out. She struck at him with a stick she had, but without result. At this juncture the four Chiricahuas forced him to turn the woman loose. She made her way as quickly as possible to San Carlos to inform the Agent of what was going on. Now the Kid and his companions went on by Peridot, where they took the daughter of one Marsil, a brave man. Marsil pursued and tried to rope the Kid, as he had no gun. The Kid shot at him, but missed, and the raiders now fearing organized pursuit, turned his girl loose, and left, down river. A little below was a canyon through which they had to pass. Here the Agent had sent his Indian police, mostly all Tontos, to ambush the five raiders. The police sergeant saw them coming, and made his men let them ride by unmolested, for what reason it is hard to say. At any rate they got safely away, but with only the one captive from Fort Apache. The Agent at San Carlos was so disgusted with his police for their action, that he fired the whole bunch.*

**Neil's Diary, San Carlos, Arizona**

Many of those I talk to here speak darkly of the Apache Kid. I even hear of the lingering fear among his living relatives that they might suffer repercussions for the crimes he committed. In the 1930s he was the most recent paradigm of Apache infamy, and my father's field diaries record conversations that are peppered with the vivid folklore surrounding the Kid.

The Apache Kid was a Western Apache who served as an army scout. Convicted of attempted murder in an 1887 brawl, he escaped en route to jail. The other convicts with him were accounted for, and the Kid disappeared alone into Mexico, where he formed an Apache outlaw gang. The four Chiricahuas with him in the account recorded by my father could have been either renegades from San Carlos or resident Sierra Madre Apaches.

Two years after hearing this story, Grennie hears more about the kidnapped girl, noting that she was the sister of a man named Hooke Smith. He writes, "Dja'okin was the name of the White Mountain tá(ha)gaidń girl who was stolen by the Sierra Madre Apache about 30 years ago. She has never come back."[3]

As frightened as people on the reservation were of the Kid, there is an undercurrent of admiration in the stories my father and others have recorded about him. The Kid was a dark folk hero, a celebrated outlaw. He was at large in Mexico, living off the land, raiding when he felt like it. It was the old Apache way.

### Grenville's Diary, cont'd.

—*Somewhere around 1908, when they were putting in a new section of the Southern Pacific, between Willcox and Bowie, there were some Apaches from the San Carlos Res. working for the railroad. A man and three women were camped at a section house along the line, by themselves. The man was working on the tracks, the women were out gathering food. About mid-morning three Chiricahua and the Apache Kid rode up. They had come from down in Mexico, to steal women. The man saw them coming and called to the women to warn them to hide. They did so, but one of them, a young girl at that time (now a medicine woman at Bylas), was seen by the raiders. They chased her, but she took refuge in a deep arroyo, and although they rode their horses right to the edge of the bank, they did not see her. Being afraid to stay around longer, the raiders went on, but did not catch any girls or women. All of them, the Kid, and the three Chiricahua, had on white men's or Mexican's hats.*

**Neil's Diary, San Carlos, Arizona**

The Kid may not have been among these Sierra Madre Apaches at all. He is reliably reported to have been killed in 1899 by two Mormon cowboys in Mexico.[4] On the other hand, there are stories in circulation at San Carlos stating that, as recently as the 1930s, the Kid was alive and in occasional touch with distant relations on the reservation. There is almost no way any longer to untangle the facts from the snarl of folklore that surrounds the Kid. It's almost as if he planned it that way.

**Neil's Diary, Mesa, Arizona**

Mesa is a largely Mormon enclave, a suburb of Phoenix, Arizona. I'm talking with Annie MacNeil Thompson, whose family history is inextricably tied to the legend of the Apache Kid. She was married to Elmer Thompson, one of two survivors of an 1892 Apache attack on the Mexican Mormon settlement of Colonia García, also known as Cave Valley. The attack was widely blamed on the Apache Kid, but the Mormons say there was no way to be absolutely certain he was responsible. I am intrigued by this story for many reasons. It is one of the most thoroughly documented of all the attacks, and it was virtually the only violent attack on a Mormon settlement. Its brutality was such that it was soon blamed on the notorious Apache Kid, although throughout the 1890s there were depredations that could have been committed by other "renegade" Apaches as well as the Apache Kid.

SEPT. 22, 1892

A small group of Apaches has been seen near Col. Juárez, edging the foothills of the Sierra Madre, going south, and it is known that they have been stealing cattle. A mixed posse of Mexicans and Mormons follow them but lose the trail and assume they have returned to the United States. Since Apaches are so infrequently seen on this side of the Sierra Madre, people think they are coming down from the U.S. reservations and that they won't linger. No warning is circulated.

The Thompsons are from Denmark. They have a farm on the Chihuahua side of the mountains in a place called Cave Valley. There are several other Mormon families settled here on farms a few miles apart. It's beautiful, rolling, fertile country with large open meadows and big stands of ponderosa pine. It's high enough so that it escapes the brutal summer heat of lowland Chihuahua and Sonora. The winters are mild — it's an ideal climate. The Mormons are the first non-Indians ever to settle here.

The Thompson family consists of Hans and Karen, the parents, six-year-old Annie (not to be confused with Annie MacNeil, whom I am interviewing), and several sons, of whom Hiram and Elmer are the youngest two. Hans is a polygamist and has another wife, Jensine, who lives in the town of Colonia Juárez in the valley about thirty miles away. He moves back and forth between the two households. In Cave Valley they have a few cows and fields of corn and wheat. Being Mormons, the various neighboring families help each other with the work.

It's harvest time, and Hans is away at another farm with the older sons. Karen is in the house. Elmer, fourteen, and his brother Hiram, seventeen, are in the barnyard doing chores. Annie is carrying a copper tub to the house.

She screams: "Hiram, Elmer. Look!"

An Indian appears at the corner of the barn and shoots Hiram. Hiram falls and begs the Indian not to shoot him again. Elmer tells his brother to be brave, not to act afraid. Elmer starts for the house where his mother is. Another Indian appears and points his rifle at Elmer. Elmer remembers his father's advice: "If someone is going to shoot you, take a deep breath — the bullet will be less likely to kill you." Elmer takes a bullet through the chest and he goes down playing dead. The first Indian shoots Hiram again. Annie runs toward the house to find Karen.

Karen rushes out of the house.

She says, "Take anything you want. Please don't shed any blood."

An Indian man, speaking in English, says, "We like to shed blood." And he shoots her in the stomach. Annie is watching.

Karen holds her arms across her abdomen and staggers to a bench just outside the house, where she sits and throws her full skirts over little Annie, hiding her. Unseen by the Indians, Elmer gets up and ducks into a chicken coop.

The women in the group find Karen sitting on the bench. They pick up big rocks and close around her, striking her head, her face, her hands. Then Karen drops to the ground and is still.

In the struggle Annie is discovered. The Indians chase her through the yard, one of the men whipping at her legs with a leather strap, knocking her down.

Annie has moxie. She is wearing an old-fashioned sunbonnet, and she snatches it off and hits back with it—her tiny rage transporting her beyond terror. The Indians laugh at her, then seem to forget about her and resume looting. They are ransacking the house, ripping open valises, smashing things.

Elmer beckons Annie into the chicken coop where they hide together, expecting discovery and then death, or worse. It never comes. Inexplicably, the Indians suddenly leave, taking two big cheeses and several horses.

In the barnyard, Hiram is still alive, though he has been shot twice. He nods when Elmer asks how he is. Elmer and Annie decide to go for help, and Elmer whistles for his horse. The horse comes, but, getting closer, smells the blood from Elmer's wound and shies away. The two children have to go for help on foot to the nearest farm, several miles away. Elmer is soon too weak from loss of blood to go farther, so Annie runs on ahead.

She meets her neighbor, Robert Vance, on the road. She's been running hard. She stops to catch her breath and can't say anything for a few moments. Vance waits.

Annie finally gets it out: "The Indians are real bad over at our place."

The people organize a rescue party for Elmer, lying somewhere by the side of the road, and for his brother back at the farm. They send someone to find Hans at the neighbor's farm. Elmer they save, but it is too late for Hiram, and Karen is dead by the house.

The pioneer Mormon community and the survivors try to pick up the pieces of this horror. Elmer is taken in by the Seveys, a neighboring family. Annie moves in with Jensine, Hans's other wife in Colonia Juárez. A doctor who examines Elmer is amazed, saying no one takes a bullet through the lung and survives.

And Hans, what about Hans, his wife and son brutally murdered while he is away, his young son and daughter scarred for life? At least the boy carries a red badge of courage. Hans is no coward, of course. He just wasn't there.

This was not Hans's first brush with family tragedy or with Indian hostility. On the trek west from Nebraska to Salt Lake, three of his children died. He took a bullet in his foot and an arrow in his side up in Utah in another fight with Indians in 1866. The bullet wound turned gangrenous, and it cost him part of his foot. His next journey—by wagon from Salt Lake to the Mexican Sierra Madre—was an epic of endurance and hardship during which he buried one of his three wives.

Within six months of the massacre Hans volunteers for a church mission back in Denmark. He leaves his devastated family in Mexico so as to convert more Danish souls to join the Latter-Day Saints in the new world. He stays abroad until 1895, at which point he returns with convert children whom he deposits with his surviving wife, Jensine, in Colonia Juárez, and then continues on into the mountains, where he spends the rest of his life, rarely seeing his family.

The record omits far more than it tells. It is hard to imagine an experience more alien for a native-born Dane than massacre by Apaches in Mexico, but, on the other hand, that's who the Vikings were: Danes, born to go far from home and fear nothing.[5]

### Grenville's Diary, cont'd.

*About 1919 the Bylas Indians found the tracks of four Chiricahua men, who had come up from old Mexico, and passed along the north side of Mountain Turnbull, right back of Bylas. Shortly after, these same Chiricahua were seen by an Indian man, near Cibecue, with whom they talked at a distance. They said they had come, not to make any trouble, but only to get girls to take back to Mexico with them; that they had lots of young men down there, but no wives for them. The Cibecue man of course warned all the camps, and no girls were allowed off alone, so the Chiricahuas went back to Mexico no better off than they first started.*

*—They say that some white men killed the Apache Kid some years ago, in Mexico. The Kid used to have a zig-zag design, in blue, tattooed on his forehead.*

### Neil's Diary, San Carlos, Arizona

Whether it was the Kid and his gang or other Apaches from Mexico who made the 1895, 1908, and 1919 visits to the American reservations, it is puzzling that they were coming to steal women, claiming that they had plenty of young men, but no women for them. In none of the attacks on Apache Juan's band were any young men killed or observed. Where were they? As Lupe told Ingstad, her band was mostly women. She added, intriguingly, that they were visited from time to time by men who did not live with them. She also told him that there were several widely separated bands, so these Sierra Madre Apaches who visited San Carlos may well have been groups different from hers. For all their trouble, they were remarkably unsuccessful in their kidnap attempts. They stole only one girl (in about 1895) that my father hears of. Lupe's mother and cousin (who were stolen in about 1900) make three.

Perhaps they were coming for horses as well, as they had in 1929, according to my father's conversation with an Apache policeman at Fort Apache. During the early decades of the century there was an abundance of wild "Indian ponies" on San Carlos.[6] These, in fact were, according to Apache oral history, descended from the small horses brought in over many years from Mexico, and were treasured for their stamina and surefootedness.[7] There were so many of these horses on the reservation that the BIA undertook to round them up and remove them in the 1930s, as they were said to be overgrazing the range. Prior to that time, the number of horses on the reservations was certainly common knowledge among the Apaches of the Sierra Madre. Although a trip from Mexico to San Carlos may seem a very long one to make just for horses, some of the Sierra Madre Apaches might well have seen some advantage in stealing horses from the reservation rather than in Mexico. At least on the reservation the wild horses would not have been missed.

## 14
# Close Encounters

**Sept. 22, 1931, Douglas, Arizona, Grenville's Diary**

*Through at Bylas for the time being, so came down here in hopes of getting down to Mexico with Bill Curtis. Found him all right, and we—Bill, his wife, another man, and myself, all go back down to Colonia Oaxaca, where Bill is now living, by way of Chihuahua.*

**Neil's Diary, Douglas**

In Grennie's second trip to Mexico lies the ethnographic heart of his diary: the exploration of two recently abandoned Apache camps. To rediscover one of the camps using the diary was first on my agenda when I began this journey in 1976. Finding the camp was for me a trial, a test, a labor, which, if I could accomplish it, would entitle, even compel me to continue.

**Neil's Diary, Colonia Oaxaca**

Barney, Tom, Misse, and I have driven due south from Douglas down the Bavispe River Valley to our first campsite only a short distance from Colonia Oaxaca. From what Grennie says, he and Bill plan to come in another way—via Chihuahua. This probably means driving east along the border from Douglas to the remote, often unmanned border crossing at Antelope Wells in the New Mexico Bootheel. From there they will enter Chihuahua and go south across the Carretas Plains to Rancho Las Varas, and then cross the Pulpit Pass to its western end at Colonia Oaxaca. In view of what happens next, I think Bill wanted to take this route to avoid the gauntlet of customs officials in Douglas and Agua Prieta. Before leaving for Chihuahua, he briefly crosses the border at Agua Prieta and makes an unpleasant discovery that forces a change of plans.

**Sept. 29, 1931, Colonia Oaxaca, Sonora, Grenville's Diary**

*Bill got in trouble with the customs officials on the Mexican side, and so we had to lay over till today, that Bill might bring back his saddles, guns, harness, etc., which the line riders had taken back to Agua Prieta, when they raided his house at Colonia Oaxaca.*

*Left Agua Prieta in late afternoon, and went direct to Colonia Oaxaca, getting there about 3 A.M. in the morning. It rained hard all the way down. Art and an old Mexican were at the house in Col. Oaxaca, and much excited over Bill's trouble with the Mexican line riders. It seems that shortly after Bill had left Col. Oaxaca, and gone out to Douglas this last time, three line riders had ridden up to the house where Art and old Jose, the Mexican were. They entered and searched the house for contraband, seizing everything Bill had there which did not bear a duty paid mark.*

*For the next three days they stayed at the house, officially waiting for Bill, then in Douglas, but making themselves generally at home, much to the disgust of Art, and the fright of old José, whom they quirted, and threatened to hang from the big Chinaberry tree in the yard. The quirting part was no joke, the hanging part was, but at any rate old José took both seriously. At the end of three days, the line riders left, with their contraband, for Agua Prieta, much to José's relief.*

### Neil's Diary, Colonia Dublán, Chihuahua

Mexico was in a state of political upheaval at this time. The most recent insurrection to have been put down was the 1929 Cristero Rebellion, an uprising of militant Catholics against the harsh anti-clerical policies of the government. Political control of the state of Sonora had just changed hands as a result of scandal and corruption at the highest levels of administration in the state.[1]

This unrest made the long, remote border between Mexico and the United States into a smuggling venue with an attractive risk-to-benefit ratio. There was an appetite for guns, ammunition, and other manufactured goods in Mexico. Prohibition in the United States added alcohol to the already-heavy traffic in marijuana, stolen cattle, and many other things moving north across the border.

According to one of Bill's nephews, the Curtis family's oral tradition identifies Uncle Bill as a black sheep — a smuggler and a gambler whose goat ranch was nothing more than a front for a contraband enterprise. Presumably he would move goods of all kinds both ways across the border, including the single item whose value the gamy old Bill Curtis would seem least likely to admire: expensive French perfumes.[2]

Apparently both American and Mexican customs officials tried to get Bill to inform for them because he knew all the smugglers along the border. Of course, if Bill had done that, his life would not have been worth a plugged nickel. In any case, he would have been caught in the middle. The confiscation of property and the three-day visit from Mexican Customs might well have been the price Bill had to pay for noncooperation. On top of that, I expect the officials who visited Bill thought they might be able to shake him down for a mighty bribe.

### Oct. 3, 1931, Colonia Oaxaca, Sonora, Grenville's Diary

*—Yesterday an American, by name of Stewart Hunt, came in from Chihuahua with a team and wagon, on his way back to his ranch in the upper end of the S. Espuela. It was he whose man was killed while packing some grub and a cooking outfit from one ranch to another. The glasses found on the edge of the cornfield were taken from this American when they killed him. When Stewart Hunt stopped with us at Oaxaca this time, he had one of this American's little boys with him, whom he had undertaken to raise.*[3]

### Neil's Diary, The Bavispe Valley

As I travel, I constantly meet people who knew Stewart Hunt well. I even spoke to his only son José not long before he died in 1997. Although José, born in 1928, lived with Stewart on the Tapila Ranch (described above by my father) from the age of four, he does not remember anything about the boy who was with Hunt in 1931, when my father met him.

Stewart Hunt was one of those American cattlemen who was drawn to the prospects south of the border around the turn of the century. He was born in 1872 in Mississippi, came West with two of his brothers, and by 1906 was sheriff of Cochise County and something of a cattle baron in both Mexico and the United States.

### Grenville's Diary, cont'd.

*—Hunt also said that about 15 years ago he was living at a ranch he owned, on the south end of the S. del Tigre, about due west of Huachinera. Across the mountain from him was a Mexican rancher. Horses from both ranches started to disappear, and each rancher suspected the other of stealing. Hunt, who had some good hounds at his place, noticed*

that they were restless, and barked more than usual. One day when he was riding through the mountains nearby, he came on a freshly made mound of earth, from which steam was rising. He opened it to see what it was, and found mescal in process of roasting. This he left unmolested, and kept on his way.

Some days later when out again, his dogs took a trail which at first he thought must be a lion. On following it up, he found his dogs holding an old Apache woman at bay, under a small ledge where she was trying to protect herself. Hunt took her in to his ranch, and gave her all she could eat, afterwards turning her loose. She had not been scared of him at all, but was much frightened of his dogs. Even though at a cold time of year, this old woman was wearing only a gee string, a sort of small buckskin cape about her shoulders, and a good pair of high moccasins.[4] She had been gathering a species of small, wild onion, of which she had about 2 double handfuls in a little sack.

Another day one of his dogs took up a trail. Hunt called him off, but the dog sneaked out again. He never showed up again. Later on, Hunt came on the same old woman again. She was in the bottom of a little canyon. Close by was lying one dead horse, and she was just preparing to kill another belonging to Stewart Hunt. The way she killed them was to lance them in the chest with a long, sharp stick, thus piercing the heart.

This time Hunt took her into jail at Moctezuma. While there, a man by the name of Bennett, who had been a govt. scout, and spoke some Apache, talked with this old woman. She said that she had been sent off by her people to get food, and was going to make jerky out of the horses she killed. She admitted that her people had killed one of Hunt's dogs (the one that never came back). She said she had been many times to the corn fields about the Mexican town of Oputo, by night, to steal corn. Also she claimed that her people could have killed Hunt many times when he rode through the mountains, but had refrained from doing so because he was a good man. Later on this old woman killed herself by falling from the jail house wall in Moctezuma,[5] from which place she was trying to escape.[6]

Eventually Hunt found the cave in which these Apaches had been living, and it was at quite a distance from where he caught the old woman. The entrance was a small hole in a bluff, and did not appear big enough to amount to much, but inside it was large. Here he found *three horse hides belonging to him and his neighboring Mexican rancher, still bearing their brands. Other things they had stolen were in the cave also. The Apaches had been camped out on a point of the bluff, above the cave, in a well concealed place. Oputo was plainly visible from this place.*

### Neil's Diary, Huachinera

I'm with Barney and Nelda. Simon Rodriguez is ninety-two, the oldest man in town. We have found him in the shade in front of his house. He wears an undershirt and is brandishing a blue flyswatter.

Simon is a fierce old citizen with bloodshot eyes. His leathery hide is loose, as if it were a size too big. His voice hoarse and rasping, he bellows thinly, so as to hear himself through layers of deafness. He leans, scowling, locking Barney and Nelda with a ferocious red eye.

Because Huachinera is the town closest to the ranch Stewart Hunt had in 1915, we have guessed that the oldest man in town would remember the capture and dramatic death of the old Apache woman caught and jailed in Moctezuma. Don Simon Rodriguez does, and then some.

His memory for detail is extraordinary. As if it had happened only yesterday, he recites without a moment's hesitation the names of the five cowboys who caught the old woman who was stealing horses. When he adds the fifth name it is an exclamation: "Audutio Rodriguez! *Mi padre!*"

The oral history of this valley is like a great river. It joins the people together, and because it has swept up Simon Rodriguez and his father it joins me with my own father. This time, close to shore, we have found a deep, swift, cold current that feels as if it has come nearly undiluted from the source.

Barney, not wanting to ask leading questions, wanting to make sure Don Simon is remembering the right event, just asks who the horses belonged to. The old man needs no time to think, but shouts, one digit skewering the air between his face and Barney's,

"*Estuart!*"

Stewart Hunt. It is wonderful.

He remembers that when the old Apache woman was taken to Moctezuma, no one could talk to her, but that there was an American there who could speak Apache and interpreted for her, just as

Hunt told my father in 1931. She told him, says Simon, that she had four sons. "My sons are good sons," she said to the interpreter.

Stewart Hunt said that the interpreter was a man named Bennett who once campaigned with the Apache scouts in the U.S. army. He says no more about Bennett, but, in all probability the only man this could have been was one Frank P. Bennett, who served in the Apache campaigns in Arizona and New Mexico from 1881 to 1886—for part of that time as chief of scouts. He might well have picked up some Apache vocabulary that would have enabled him to communicate with the captive woman.[7]

Don Simon goes on to say that after the old woman's death her four sons went east, deeper into the Sierra Madre, to join Apache Juan. Don Simon raises the intriguing possibility that the old woman may fit into the Apache Juan story. The scattered bands of Apaches were almost certainly in some kind of contact with one another. Could the back-to-back captures of Lupe and the old woman—both of which took place around 1915—have ignited in any of the Apaches some kind of inclination for vengeance? Since about 1900 there had been fifteen years of uneasy standoff between the Apaches and the Mexicans of northern Sonora and Chihuahua, but within a very few years of 1915 the violence and raiding began again leading to its explosive climax in the late 1920s.

During the 1920s and '30s Simon's Rancho el Salto in Puerto de los Guacamayos—Parrot Pass—was one of the very few ranches in the mountains. He spent a great deal of time looking after his cattle, so he was no stranger to the Apache presence. They were all over the El Tigre Mountains, west of Huachinera. He saw their camps in many places, and they stole cattle from him once. They made houses of bent oak limbs, covered with beargrass. There was one bed in each house. Some rancherias had six houses—others, four; still others were cliff dwellings or in caves. Lots of bones were found in the camps, and these people ate their meat with salt. They wore trousers and shirts of buckskin.

Barney asks him, "Weren't you afraid of the Apaches?"

"No!" he bellows. "No! I had a good gun and a good pistol. My rifle was a .30 and my pistol was a .38."

He names all the places where he saw Apache camps, the names rippling out as if he had just been there: El Cajon del Salto, Arroyo

Taste, Sierra de la Nutria, Arroyo de los Jucoros, Rancho Santa Anaute.

Twenty miles to the southeast in the Sierra Madre there is a mountain that once had no Mexican name. Now it is called the Sierra Tobacco because that is the name Don Simon gave it. It was where he found a buckskin bag filled with tobacco left there by the Apaches.

As is the way with all folklore, there is another story about this place. Cliff Bowman, a Mormon hunter and guide who lives on the other side of the Sierra Madre, tells us that a man named Cirilo Perez gave the place the name Sierra Tobacco, because that is where he lost a pouch of tobacco sometime shortly after 1925. I relish the possibility that Don Simon had found Cirilo's pouch, making this a place that had been named twice for the same tobacco.[8]

There is another place that Don Simon says never had a name until it was given one by him: Cerro del Caballo — Stallion Hill.

Around 1930 the Apaches stole fifteen mares and one stallion from a spread called Rancho de las Villas. The stallion was a mean black stallion. After stealing the horses and taking them into the mountains, the Apaches lassoed the stallion with a horsehair rope and passed the rope over the limb of a tree, and hung him from that tree. They then killed him and butchered him, taking all the meat and leaving the skeleton hanging from the tree. Simon found the hanging skeleton and so gave the mountain its name: Cerro de la Caballo.

### Neil's Diary, the Next Day

Don Simon instructs us to pay a visit to Doña Lola Barela. By now Lola is an old friend, for she has already told us about the Apache captive girl, Maria Samaniego, mentioned in Grennie's diary. We find Lola at home, and, as usual, she wants to talk outside the house so she can keep an eye on things.

An occasional pedestrian or rider goes by, but it is Sunday and quiet for a Mexican village. The noises are swallowed by distance and sky today, blurring the roosters, dogs, burros, car radios with blown-out, overdriven speakers into a mutter. Lola tells us the kind of story I treasure: a melodramatic, operatic evolution of the same story my father heard from Stewart Hunt in 1931.

Lola says, "There was an Apache, a woman who was caught at La Cueva de la India. The woman had stolen and then killed a horse.

The woman was captured and taken out to Moctezuma. While in jail she cried, and said that her brother Juan was a good man. She said that she did not want to die.

"She had money, and she called for mescal and whiskey to drink. The woman asked if musicians could be brought in so she could dance. They were, and they played music while she danced. She drank the mescal, and prayed in her own religion. It was as if she was performing a ceremony, a religious ceremony.

"She said that she did not want to die, but she had many drinks, then while dancing, she made her way to the roof and jumped off to her death.

"When the local authorities examined her for burial the old woman turned out to be a man."

In a version told by another, the old Apache woman rammed her head into a stone wall in the jail cell, killing herself. I have heard that the Mexicans called her "Salome."[9] The name caught my attention because it made no sense—until Lola told us about the death dance. It is hard to imagine how a cross-dressing doppelganger also found his way into this story. The original Salome was all woman.

What Stewart Hunt tells my father about her is probably as close to the truth as I will get. She made an unforgettable impression on Hunt: a gaunt old woman who caught and killed a horse he remembered as almost too wild to handle; an old woman who had the defiance to tell him she knew his every move and could have killed him many times, but did not because he was a good man. Was she looking for mercy, bargaining for her life, or telling him what would be in store if he were to harm her? An old woman who would rather risk her life and lose it than stay in the Moctezuma jail.

### Oct. 6, 1931, El Paso Púlpito, Sonora, Grenville's Diary

*—There is an old man, an uncle of Ramon Vegas, Bill's cowboy at the caves, living there with him. He had a pair of high moccasins, like those of the Apaches, which he was making for himself. He said he had learned how to make them from the Apaches, who took him captive about seventy years ago. This happened when he was a boy of about ten years, near the town of Ures. He was gathering Chilicothe beans near his home, when the Indians came on him. For 11 months he was with Chi's people, and then for 9 months with Geronimo's people. One day the In-*

*dians were going to a Mexican field near Ures. In the corn were some Mexican women and a man. The Indians came on them suddenly and were so startled that they ran off, leaving their Mexican boy captive behind. The Mexicans saw him and called him over. This way he was returned to his own people.*

### Neil's Diary, Mescalero, New Mexico

At first I thought *Chi* might be a reference to Juh, the Ndéndaa'i leader. Now I am not at all sure. In Bavispe we have heard Francisco Zozaya refer to an Apache by the name of "Chis." But while talking with my Chiricahua friend, Berle Kanseah, at the Mescalero Apache Reservation, I learn that *chish* means "wood" and that it is one of the roots of the name Cochise. In fact, "Chis" is the name by which Cochise is known in Mexico.[10] Berle goes on to say that a similar-sounding word, *dich'ish*, means "rough" or someone who is rough-textured—leathery and uncouth—as if he lived out of doors. Soon after this visit I hear from Nelda Villa, my historian friend from Mexico, that *chis* (probably the Mexicanization of *dich'ish*) is an expression in local Mexican usage, meaning "hombres del bosque," or people who live in the out of doors. The expression *shis inday*, which means exactly the same thing, appears in both Ingstad's and Lumholtz's books.[11] Though local Mexicans do not know the origin of the expression, it is certain to have been borrowed from the Apache *dich'ish nde*, meaning "people of the forest, of the bush."

### Oct. 9, 1931, El Paso Púlpito, Sonora, Grenville's Diary

*Marcos, the son of Ramon's wife, by a former husband, is going to the Apache camp on Chita Hueca with Art and I, as he has been there before, and knows the way. I guess we will leave after shearing.*

*— The day before yesterday, Art and I went up to the caves to get some chili and corn. On the way back to the adobe house we met a man from Bavispe, on horse who said he was headed for Las Varas. Yesterday morning Ramon's brother in law stopped in on his way to Col. Oaxaca, and said that this man from Bavispe had shot himself in the leg while getting off his horse at the caves. The gun had gone off when it fell from the hitching rack to the ground. Marcos had gone for his father, the wounded man's, at Bavispe in the night, and they expected the father back this afternoon.*

*Yesterday afternoon Art and I went up to the caves, and saw the wounded man. The ball was still in his leg and he was suffering pretty much. His father got in all right.*

*The goat herder went up to the caves and spent last night there, coming back this morning with lots of news from Bavispe. It seems that two Americans, part of a bunch of five, all well armed, and with good outfit, who have been camped on the head of Pulpit Creek, had been put in jail at Bavispe, along with Chy. Six* ofiscales *had come into town, from a tip-off, and found 8000 rounds of ammunition, 3 saddles and two rifles, all in Chy's mill. All these they had confiscated, being contraband, and belonging to these two Americans, who were staying with Chy. The* ofiscales *had turned the two Americans loose finally, and they had immediately left those parts. Chy only had been kept in jail, and was now being taken to Agua Prieta, on a lead mule, tied and handcuffed. He apparently had talked too much.*

### Neil's Diary, Colonia Dublán, Chihuahua

Beula MacNeill is telling us that it was actually her husband, Wayne, who owned this mill, and that Chy would only have been operating it for him. When we ask her whether Chy had ever done any smuggling, she says with a grin that she doubts it very much. Why was he arrested, then? Beula hasn't thought about her checkered past for a long time, but it comes welling up now, to her vast amusement.

"Maybe Chy went with Wayne a trip or two, but my husband was the bootlegger, and I actually went with him smuggling. I lay down on a fender of the car, and him driving with me flashing the flashlight. We couldn't put our car lights on because they'd see us, and we'd cross near Antelope Wells. My husband smuggled silver. I remember great big beautiful pieces like this of *plata* that he took to the United States. Native silver. They tied it underneath the bottom of the car to smuggle it over."

As Beula talks, I wonder if there is a chance that Chy could have been taking a fall for Wayne. Like the mill in Bavispe, the ranch at the head of Pulpit Pass where the five Americans were camped is Las Varas, at the time owned by Beula's husband, Wayne MacNeil.

### Grenville's Diary, cont'd.

*—This morning they took the wounded man out to Agua Prieta in a truck, to a doctor. I doubt if he has much of a chance to save his leg.*

### Oct. 10, 1931, Col. Oaxaca, Sonora, Grenville's Diary

*Art and I went down to Oaxaca today, and we spent the night here. It turned out that Chy had been taken to Agua Prieta all right, but not in irons. He and his escort had stopped off here on their way out, about two days ago. Old José had immediately taken to the brush on seeing the* ofiscales, *and did not return till they left. He hadn't forgotten his proposed hanging by the* ofiscales *who had raided Bill's place in Sept.*

*Bill, who had gone out to Agua Prieta a few days ago, came in with a load of Mexicans from Nacozari mines, which have closed down. He is taking them over to Casas Grandes tomorrow.*

### Oct. 13, 1931, El Paso Púlpito, Sonora

*Bill came back from Casas Grandes today, with some grub, which we needed badly. He took a load of goats on out with him. Art and I missed him as we were hunting around the north end of Pulpit Rock. Marcos got back today also, and I guess we start for the Apache camp, on Chita Hueca, the day after tomorrow.*

### Neil's Diary, Sierra Chita Hueca, Chihuahua

The Chita Hueca Apache camp was discovered in 1929 by cowboys from the Gabilondo Ranch. It was the first one Grennie went to, and, because it is in country that Barney and Tom know well, it is the one we have decided to try and find first. We break camp where we have spent the night at the head of Pulpit Pass, not far from where Bill's adobe house was in 1931. On the way through the pass I keep looking for any feature, any landmark that my father may have mentioned in the diary.

We enter the lower end of the pass through which Pulpit Creek flows. In fact there is room for little in the bottom of the pass except the creek, so much of the time we drive along the streambed. It makes a better road than some we have seen. We try to spot Bill Curtis's house, but although there are one or two adobe ruins to be seen, we can't be sure.

This is one of only three similar thoroughfares across the Sierra Madre in a region running south from the U.S. line for three hundred miles. It is as if from the Canadian border to Long Island Sound there were only three east—west roads of any kind through New England. These three twisting tracks through the Sierra Madre are all main roads and carry a good deal of traffic, which crawls over the ruts and boulders. There are, of course, no road signs, though there is one official plaque that was installed by the Mexican government declaring that the road was improved in 1936.

We're climbing now, corkscrewing through sharp switchbacks until we top out at the head of the pass, where we pay our respects to a small travelers' shrine: a peso a head and one for the car. Miles later, we arrive at Rancho Santa Anita, the Gabilondo headquarters—a tight gathering of low white buildings on the plains of Chihuahua, surrounded by the only substantial stand of trees for miles around.

The main house is not old but large and comfortable, almost baronial. In spite of the land reforms, a kind of feudalism survives on the big haciendas. When we arrive a man rolls out from beneath a gutted tractor, and we exchange courtesies about the nature of machines, the weather, the growing season, and then ask him about old vaqueros who might know about Apache camps. We are directed inside to the foreman for permission and information.

As is the custom in Mexico and the Southwest, welcoming strangers after a long trip is a solemn undertaking. Good manners are a mark of character, and the foreman is generous, attentive, and serious—almost grave. He assumes the responsibility of host and temporary advisor for our search for Apache camp remains. We spend much time talking to him and other cowboys that he sends for. Soon there are several men poring over the diary, the photos, and the maps, discussing them with increasing animation and puzzlement. Tom's rapid, fluent Spanish marks him as a border native, like them.

It is curious what a short half-life oral history has on the east side of the mountains. These immense sprawling ranches are empty, unpopulated space. The stories have dissipated like water from a rock tank. The human intercourse in the Bavispe Valley across the mountains will not allow the stories to disappear. They crystallize, take on a life of their own, and bind the people together.

The cowboys all agree that there is one who would know most about the Apache camps, but add that he is out administering artificial insemination to a cow. Without his advice, they can think of only one place we ought to consider—an old mining camp—and one man offers to go with us as a guide.

He takes us up the east flank of the Azules (Sierra Chita Hueca in the diary) near the north end, to an old manganese mine, but it is clearly not right—none of the landmarks fit. We drop the man back at the ranch and return to the base of the mountains, where we make camp in an arroyo near the ruins of the old Ojos Azules Ranch that Gabilondo's men built in 1925–26. It was when this outlying ranch was being built that the Apache camp was discovered. We decide that the only way to find the camp will be to study the mountainside from below in the morning, compare it with the maps and photos in the diary, and try to match up landmarks.

# 15
# An Apache Camp

**Oct. 15, 1931, Apache Camp, S. Chita Hueca, Chihuahua,**
**Grenville's Diary**

*Left the Pulpit this morning with one pack mule, and riding two horses and a mule. Came by a trail across the hills, and struck in above Las Varas, and to the south. Passed Ojos Azules, one of Gabilondo's ranches, in the after noon and struck in towards the side of S. Chita Hueca. The horses and mules were pretty tired as we had come at a pretty fast pace.*

*—This side of S. Chita Hueca slopes up steeply to a rim, the top of the mountain. The slopes are covered with blue oak, manzanita, silver leaf oak, New Jersey tea, a little Chihuahua pine, and some yellow pine, black locust, and a few aspens in the northern sheltered draws. The soil here is extremely gravelly. Along the foot of the mountain, and running out to the east for about five miles, are rolling hills which terminate in the* llano, *a level, grassy, open plain, stretching for a great distance to north, east, and south.*

**Neil's Diary, Sierra Chita Hueca**

I wake early and take the diary and binoculars to a spot just above the arroyo where our camp is.

The big problem is to find some key feature, a positive locator. This small range is perhaps six miles from north to south, but the east side here is one of steep relief cut by abrupt canyons and gullies. Unless we are able to go right to the old Apache camp, we might spend days finding it.

My father's map shows a prominent knob at the south end of the Apache camp, separated from the mesa by a saddle. As I slowly scan the slope above me with binoculars, I see only one place on the entire mountainside corresponding to that feature.

The early-morning sun casts a distinct shadow that might not have been there at all later in the day. The other features fit in generally with the diagram, but from where I stand it still takes optimism to match the map to the mountain. Yesterday when we made camp Barney and Tom insisted that this is the mountain. The locals don't even use the name "Chita Hueca" any more. The mountain is called Sierra Azul. Barney and Tom could be wrong—we could be miles away.

Nevertheless, when they get up there is a general agreement that the location of the camp is as likely to be next to the knob and saddle I have been watching as anywhere. We pack up camp and move off past the old Ojos Azules building and over into the next valley, where we find quite a good road that leads up the canyon. The ground is littered with softball-size chunks of volcanic debris.

Near the end of the road we encounter an old cowboy, Guadalupe Quesada, with whom we spend some time. He knows nothing of the Apache camp here, but says that his uncle had long ago told him of one on the west side of the Azules. His uncle had apparently seen them and had talked with them. The trail freshens.

Guadalupe is wearing an ancient baseball cap, chaps, boots, spurs, and a tattered jacket. He rides a small shaggy horse that tossed him off earlier that day, landing him shoulder first on an oak snag. He is still stiff and sore, and all his movements are cautious and experimental.

We move off on foot. The hillside is brushy, and the volcanic debris makes footing treacherous. Barney gets separated and reaches the ridge at a higher point than the rest of us. After stopping for lunch at a lower point on the ridge of rock, Barney says he thinks it more promising higher up the ridge where he has already been. We spend a long time reexamining the maps, photographs, and the notes, trying to reconstruct the camp.

So far we have seen no real sign of it—which is not surprising as it had always been well hidden. What's more, the brush is thick everywhere, and forty-five years have elapsed since my father was here. The ridge we are on still looks to be the most promising one, judging from Grennie's photos and maps. In one of his two photos, there are two unmistakable outcrops of rock where the camp was; we appear to be on the lower one.

We split up and resume searching. I head up the hill with the diary. I pick up a small bit of sheet metal that appears to have been an implement of some kind. There are bones here and there, but so far no sign of the stone foundations of the huts. By now I am very high up the ridge. After passing the second outcrop, the going becomes steeper and steeper, the brush somewhat less thick, the groundcover trending more to the grass that feeds the Gabilondo cattle that roam all through these hills.

I hear a shout from below—unintelligible, but I start down. There it is again—Misse is yelling—and a few minutes later I find them all sitting around the stone foundations of the old houses.

I must have nearly walked through them on the way up. There isn't much left—only the low rock walls of the foundations of one of the houses, bits of coiled wire that had held the fencing together (now all rotted away), a bottle, an old Prince Albert tobacco can, a metal bucket rim, and a stone metate.

I stare at the metate and experience a powerful but fleeting sensation I have sometimes when I am somewhere for the first time, but everything's familiar, as if I'd been there before. I sit and open the diary, looking for pictures. There it is: a photograph taken by my father forty-five years ago of the same metate resting on the old foundation wall in the same position it's in now. It makes me lightheaded to see it, and when I shut my eyes there comes a vivid, unbidden image of my father busily surveying the scene, walking through the brush toward me, intent, slightly out of breath, measuring distances, taking more pictures, making diagrams and maps and drawings of the houses, cataloging, indexing, listing everything. He seems exhilarated, breathless, serious, very sure of what he is doing. He's hatless, lean, fit. He looks just a boy.

He never imagines that a lifetime later his own son will come back, guided by his doggedly thorough directions, and will try to imagine what that day in October 1931 had been like for him.

My mother says he was sort of psychic.

Years after finding this camp, Barney told me: "Grenville once called to me."

This is what happened. Barney was driving east of Tucson down a side road through the desert to visit a friend. He remembered that my father was buried somewhere east of town. Feeling drawn—as if, he said, he was being beckoned—he stopped, got out of his car, and began walking east through the thick mesquite and cactus underbrush. There was nothing to guide him, nothing to see ahead. He was just walking. Within ten minutes he was standing by my father's grave. He just walked right to it. It is not in a cemetery, but alone in the desert, on the ranch we had when I was very young but which Barney had never seen. Barney felt blessed, but his mind was reeling. It is the kind of encounter after which nothing is quite the same.

Barney does not go looking for experiences like this. He doesn't cultivate the spiritual, but he is ever at ease and at home in terra incognita. He is never lost. Better yet, unseen places and unknown people seem to summon him, and then he finds the very thing he never thought of finding, the thing he never knew was there, or the thing he never knew existed.

An old woodsman in the Adirondacks named Henry Houghton once told me my father had an uncanny sense of direction. When they were young they used to go for miles cross country in the deep forests of upstate New York. They'd try to get lost. Then they'd stop and the question would be:

"Where's home, by a different way from how we came?"

Henry said, "Your father always got us home."

More things keep turning up: a neatly cut rectangle of sheet metal that may well have been a blank for an arrowhead or some other implement, a small piece of red hematite with a ground facet on it, a small piece of sheet metal that had been folded over and beaten to a point—similar to others that my father found here.

While examining the brush below the camp Misse comes across a large pile of bones—certainly the pile that my father had noted in 1930—mostly horse and cattle bones. We find only one burned bit of deer bone.

The discoveries accumulate. The experience of seeing these things, once photographed and described by my father, and by no one else since, is like moving through rooms of treasure, visible only to us. We have come to this forgotten, nondescript terrain, and, with the diary as the key, we are let in on its secret.

Misse finds the big iron gong that had originally been at Las Varas, a few miles from here, and had been used by Mexican troops to summon the men in 1928 or '29. The diary says that the Apaches must have seen them using it and must have taken it for similar use at their own camp.

It is a perfectly situated campsite, with a spectacular view of the plains of Chihuahua. You can see all the way to Hatchet Mountain in

New Mexico. The Sierra el Medio and Janos are clearly visible. Except for the stone foundations, everything else has long since deteriorated—even the memory of the place among the local people.

As we walk down after hours of exploration and re-photographing, we kid around a lot, but I am still giddy, stunned by our success. I can't understand it. I'm reeling with unformed thoughts and feelings; I am in a place I've never been before, closer to my father than ever.

It almost seems as if we could not have failed—as if we were drawn to the place. I think back, trying to recall every moment of my sunrise scrutiny of the mountainside: the nuances of light and shadow, the timing of the looking, the interpretation of my father's maps and descriptions, the searching for detail in the photographs—detail swallowed by grain and shadow. Watching the mountainside was like watching a photograph develop—relief and detail appearing as light bathed the rocks and ridges.

I treasure the fragile, secret certainty that he spoke to me then. We were lost, and my father showed us the way. It is like a benediction.

### Grenville's Diary, cont'd.

—*We came into the rancheria on the main trail from the llano, and entered the lower pasture gate coming up through the main camp, and on south, along the mountain side, to the spring, and reservoir which the Apaches had built, about 1 miles from the main camp. Turned our stock loose, hobbled, to graze on a little hill just above the spring.*

*Marcos was saying tonight that he worked for Gabilondo at Ojos Azules, three years ago, when it was being built, there having been no ranch there previous to that time. Then, of course, the Mexicans had no knowledge of the Apache camp, nor even a suspicion that there was one on the mountain Marcos and another Mexican, Patroncito, working with him, were camped right at Ojos Azules. One night, as they were getting ready to leave for a trip to Las Varas, they heard many owls calling, around their camp. They left for Las Varas well after dark, not thinking any more about the owls. When they came back all their pots and pans had disappeared from their camp as well as a good set of harness.*

*—Another incident which happened about the same time [1928] was this. The Carretas ranch and another ranch close by were putting out salt for their stock, which kept mysteriously disappearing. This salt, or some of it, was found stored in a cave near the Apache camp, shortly af-*

ter it was raided. At the same time the Carretas ranch had some 200 good mares in their pasture, which they were going to sell in Casas Grandes. When they came to round them up to drive them on to Casas Grandes, some sixty were missing. They never found any trace of them, or how they could have gotten out of the pasture. But when the Apache camp was raided, there were several horse hides found there, with the Carretas brand.

— Marcos said that at that time there was a little, stocky old man, an American, who was trapping at Ojos Azules. This man used to go off in the mountain for two or three days at a time, and told the Mexicans he went to trap bear. However he never took any thing with him when he started on his trips, and moreover never came back with any bear. He had not trapped much at Ojos Azules either. Marcos suspected that he used to visit in the Apache camp and keep them informed.

— This camp was discovered by Patroncito in Dec., 1929. He, Reyes, Jose Ben Coma, Marcos' brother, Louis Grajera, and the Cordada of Chihuahua who had been sent for, raided the camp shortly after.[1] These men approached the rancheria from Ojos Azules. The Apaches had found out what was up, and had left the place quite some time before the raiders got there. Reyes, Gabilondo's foreman, said he would wait at the foot of the mountain while the others went up it, in order that he might get a shot at the Apaches if they should run down hill. He hid behind a large pine tree, and stayed there till the others had determined that the Apaches had already fled, an action which shows his character very well. It was not until this party got above the main camp, and were able to look down on it, that they discovered its location. The Apaches had time enough to get together most of their belongings before they left, so that not much remained in the camp in the way of booty.

About a month or so after the raid, Reyes came back to the main camp, and burnt all but one of the houses, so there is little left for the Apaches to come back to. However the Apaches have come back through this camp, at different times, since the raid, on their way to the Espuelas. We found several fairly fresh cut twigs, small rocks piled one on another along the trail, and a clump of bear grass tied in a knot, right beside the trail, from the main camp to the springs.

### Neil's Diary, Douglas, Arizona

In all the time since the death of Gerardo in April 1930, a year and a half earlier, there has not been any recorded contact between Apaches and Mexicans. There have been no reports of stolen livestock, no accidental sightings or chance encounters. The Apaches have gone to ground, but that they are in the mountains there appears to be no doubt. Grennie has seen unmistakable signs.

I'm visiting with an old cowboy named Walter Ramsey, and we're sitting in the shade outside his house in Douglas. He knew Stewart Hunt well, worked with him for a while at "El Tapila," the ranch he had when my father met him. It was just south of the border, and thirty miles directly north of the Apache camp in the Chita Hueca.

Walter smokes too much, and you can hear it in his voice. His face is pinched and seamed—doesn't seem to have quite enough flesh. He's been cowboying on both sides of the border for most of his seventy-four years, and he's a good storyteller. With the life he's led, he doesn't have to make anything up: just telling the truth is enough.

Walter remembers that in the 1920s Hunt saw Apache signs so frequently that he came to know their favorite routes through the Sierra Madre and their favorite points for border crossings. Tapila, his ranch in the Espuelas, backed up to a drainage called the Cajon Bonito. It empties northward into the Animas Valley of New Mexico and provides an easy, yet remote, passage between the United States and Mexico. These strange tracks could have been smugglers', of course, or illegal immigrants', but Hunt was convinced otherwise. The Apaches, said Hunt, preferred to travel on foot, and when they did so as a group they walked single file, and each person stepped exactly in the footprint of the one before, so no one could tell how many of them there were. Based on observation of the tracks, which he used to follow for some distance, Hunt was convinced that they met other Apaches from the U.S. reservations in remote areas along the border for weapons and ammunition resupply.

The tracks Hunt saw may well have been made by the Apaches, but, if they had been, which Apaches? The remnants of Apache Juan's band? They could easily have moved north from the Tres Rios area to the Tasahuinora or the Espuelas, or even beyond, to get as far as possible from Nácori Chico and from the manhunt dedicated to their destruction that was still under way.

Fimbres and the people of Nácori have been combing the mountains, but in vain. Fimbres even goes to the governor of Sonora for help, but is not warmly welcomed. He meets only with an aide of Governor Elias, Abelardo Sobarzo, who reminds him of the money and weapons already given by the governor.[2] The governor will not send troops, but will turn a blind eye on whatever it takes to reduce the Apaches. Open season in the Sierra Madre, already beyond the law, will eventually turn it into a killing ground.

### Oct. 16, 1931, Apache Camp, S. Chita Hueca, Chihuahua, Grenville's Diary

*This morning Art got a young deer. After eating, and after watering the horses all three of us set out for the main Indian camp to explore. I spent all day there. Art and Marcos went up on the rim, top of the mountain, and got back to the springs a short while before I.*

*In the main camp we found a lot of scraps of tanned leather made from cow hide, some rawhide, some sinew, some real leather apparently picked up or stolen from Mexicans or Americans, cloth of the same origin, a few corn cobs, mescal wads, a luger cartridge, empty, a few tin cans, one or two of which had their leaks caulked with wads of cloth, a couple of bottles, some grinding stones, the remains of three very roughly made burden baskets consisting of frames only tied together with yucca, a wooden trough cut out of a pine log, and a forked pole used for scraping hides on.*

*Above the main camp, in a shallow cave, there was a rope twister.[3] At the springs we had found a crude pack saddle, some rawhide thongs, parts of a pair of khaki trousers, part of a white shirt, a piece of patch work quilt, and a spoon, all probably stolen from Mexicans, with the exception of the pack saddle, which they appear to have made themselves. Everything else that the Apaches had left, had been picked up, or eaten by pack rats, etc.*

*Tomorrow am going to try and make a survey of how the whole rancheria was arranged. It is a mighty interesting camp all right, but, except for things [i.e. artifacts], does not look like any Apache camp I ever saw on the reservation.*

### Neil's Diary, Fort Apache

Without a doubt, the most unusual things about this camp are the little houses made from stone, adobe, and logs. My father says they are utterly unlike any houses the Apaches build on the reservations. But, four years later, in 1935, he sees very similar structures used for food storage at Fort Apache, and when I go there myself in 1997 I see the very same ones.[4] In fact there appears to be ample evidence that the Apaches were masons when they needed to be. On a trip to remote areas of the reservation, John Welch, the Fort Apache tribal archaeologist, shows me other examples of Apache masonry: small fortifications, several low circular walls two or three courses high.

In 1976 a man named Chester Davis told me that in the camp where Lupe was caught, some one hundred miles south of the Chita Hueca camp, there were houses with rock walls. They had no roofs, he said, so that when the Apaches built fires inside them they couldn't be seen at night. Chester's first cousin, Lloyd, tells me in 1997 that he remembers a small stone house on his ranch near the place where Lupe was caught. Francesca Mendoza, an elderly woman of Casas Grandes, tells us in 1987 that the Apaches sometimes plastered their houses.

Although only a few people remember such dwellings, many remember the Apache security system. It was used in these northern camps as well as in camps one hundred miles or more south of here. Sometimes made of braided or twisted horsehair, sometimes of thin leather thong, a long line would run from a sentry position with a view of all the approaches to camp to one or more cowbells or similar alarm devices.

When Lupe was caught at Pico de la India, she was the lookout, says Nelda Villa, our historian friend from Colonia Juárez. Lupe was on a high place and held a long string that was attached to a cowbell in the main camp. When she saw danger she pulled on the string. All the others got away because she was able to warn them, but she was trapped and could not escape.

The big iron gong hanging from a tree when Grennie was there, fallen to the ground by 1976, was the alarm for the Chita Hueca camp.

### Oct. 17, 1931, Apache Camp, S. Chita Hueca, Chihuahua, Grenville's Diary

*This morning we found a lump of beef tallow thrown under a bush near our camp at the springs. It had not been there very long, and was probably left over from the last time the Apaches traveled through here.*

*Marcos left for the caves in Paso Púlpito this morning.*

*This day I spent in taking pictures, following fence lines out, and plotting the rancheria in general. . . .*

*On a little rocky knoll, below the little corral, the Apaches have camped, the remains of their temporary brush shelters still being there. At this knoll there was a great quantity of cow, horse, and mule bones. Right off this knoll, in the draw, are two or three large rock tanks, full of water. At one of these was half a barrel, which had been used as a tub, and a dilapidated tin pan, which had a big patch of canvas on the bottom.*

*Up the draw from the springs, on its left hand side and at about 3/4 of a mile distance, is a small cave, located in a white sandstone ledge there. In this cave was found some salt. Right in front of this cave was a patch of soft ground, and at the time we were there, some horse tracks showed in it which must have been made within the last month. These tracks were most likely made by ridden Apache ponies, as they were flat bottomed, and left an impression as does a horse shod with rawhide in the Apache manner. . . .*

*The color of the rocks here is dull gray, they being of a sort of tufa formation. As the wood in the stockade of the camp has weathered to the same color almost, it is extremely difficult to distinguish the camp from any distance, unless you know right where to look for it. No one would ever suspect a camp there, looking from below, or even from above. Right on the edge of this point are some good sized yellow pine, and other trees, which completely conceal the camp from below.*

*There is a small level place where the houses rested. The whole place was in a tumble-down state, but enough was left to get a good idea of the arrangement. There was a good picket fence surrounding the place, well made of poles about 2 to 3 in. in diam., about 7 feet tall and set closely together, upright, in the ground where not too rocky. These upright poles were lashed together with horizontal poles running along in lines, and tied securely with strips of rawhide. This picket fence, or more truly stockade, guarded the camp on the downhill side, and ran up to the rocks, on the uphill side of the camp, thus forming a regular little fortified village of the place. . . .*

*In the enclosure were seven houses originally, all of similar appearance and structure, except for the largest cabin, the only one still retaining its roof. . . .*

*Six of the houses had a fire place and chimney, built in one of its corners, against the logs, and of rocks and mud, the enclosed chimney part not beginning till about 4 feet above the ground, and being very narrow at that, The chimney did not come vertically up out of the house, but came out through the end of the houses passing through the side of the stone partition between log wall and roof. . . .*[5]

*These cabins must have been very snug in cold weather, but could not possibly have held more than 3 sleepers. The largest house appeared somewhat newer than the others, and had no fireplace or chimney, and no attempts had been made to close the ends of the house up, between logs and roof. . . .*

*Right beside the first house, mounted on a stout pole frame, was a large, flat circular piece of iron, about 2 feet in diam., a part of some machine [I think this was the "cow-bell" described in my father's Nov. 21, 1930, entry]. Marcos said it had originally been at Las Varas, where the general called his troops together by beating on it, when the soldiers were there during the revolution of 1928. The Apaches had probably lain and watched this crude gong used, and when the troops left, had taken it away to their own camp for a similar purpose.*

*. . . Right above, on the same ridge as the main camp, were two beds of brush, laid flat on the ground, on which hides had been pegged out to dry. The pegs still remained in the ground, although the hides had been taken up. . . .*

*Right below the main camp, at the bottom of a little cliff, were strewn many bones of animals. There must have been the remains of at least 150 head of horses, mules and cattle. There were very few deer bones, which may indicate a lack of ammunition or rifles, or the fear of making a noise by shooting. . . . I found part of a saddle, and some hair, braided, which appears to be human.*

*The remarkable thing about all the work done in this rancheria, is that all brush or timber which these Apaches have had to cut by ax for use in fences or houses, etc., has been cut so carefully as not to show any traces of the work on the slopes of the mountain. . . . There is a good plain trail coming up from the llano to within a mile of the brush fence of the pasture where it plays out, and does not again become evident till within the pasture. This seems to have been the only precaution taken to conceal the entrance trail.*[6]

### Neil's Diary, Chita Hueca Apache Camp

The camp may have been hidden, but it was also surrounded. These people were trying to conceal the location of their camp, but they could hardly expect their presence to go unnoticed. They were stealing large quantities of livestock, as they had since they first saw Spanish horses—a time when they had the Sierra Madre to themselves. But in the 1920s they played cat and mouse: stealing at will everything from livestock to pots and pans. They toyed with the cowboys' nerves by leading them on wild-goose chases in the mountains and making bird calls at night around their camps. But the Apaches must have known that a reckoning of some kind was bound to take place; that was only a matter of time.

From this camp you can see far out across the plains of Chihuahua—the Apaches' breadbasket. Directly below is the Gabilondo Ranch, just beyond that the San Pedro Ojitos that used to belong to Curtis Morris, and, before him, to Lord Delaval Beresford, a ne'er-do-well Irish baronet. Slightly to the south are Gordy Boyd's Carretas Ranch and Joe Fenn's El Oso. There are smaller ranches to the north and the south, and due west fifteen miles away over the mountains is Colonia Oaxaca.

I do some simple arithmetic based on my father's estimate of the number of animals represented by the bones in the camp's midden. If the Apaches came here in 1929 only after abandoning the Sierra Espuelas camp to the north in 1926, they were here for a maximum of three years. Say fifty head of stock, or about one per week, were killed each year, and each animal yielded one hundred pounds of meat, and each person ate one pound of meat a day, or seven pounds a week. Then those hundred pounds divided by seven pounds means that at least fourteen people could have been living in the camp. A remarkable act of concealment, while it lasted.

Quinn Boyd, the son of Gordy Boyd, who was the owner of the Carretas Ranch in 1929, recounted to me a piece of oral history as affecting as any I have heard about these people. Gordy had been raised on the Carretas Ranch but had a lifelong interest in aviation. During World War I he was a combat pilot in Europe. For a period of time he worked at Ryan Aviation in San Diego and helped build the Spirit of St. Louis. He engraved the initials and the birthdate of his son Quinn on the back of Lindbergh's fuel gauge.

In the late '20s some Mexican entrepreneurs started an airline that flew between Sonora and Chihuahua, and Lockheed Vegas made weekly flights across the Sierra Madre over the Carretas Ranch. The planes flew so low you could see them easily.

In about 1930 Gordy Boyd found a recently abandoned Apache camp on the Carretas Ranch a few miles farther south of the Chita Hueca camp. In the camp, Quinn tells me, was a nearly life-size replica of the Lockheed Vega that flew low over the mountains once a week. I am at a loss for words or understanding, though the "cargo cults" of the South Pacific come quickly to mind. Quinn continues calmly: "My father knew airplanes, and there was no mistaking what he saw. He would never make up something like that, and neither would I. The only thing my dad could think of was that the Apaches thought that if they made one of those flying machines, they could fly too." [7]

### Oct. 18, 1931, Apache Camp, S. Chita Hueca, Chihuahua, Grenville's Diary

*Today Art stayed around camp. I left there and went up the mountain, striking summit above the main Apache Camp, and traveling to north end of mountain; thence back along top to a place just above the springs, and then back down to our camp. Killed a small buck deer on the way back. He was one of these Sonora pygmy white-tail I think. The deer are not very wild here and we saw quite a few. There were some bear signs on the mountain about 2 days old.*

*Just off the north point of the mountain, in the heads of some draws, right under the rim, are a few firs, but this is the only place I have seen them so far. The slopes of the mountain are very brushy, except for those having a northern exposure, these last bearing a good stand of yellow pine in places. At this time of year all the ash trees on the sides of the mountain are turning yellow. On the top of the mountain, where there is any space, an open pine forest stands, with grass growing almost to your knees, and no brush, etc., except for a few wild cherry trees and some blue oak.*

*There are three or four of these timbered flat places, connected together by very sharp brushy ridges, the whole outlay proceeding along the general line of north to south. There was some horse sign on top of the mountain, but this probably came from the Oaxaca side, which is not so steep. However it would be possible to get horses up the east side in places.*

*The altitude of this part of Chita Hueca must be around 7000 feet. From here you can see far to the south, over ridge after ridge of the Sierra Madre, which spreads out considerably below here. The country appears very rough, and all the higher mountains are black with timber. It is really a big country in which these Apaches have to live. To the east, north-east, and south-east the llanos spread out seemingly indefinitely, with one or two dim ranges showing up far away. To the north lie the Espuelas, very rocky and broken, and further on yet, the Chiricahua Mountains could be seen, as well as the Bisbee Mountains, Pedrogosas, Huachucas, and old San José Mountain near Naco.*

*Carretas and other ranches can be seen easily from the top of the mountain, and one can easily imagine the sense of security the Apaches must have had in this location. They probably came here after being run off the S. Espuelas by Bill's raiding party, some 5 years ago, and might still have been here if it were not for Gabilondo taking it into his head to build Ojos Azules ranch almost on their front door steps.*

### Neil's Diary, Chita Hueca Apache Camp

It was their bad luck to be discovered. That there were Apaches somewhere deep in the mountains was common knowledge, but, in spite of missing livestock and mysterious thefts, these ranchers never thought that the Apaches were anywhere near the Carretas Plains. Neither this camp nor the one farther north, to which Bill would next lead my father, were discovered during the course of an active search for Apaches.

To build a rancheria as elaborate and well appointed as this was an act of confidence that combined both caution and reckless defiance. The occupants had an ingenious alarm system, were ready to leave at a moment's notice, had concealed all evidence of brush and wood-cutting anywhere near the camp, and had a way of dissipating smoke from cooking fires. On the other hand, the Apaches were stealing heavily from neighboring ranches, and there was a wide trail leading in the general direction of the camp across the plain to within a mile of the place.

The Apaches invested so much time in building the camp that it is hard to think of it as seasonal. For as long as it was of use it seems most likely to have been occupied full time. The fact that my father and others saw tracks passing through this camp indicates an Apache presence of some kind either to the north or to the south of the camp—or both.

### Grenville's Diary, cont'd.

*—There were no Apache signs on the summit at all, but there were two piles of rock, some distance apart, which may mark the Sonora Chihuahua boundary line, which is supposed to follow the summit of Chita Hueca. However between here and the U.S. line there are three different boundary lines surveyed between Sonora and Chihuahua, each of them valid, so it is often difficult to tell which state you are in.*

### Oct. 19, 1931, El Paso Púlpito, Sonora

*Left our camp at the springs on Chita Hueca early this morning, and made it home to here in late afternoon. We met Reyes near Ojos Azules, on the way out, and he said that 6 of these Apaches passed through their camp about four weeks ago, bound north toward the Espuelas. He had seen their tracks, and the tracks we saw while in the camp were probably of the same party. Reyes also said that when the camp was raided, a can, full of Springfield shells, was found in one of the houses.*

# 16
# Booty

**Oct. 20, 1931, El Paso Púlpito, Sonora, Grenville's Diary**

*Looked over what we brought back from the Apache rancheria on Chita Hueca. Our booty isn't much. There is one pack saddle, one pommel and horn of a riding saddle, one rope twister, three other worked sticks, use unknown, one of them shown, some rawhide strips used in lashing fencing together, the covering of one side of the cantle of a saddle, a piece of Gabilondo's horse collar stolen from Ojos Azules, two small grinding stones, a woman's moccasin sole, a child's moccasin sole, three pieces of buckskin which appear to have been parts of some garment or sack, etc., one tin can used for cooking, one sardine can used for a dipper, some corn cobs (it should be here mentioned that there were still a few corn stalks in the ground, within the enclosure of the main camp), a lock of hair, some odd pieces of rawhide and leather, a wire nail which the Apaches had made by flattening one end for a point, two pieces of cloth, one being part of a homemade shirt or blouse, one luger pistol cartridge, and one Springfield cartridge, both empty, one bundle of sewing sinew, and one spoon.*

*—Art went down to Oaxaca this afternoon to see what Bill is going to do next. Bill's goats are kidding now, so things are liable to be a little busy here for a while.*

**Neil's Diary, Bavispe**

When Francisco Zozaya, our historian friend in Bavispe, tells us about the description of this camp given by his old cowboy friend, Agustin González, the inventory of articles he found sounds almost as if he were reading out of my father's diary. There are the blocks of salt, the alarm system that he calls a "telephone" just as my father does, the saddles, the harness, the cartridges, the leather tanning vats. He also mentions the fact that the Apaches used harnessed steers as draft animals.

As my father lists all this material, he makes no comment, but it must have spoken volumes to him about how the people lived. In fact it might have been a welcome change after hearing so much about the popular image of the Apaches as violent outlaws. Although there is no denying the violence and the mischief that the Apaches authored, they also, in their own way, lived everyday lives, normal to them, if utterly unfamiliar to us.

There was much leather, so they had time for skinning the animals and tanning the hides. There were moccasins for a woman and for a child, so it can be assumed that there were one or more families of men, women, and children. They made use of tin cans for implements—tin cans that they had to scavenge from somewhere. They had the time to work on skin and cloth clothing; they planted corn, so they would have had to be there in the early summer and the fall, if not permanently. They may have had a Springfield rifle and a Luger pistol. Among them were skilled masons and woodsmen who made warm, weatherproof huts.

The band created this refuge and peopled it, making a tiny fugitive community, isolated from the surrounding population so universally arrayed against them. The Apaches that lived here in a secret, separate world were remarkably busy. They were rustling, scavenging, gathering, planting, cooking, house-building, fence-building, corral-building, herding, butchering, jerking, skinning, tanning, and mending; they were making clothes, moccasins, toys, bows, arrows, ammunition, baskets, implements; they were marrying, coupling, birthing, caring, praying, and watching, always watching. And they did it, as my father notes, for three years, if not longer, without ever betraying the location of their camp to the ranchers, prospectors, hunters, trappers, cowboys, and smugglers that were pressing ever closer.

An unsuspected presence themselves, the Apaches would have known everything that went on in the mountains. They would have known just how many goats Bill had and might even have been watching as Grennie methodically surveyed the camp and rode back to Bill's ranch.

### Oct. 25, 1931, El Paso Púlpito, Sonora, Grenville's Diary

*Bill's goats are dropping from eight to sixteen kids every day now, and the place is alive with hungry young goats.*

*—Rode down to Oaxaca today to see what was keeping Art so long.*

*Art and the rest had all been harvesting the beans and maize there, and had only just got through. Bill and Art were busy packing up to start for the Apache camps in the Espuelas, so we go after all. The three of us rode back here to the adobe house this afternoon, and we leave for the trip to the S. Espuela tomorrow. Its hard to tell how many goats there will be here when we get back. The goat herder is greatly excited about this increase in population.*

### Neil's Diary, the Carretas Plains, Chihuahua

With the harvest out of the way, Mexican Customs off his back, and the goat herd growing by leaps and bounds, Bill must have welcomed a chance to go on what amounts to a vacation: a pack trip in the mountains.

For my father it was an opportunity virtually unheard of in Apache ethnography. He has just had a taste of something he must feel he has been preparing for all his life: a piece of completely original field research. He's just seen one Apache campsite no other ethnographer has ever seen or even dreamed of seeing, and now he's about to see another.

# 17
# Apache Gold

**Neil's Diary, the Carretas Plains**

Grennie now heads for the second of the two camps. This one is thirty miles to the north of the one he has just explored and is hidden deep in the Sierra las Espuelas, a range within the Sierra San Luis, the northern rampart of the Sierra Madre.

The Sierra las Espuelas was one of the stops on a favorite Apache route in and out of Mexico. In retelling his experience of scouting with General Crook, John Rope, an old Apache scout my father knew, mentions the Sierra las Espuelas again and again as the command crossed and recrossed this rugged range in pursuit of Geronimo in 1883.[1] The Chiricahuas evidently knew this part of the Sierra intimately—every tank, every cave, every canyon, every bolthole.

When Geronimo agreed to discuss a cessation of hostilities at a conference with General Crook in March 1886, he chose a place in the western foothills of this mountainous massif called Cañon de los Embudos. Geronimo had ridden north from strongholds far to the south, keeping to the height of the land, as Apaches always did. He and his people came unseen through the Sierra las Espuelas until they came to the head of Cañon de los Embudos. Then they filed down the narrow canyon to their historic meeting. This small band of Apaches had at their back an escape route into the Espuelas and its maze of ravines into which no one could pursue them with any success. Geronimo himself might very well have spent the night before his arrival at Embudos, encamped in the place where Bill is about to take my father.

Bill and Art and Grennie pack enough food for a week: flour, beans, coffee, salt, sugar, dried chilies, cornmeal, dried meat, and a few other staples. They can hunt for what else they need. Each of them is armed. My father has his 30-30 Marlin, Art's got a rifle, and Bill packs a six-shooter as well as a rifle. It simply is not safe to go unarmed. Apaches are known to be in the mountains, and, as had always been the case, smugglers and other ugly characters are still drawn to the border and its remote mountain approaches.

Bill did not go with Grennie to the other camp, the one in the Chita Huecas, but Bill is going on this trip. He and Moroni Fenn discovered the camp in the Sierra las Espuelas, and Bill probably could have told Art and my father how to find it, but this camp is a very large site, and only Bill will know all its parts and features. As the author of the camp's discovery, he would want to be the one to take my father there.

It is not hard to imagine them going to the Apache rancheria. Curtis is a master storyteller, and while they ride horseback or camp in the evenings—it takes two days to get there—my father listens to his inexhaustible narrative repertoire. They will cross the Pulpit Pass, as they did to go to the Chita Hueca camp, but they will turn north toward the Sierra las Espuelas when they emerge at the east end of the pass.

### Oct. 26, 1931, Near Las Varas, Chihuahua, Grenville's Diary

*We left the Pulpit about noon, and camped here at Gabilondo's tank. A few years ago, when Las Varas was owned by an American named MacNeil,[2] the Apaches had passed across a ranch nearby, and cut a wire fence in order to get through. Everybody in the locality was on the watch for them. This MacNeil, and a couple of other Americans living with him, had been trying to track down the Apaches. He was camped right at the foot of a big hill to the east of Las Varas, which was then not built— that is the ranch house. There was a good spring at this place, and it used to be a favorite camping place. The top of the high hill nearby was covered with juniper and blue oak, so as to afford good shelter. About 3 days after MacNeil and his two friends had been here, one of them happened to walk up on to the top of the high hill. There he found the Apache camp, much to his amazement. The Apaches had only just left there that morning, and from signs it was evident that they had been there for the past four or five days, looking right down on the three Americans all the time. It is needless to say that the Americans left there immediately, and gave up hunting Apaches. This hill can be seen in the lower right hand picture, on page 57, and lying in the center background.*

### Oct. 27, 1931, Las Piedras Canyon, Chihuahua

*Rode by Las Varas ranch, where a large mescal outfit is being put up, and turning north there, followed up Alamos Canyon for about 7 miles.*

*From here we went up over a little divide, and down on to the* llano *along the edge of the mountains, in Chihuahua.*

*These plains have very little brush on them here, except for some places in which mesquite, desert willow etc., grow along the arroyos. We hit the llano near a place called the Vacas, where there is water, and a large prehistoric ruin. From here followed along the foot of the mountains, stopping at some windmills on the flat for noon, from which place we could see a lot of smoke rising from one of the high peaks of the S. Espuela.*

*Not long after, we left the llano and turned up Las Piedras Canyon, heading back into the S. Espuela to the west. There is a road up this canyon for about 6 miles, over which the Nogales ranch outfit used to haul fence post which they cut in the canyon.[3] It is in a fork of this canyon that the Apache Rancheria is situated. The hills bordering Las Piedras Canyon are covered with a good stand of Emmory's Oak, and lots of grass.*

*— We rode up to the mouth of the branch canyon in which the Apache camp is, and here had to make a dry camp, as it was getting dark, and none of us three cared much to travel that country after dark. The mountains in this locality have little water except in the rainy season.*

## Neil's Diary, the Carretas Plains

I picture the three of them on the ground by a campfire in the dark. Bill reminds me of the Walter Huston character in *The Treasure of the Sierra Madre*—crusty, grizzled, experienced, dependable, and shrewd. But, unlike that character, Bill has no nose for gold.

## Grenville's Diary, cont'd.

*— Riding up this afternoon Bill told Art and I how he and Moroni Fenn came to run on this Apache camp here. They were looking for a lost mine, and the story about this mine is rather interesting.*

*It seems that back in the nineties, sometime, a party of Frenchmen, of whom there were a good many in Mexico at that time, were prospecting in this part of the country.[4] They had been warned before of Apaches being in the Espuelas, but had apparently disregarded this information. After some time these Frenchmen ran onto a rich gold-bearing ledge, and started in to work it. They had worked here for about a month, when they ran out of grub. One of the party was sent out to get provisions, and* when he returned he found all his companions killed by the Apaches. He immediately left there with what gold he and his partners had cached, and made his way to California, where he lived the rest of his life. Here he made friends with a man, and to this man he told his story of the mine, etc., also giving him a map of the mine's location. This man, in turn, gave the map to his son, an electrician.

In about 1914, this son, and a friend of his, an engineer of some sort, decided to spend their summer looking for this mine. The two friends came down, and crossed the border below Columbus where they hired a Mexican to take them to the mouth of the canyon in which the mine lay. Here they paid him off, and he went on south to Carretas. The other two came on up the canyon and found the mine. Here they worked for a while, panning in the wash below the ledge. One day they came back to their camp to find everything gone, taken by the Apaches.

(I forgot to say that about a mile or two below the mine, in the bottom of the canyon, the two friends had come upon an Indian camp, on their way up. There was only one very old man in the camp with whom they were unable to converse. So being afraid of the place, they gave it a wide berth, circling around it, and proceeding on up the canyon.)

After their camp had been raided by the Indians they had to leave, so took out over the mountains with two large nuggets, and some smaller ones which they had cached. The two fugitives came out finally in the Animas Valley, New Mexico, half starved, and about played out. From here they went on back to California where they deposited their gold at the mint in San Francisco. The two never returned to the mine. The engineer was killed, and the other was badly crippled by high voltage in a power house. This crippled one, however, made friends with an old peg-legged man, whom he in turn told about the mine. The map had been destroyed, but the cripple gave directions as closely as possible, and the peg-legged man set off on his search. But he never could find the mine, and as the electrician was unable to go with him, he had to rely entirely on directions by letter, etc., which were not very satisfactory. Moroni Fenn helped the peg-legged man look for this mine, and it was this that led Bill and he to the Indian Camp, after both peg-leg and electrician had died.

The location was described thus: "You strike a canyon in the mouth of which is a marshy area. This may be passed on either side. Up this canyon goes a road for some ways. After a while a side canyon takes off to the right, and following on up this you strike the Indian Camp in the bottom of the canyon. About a mile above this canyon is a brushy flat, about 1.5 acres in extent, and on the left side of the wash. At the upper end of this flat is a rock which looks like a monument. Right across, and up on the side of the canyon is the mine, the shaft passing into the rock ledge for about 15 feet The only place you can pan gold is right at the flat."

Bill and Fenn knew that the mine lay some place between Carretas and the U.S. line, and as Las Piedras Canyon filled the description almost perfectly, they went up it, and this is how they came on the Apache Rancheria there, but never found the mine, as have no other people either.

Bill says he had heard of there being wild Apaches in these mountains, but had never really believed till the time he came on this camp. He had met an old American prospector in San Miguel, Sonora, who claimed to have seen them one time. This prospector was up in the Sierra Espuela. He had run across two human skeletons, and started to find Indian tracks on top of his own. One day he saw two or three Indians, but was not able to parley with them. This was enough for him, and he left the mountains right away. He told Bill they looked more like Apaches than anything else.

—Years ago the Mormons followed a band of Apaches who had stolen a bunch of horses from one of their Chihuahua settlements, near Chuhuichupa. After five days they had come up on the Indians, who had taken refuge in a cave on the side of a canyon, from a snow storm then in progress. The Mormons on the opposite side of canyon shot into it, and got all the Indians inside, which they claimed numbered 25.

## Neil's Diary, Colonia Juárez

How often Barney and I hear stories from our Mormon friends like this one—and they always take place near Chuhuichupa. We're sitting on the shaded lawn of Marion Vance's comfortable house in this old Mormon settlement. He's telling us that in 1927 some horses were stolen from his father, who had a ranch near Chuhuichupa. A posse was gathered, and it followed the stolen stock for several days, coming on successive camps. They were certain the thieves were Apaches, but, in the versions I hear, they never make contact, let alone kill twenty-five people. Only one horse was recovered.[5]

**Grenville's Diary, cont'd.**

*Another story told is that the Apache Kid was supposed to have been killed by two Mormon boys near Chuhuichupa, a good while ago. The Kid was riding up a canyon with some other Indians, and was in the lead. The Mormon boys who just happened to be in ahead of them, and lay in wait, having seen them. When the Indians got close, one boy fired a charge of buckshot at the Kid, but this did not seem to hurt him. The other boy fired at him with a .44 rifle, and the Kid fell from his horse. The other Indians got away. The reason for the buckshot not hurting the Kid, was that he had on 13 thicknesses of buckskin, in the form of a shirt. There may be some truth in this story, even though it sounds fantastic.*

**Neil's Diary, Tucson, Arizona**

Lloyd Davis, eighty-five years old, is a master saddlemaker now living in Tucson. He grew up in the Mormon mountain colony of Chuhuichupa, about fifty miles south of Cave Valley, the site of the 1892 Thompson Massacre.

It's ten in the morning, and I find Lloyd chain-smoking in the saddle shop. His son Brian is bent over a beautiful saddle, tooling designs into the cantle. The place smells of beeswax and leather. An old Tanya Tucker number spills out of a radio that sits between cans of contact cement and neat's-foot oil on a shelf. Lloyd is talking with a customer about a revolver holster. His face is gray and drawn, and his breath rattles in his throat.

When I ask Lloyd how he's doing, he says, "Not too good."

He says mornings between seven and nine are usually pretty rough. He has high blood pressure, probably emphysema or worse, and seems to be in pain. Even so, he wants to talk and tell stories, so he leads us into the house where he can lie down. When he's out in the shop he chain-smokes, but his wife forbids it in the house. It's bad enough to know he's probably killing himself; she just doesn't want to watch. Once in the house he heads for the couch, lies down, pulls a blanket over himself, and the stories roll with an almost desperate energy.

His voice is strong, and he is a natural, compulsive storyteller. It hurts him to laugh, but that doesn't keep him from telling stories, drawing on all of his dry cowboy wit, his laughter turning to searing coughs.

Lloyd knows the story of the death of the Apache Kid well, having heard it from boyhood. It is the same story whose bare bones my father heard from Bill Curtis.

Martin Harris is a farmer in Cave Valley, where the Thompson Massacre had taken place in 1892. One night in November 1899 Harris's dogs begin barking, and rocks rattle down on the roof of the house. Harris, an old Indian fighter, suspects a trap and stays put.

Come daylight, he finds that his fields have been robbed of corn and potatoes. He grabs a ten-gauge shotgun and a nosebag full of shells, and enlists his neighbor, one Tom Allen, who gets a rifle. They go off on the trail of their night visitors—more to find out who is guilty than to attack them.

The trail leads to an Apache camp with a group some twenty strong. Harris and Allen hide beside the trail with no thought of attacking the Indians, but the Apaches mount up to leave their campsite and come straight for their hiding place. One of the Mormons makes a noise, and the Apaches see them instantly. The Apache in the lead tries to pull his rifle out of its scabbard, but the gun is stuck. Harris gives the Indian one barrel of buckshot, but it does the Indian no harm because of the many layers of buckskin he is wearing. His horse bolts, but the Apache reins him in and comes back still trying to get his rifle out. Tom Allen, who has a rifle, shoots at the man and hits him in the throat, killing him as well as a baby he carries on his back. There are several women on horseback right behind the Apache man. They are so close it is too late for them to run, so they ride on by Harris and Allen. The one in the lead is a tall, handsome woman, still as a statue, who never takes her eyes off the Mormons as she rides by.

Mexican and Mormon authorities come to inspect the scene. Some of them knew the Kid in Arizona, and they are certain that Allen and Harris have killed the Apache Kid. There is a bounty for the Kid offered by the Governor of Sonora, but he isn't satisfied with the identification, and no bounty is ever paid.

### Grenville's Diary, cont'd.

*When they were cutting posts in Las Piedras Canyon, the Mexicans there had their camp completely cleared by the Apaches in broad day-*

*light.[6] These Mexican post cutters moved out right away, and started cutting in another canyon, some distance to the north of here. The same thing happened in this canyon again, and all post cutting was postponed indefinitely in that locality. But the exact location of the Apache rancheria here was never known until Bill and Moroni stumbled on it.*

# 18
# The Hidden Camp

**Neil's Diary, the Carretas Plains**

The Sierra las Espuelas is one of the few places we have not combed, and I feel that the big Apache camp up there holds one of the keys to the story. We have been so busy trying to find and interview aging people that we have postponed a search for this camp, but now it's time. My father was there so soon after the Apaches abandoned it that the outlines of a whole way of life might be inferred from what they left behind for him to see. Not only had there probably been Apaches in the Sierra las Espuelas for hundreds of years, their presence there in the twentieth century is as strong as it is anywhere. In this Sierra Madre backwater they survived the European invasion that had surrounded but never quite dislodged them.

Twenty years have passed since our rediscovery of the first camp in 1976. I had always hoped that the four of us, Barney, Tom, Misse, and I, might complete the circle by discovering the second camp together, as well as the first. But by now Misse has moved on to marriage and the legal profession in Vermont. Tom, the closest friend Barney ever had, is gone, having been killed when he was thrown from a horse near Tucson on April 30, 1990. As I travel with Barney in the years that follow, hardly a day goes by that he does not mention Tom: If only we had Tommy's sense of direction, Tommy's fluent Spanish; Tommy would know . . . ; Tommy and I . . . ; remember when Tommy . . . ? I know it is a comfort to Barney. In a way it is a comfort to all of us to know that Tom is still there because Barney won't let him leave.

Barney, my son, Seth, my friend Don Metz, and I have been in Nácori Chico for a week. We are coming north and decide to cross to the eastern flank of the Sierra Madre via the Carretas Pass so as to swing near the Sierra las Espuelas and check out the approaches to the Apache camp located there. It is probably on a private ranch, and it may take time to find the owner, dispel his suspicions, and secure permission to explore. Many of the ranches close to the border have been bought up by *narco-traficantes*, for growing, for smuggling operations, or for money-laundering, so our arrival might not be welcomed.

We get to the town of Janos and then head west on pavement. We find a dirt road going south into the wind and dust in the direction of Las Piedras Canyon. Just at the turnoff there is the wreckage of some abandoned buildings: tumbleweed in a corral, a collapsed door frame, tattered plastic whipping in the wind, a disemboweled mattress, bedsprings, a parched tire, a rubber boot sole, broken glass. There's nothing more as we go south through the dust, past the Sierra el Medio.

We come to a ranch about ten miles and an hour's drive south of the pavement. This is the bleakest place we have seen. It's a long, low house with two or three stunted mesquites, a few horses tail-to in the driving dust. There is a chain-link fence around all of this. Two cowboys come out to meet us. They have greasy caps crammed low on their heads; their jackets are buttoned up tight because the wind is cold and dust is everywhere. Two pit bulls come circling out of the house, inquisitive, moving half sideways, massive heads low. Here they breed the dogs for fighting. We ask them about Piedras Canyon. One of the cowboys tells us that it's on the neighboring ranch. The headquarters are farther down the valley, and the owner should be there. He's pretty sure the canyon has a locked gate.

Barney is direct: "Hay problemas con los narco-traficantes en la sierra?"

"Ay, no. No por aquí hombre."

Barney mutters to us as we leave: "Yeah. Right."

The next ranch is quite a different place. From a distance we can see elegant whitewashed walls and a red tile roof. Cypresses swaying in the wind. A big TV dish. There are only three very young cowboys — one can't be more than twelve or thirteen. Barney hunkers in the dust with them. They draw maps in the dirt with sticks. The owner is away in Ciudad Juárez, which faces El Paso from across the border. He's seventy years old and likes to keep everything locked up in the valley.

We're as close as we're going to get for now. Barney feels we will have to approach the owner of the ranch carefully in order to get permission to explore. So much security is unusual. The ranch itself is almost baronial. It is entirely possible, we all think, that the owner of the ranch does not want strangers in the mountains.

We cross the border that night, already planning another crossing in two and a half months.

### Neil's Diary, Sierra el Medio

We think there is a good chance of a chilly reception from the owner of the ranch. So during the late fall and early winter Barney spends a great deal of time on the telephone laying the groundwork for contact with him, lining up mutual acquaintances, researching neighboring ranches. Barney finally reaches the owner and describes the Apache camp we are looking for.

The owner's courtesy is disarming: "Oh, you mean those little stone houses. Oh yes, I have seen them. They are right there in the canyon, and some on top." Barney grills him, making sure he understands the location of the camp. There seems to be no doubt, but I am deeply skeptical. The houses at the Chita Hueca camp were obliterated by time and looting; there was hardly anything left when we found the place. The Espuelas camp was burned and looted several times, according to my father's diary. How could any of the houses outlast sixty years of wind, snow, rain, gravity, cattle, and cowboys?

No, I think. It's not going to be that easy. When we found the Chita Hueca camp we were somehow guided, we could make no mistake, our enterprise was charmed. Now we're going to have work for it.

The owner of the ranch says we are welcome to come and that he will set things up with his foreman so that when we arrive there will be no surprises.

Our Mexican friends in Agua Prieta have told us we are crazy to be going to Chihuahua in January. We'll freeze, they say. Margot, Kathy, Seth, Barney, and I follow the familiar route down the Bavispe Valley and cross the Carretas Pass in Barney's veteran Suburban. As we drop out of the mountains into the table-flat Carretas Plains we can feel the temperature slipping. A gale rushes down the valley from the north as it did in the fall, but now it's colder, has more bite than before. Looking north to the Espuelas we can see a stark white skirt of snow at the four-thousand-foot level. Above that the high ridges and peaks disappear into the clouds.

The ranch we want is about thirty miles to our north, and we approach it through scrub and cactus. The rutted dirt road plunges through arroyos, alongside barbed-wire fences, through cattle gates, and across cattle guards. We pass a steer carcass, and a vulture wheels overhead.

Up ahead there's a windmill, its vanes locked, motionless and humming in the strong wind. Below it a bellowing diesel engine drawing water from a deep well. Next to the diesel are two men and a pickup truck, not in the least surprised to see us. Barney's van is battered enough to look as if it belongs there.

The good news is that the man we have found is Alfonso Gómez, the foreman, or *mayordomo*, of the place, so we won't have to go blundering around the property looking for him. The bad news is that, in spite of all the telephoning Barney has done, the owner of the ranch has not told Alfonso we were coming, and until Alfonso talks to him, we don't do any exploring.

Mexican manners never turn a traveler away, but Barney takes no chances and soon has told Alfonso our entire story. He keeps pointing at me as he tells about my father's travels through this valley in 1931. He opens the diary and goes through the pictures and the maps and, as he points to the photographs of the stone houses at the camp, Alfonso tells us that he too has seen the little round houses. Until now, he never realized who built them, but if it was Apaches, he can't imagine why anyone would be interested in them.

Alfonso remains grave. I think it is his way, but the ice seems to be broken. He says he will try to contact the owner on the radio, and in the meantime, we can camp at the ranch headquarters.

The building is a simple concrete block box with a long, narrow anteroom where we place all our gear from the van. Seth and Kathy survey the supplies and start to think about the next meal. Margot gets out the video camera and turns it on as we begin to take stock of where we are and how we might find the camp.

Alfonso studies the map and after much discussion places the camp. His callused forefinger leaves a smudge of soot on our map where he finally says the round stone houses are. But there are problems. It is not where we expect it to be, which is to say it does not agree with my father's description. Even that is confusing as we tease it apart. Alfonso does not place the camp as far up the canyon as Grennie does, and it's on the north slope instead of the south.

What's more, we still can't get through to the owner, and if we don't soon, the search may end right here, at least for a while. The weather is a factor too. Canadian cold and Pacific moisture are about to collide directly overhead for the second time this week, and we now see that the camp is almost certainly at about seven thousand feet and could get buried under deep snow if this system does its worst.

A woman feeds the men in the next room while Seth and Kathy work wonders with canned chili on the Coleman stove. The cowboys move into the big room off the kitchen. It has a bloated plastic easy chair and a double bed, a blinding bare bulb in the ceiling, and a big TV set up on a bureau. The cook's husband drops into the easy chair. Alfonso takes off only his boots, and gets under the covers on the double bed. They watch *Wagon Train* reruns in Spanish.

### Neil's Diary, Rancho las Piedras, Chihuahua

As soon as we are up this morning, Alfonso tries to radio the owner of the ranch. He gets through and we are OK'd for access to the canyon where the camp is supposed to be.

We pack the truck and go over the directions some more. As we leave the headquarters to cross the valley, it begins to snow, and by the time we get there we're in a near-blizzard. We come to an outlying ranch house where Alfonso has told us we can stay. There is a cowboy who lives here with his wife, and we find him unsaddling his horse in the blizzard. It is already about ten o'clock, so we say hello without unloading, and keep right on going, navigating canyon by canyon until we get to the mouth of the one we think is right.

Visibility is poor, and the going is about as bad as it gets once we turn off into the Apache camp canyon which has a primitive road. The only landmarks we have to go by are the branching canyons, which we count to keep our bearings. Low clouds hang over the ridge-tops, so it is almost impossible to distinguish real canyons from shallow draws. Alfonso has placed the stone house at about a mile and a half up the canyon. My father said it was three miles, so we feel we cannot rely on mileage but will have to find it by landmark.

Seth and Kathy are navigating in the back seat. A mile and a half up the canyon we come to what seems the right place, judging by landmarks—arroyos on the left and on the right almost facing each other. We stop and sweep the area on the east side of the canyon for a while in the snow, but it simply does not look right.

We move farther down the canyon to a place where there is a deep level terrace. It is a gentle grassy slope, fairly open, with scattered oak trees. There is frequent bear sign in the road, big bear sign — black bears feasting on quantities of juniper berries when they should be sound asleep.

It looks promising here. Margot films us as we spread out and sweep the terrace in the snow and rain. The drama of finding the camp in a near-blizzard appeals to the filmmaker in me. Margot and I trade off, turning the camera on each other and on the others as we comb the hillside, looking for the remains of stone walls, corrals, fences. The snow becomes rain, and soon we are all soaked, but we make one more sweep of the terrace, finding nothing. It is clear from this preliminary probe that we do not know enough. We are in a blind search and will never find the camp this way. I tell Margot again about the almost mystical way we were drawn to the first Apache camp twenty years ago, before we knew each other, and I wonder if it will happen the same way again as it did then — almost without warning, like a gift.

We labor back down the arroyo to the little ranch. The compound lies exposed in the mouth of the canyon, just in from the *cienega*. The four-room house is surrounded by a stout hurricane fence, meant to keep out wild animals and livestock.

On the job for only three days, Efrain Rios is the young cowboy who lives here with his wife, Maria. There's a solar panel on the roof — probably for heating water. They occupy two of the four rooms in the house. In back is a small bedroom, and in the front room there is a big wood-burning stove that heats and cooks. Hung from a nail on the wall is a portable radio with blown speakers blaring Tejano and mariachi music. By the door are rain-soaked clothes, dripping on the concrete floor, and two pairs of mud-caked boots.

Maria is wearing a gold and black San Diego Padres warm-up jacket. Efrain's got on a Baltimore Orioles cap. In the other, unoccupied half of the house there are two empty rooms, which he shows us. He hazes a cat and dog out the door and says we can move in. The wind is picking up outside, driving the last of the rain sideways as we empty the truck and settle into the frigid concrete box. Seth and Kathy and Margot and I spread our bedrolls in the back room, hang soaked clothes on nails in the wall. Barney's in the kitchen, where the two-burner Coleman stove is in a losing battle with the cold.

I have been reading the diary and poring over the photographs, looking for clues. Having been up the canyon once already, the features in the photographs take on a new reality. Rising above the main camp in the canyon bottom is a camel's hump skyline with a wide band of rock across it that I had not noticed before. The skyline and this rock outcropping are so distinctive that if we can see them, we will know we are there.

### Neil's Diary, Rancho las Piedras

We get off to a slow start, basking in the sun like lizards to warm up and dry out. Alfonso Gómez drives up in a pickup with another cowboy. He says he has come to take Efrain Rios and the other man to the Gabilondo Ranch. He may also want to check up on us — to see what we are doing.

We tell him we are having trouble finding the place and ask him to go over the location again. When we tell him what we did yesterday, he says we did not go far enough up the canyon. We must go to the end of the bulldozed road and then walk another half mile, and we are there.

We drive past yesterday's farthest advance. I watch the odometer. As we labor up the road, it approaches three miles, as Grennie said it would, and ends. We get out and walk up the streambed, climbing through a dense forest. When we emerge in the open, it is at once obvious that we are at the end of a long search. There is the camel's hump skyline, and below it the band of rock my father photographed in 1931. This is the hill at the base of which lies the Apache camp.

Using the pictures from the diary, we are able to see exactly where we are. Seth and Margot and I scramble up the slope to the right to find the place from which my father took the picture. As usual there is that lightheadedness that comes from knowing I stand on the same spot where my father stood sixty-five years earlier, and, as always, there is a void. As my father considered the scene there was no place for excitement — only for the witness's tabula rasa.

In 1931 virtually nothing was known about the Sierra Madre Apaches or the way of life represented by the two camps in this range. As Grennie bent to his task of documenting and surveying the place, I knew he realized that these people were the last of their kind, the last Apaches to live this way. I suspect that knowing this gave the job of documenting the camp an urgency, but he never breathed a word of that—not on paper.

As Margot and I watch Seth move easily up and down the rock-strewn slope, we notice how much he looks like Grennie: tall, rangy, graceful. He has Grennie's focus and purpose, also his openness—at once innocent and honest and guileless and trusting. There is a photograph of Seth standing next to a life-size picture of Grennie, and the resemblance is remarkable. From my mother I know the ways in which I am like my father, and these similarities have never failed to surprise me, since I never knew him. But it is always with a start that I see glimpses of him in my son, and I wonder if there are other ways in which they are alike that I will never know.

Seth takes a number of registered photographs to match those his grandfather took of the skyline above the camp, then climbs back down and walks up the canyon. We come to a split in the arroyo and, following my father's map, turn right. After he's walked a hundred yards Seth calls out from ahead, "bingo." We are there.

## 19

# A Refuge in the Espuelas

**Oct. 28, 1931, Apache Camp, S. Espuela, Chihuahua, Grenville's Diary**

*Got up here to the main camp, in the bottom of the canyon, about noon, and spent the afternoon in going up on the big ridge to the east where the big corrals are, and in looking for the small corrals on the other side, which we were unable to find. Found out that the smoke we saw coming from the mountains out on the llano is caused by a small forest fire on a mountain to the north. As there have been no lightning storms lately, and as few Mexicans or Americans ever go in this part of the mountains, there is a good chance that this fire may have been started by the Apaches. There are lots of deer and bear signs here, as well as some of mountain lion.*

*— The country right in this vicinity is very broken by steep ridges, and canyons and rocky ledges, etc. The canyon bottoms are very brushy as are also the northern slopes. The southern slopes are more open and grassy, being dotted with blue oak. There are a few ash trees in the draws, and sheltered places; a great deal of silver leaf oak, and on the high ridges and in deep draws some pinon and juniper grow, along with pine. On the highest parts of the mountains there are good stands of yellow pine.*

*— These Espuela Mountains are nothing more than a series of canyons and high ridges, with a few high peaks among them, which stand out because of the large timber growing on their sides.*

*— We didn't get back to the main camp in the canyon, which we had made our stopping place, till a good bit after dark. Tomorrow am going to get the photographs needed, and try to draw a general map of the rancheria, as well as plans of the different camps, and houses.*

**Neil's Diary, Rancho las Piedras**

Grennie and Bill and Art spend the night at the mouth of the branch canyon, only three miles down slope from the main camp. Fifty years later the arroyo bottom is still as brushy as it was in 1931, and I am not surprised it took them four hours to go the three miles. Like the camp in the Chita Hueca Mountains, this rancheria is spread out. It is two miles from end to end, and the upper camp is a thousand feet higher than the main camp, where Bill wants to stay. There are big boulders along the sides of the sand and gravel flats in the streambed. The place has become totally overgrown, but we will try to do an inventory of the site, using the diary's diagrams.

### Grenville's Diary, cont'd.

*—About 8 years ago some Mexicans were killed near Janos, by the Apaches. The Apaches took straight out, from the scene of their crimes, across the llano, by night, striking the S. Espuela, at a place just north of the Vacas, and following up a steep rocky ridge at that point, which can be seen in picture on page 110. A party of 100 Mexican soldiers and their officers, guided by Joe Fenn, and a couple of other men, took their trail. They followed the tracks of the Apaches across the llano, finding where the Indians had cut a fence to get through.*

*When the pursuers passed the Vacas, they took the tracks right up the rocky ridge, and back on to a high mountain which can be seen on page 28. The soldiers and their guides jumped the Apaches in the bottom of a canyon on the side of this mountain, where the Apaches had been camped. As the soldiers started firing immediately, and not taking much aim, the Apaches all got away, though on foot, and without their belongings.*

### Neil's Diary, Altamirano, Chihuahua

In spite of a thorough search, there appears to be no memory or record of an Apache attack near Janos, but I believe that he is writing about the attack on an Altamirano family named Molina. They were killed, not "eight years ago" in 1923, but in 1920, not far from where we are now, thirty miles south of Janos.

This is one of those Sierra Madre villages in which time seems to have stopped. There is no electricity, no telephone, and no running water. Every house—many of them log cabins—has a hand pump and a privy. The nearest town of any size is a gear-grinding, five-hour haul on one of the roughest roads we have seen. At night, after all the dogs, cows, horses, chickens, and pigs are asleep, a silence as profound as any I have ever heard settles on the place, and the Milky Way seems close enough to touch.

We're in the cemetery. All the members of the Molina family, who were attacked on the road to Casas Grandes in 1920, are buried here. Margot and Barney and Nelda and I are speaking with Socorro Molina, the daughter of Nacho Molina, who survived the ambush to live a long and happy life and die in bed at the age of sixty-five on the first of September 1968. She has come to tend his grave, as it is the second of November, the Day of the Dead. As we stand by the graves she relives her father's appalling experience.[1]

There are five in the wagon. There is a very narrow place on the road from Altamirano to Casas Grandes, with high cliffs on both sides. They call it the Piedra Volada, the Flying Rock. There is a cave by the side of the road, and there are two Apaches hidden in the cave. As the wagon passes the entrance to the cave, there are three shots. Killed instantly are Leonardo Molina; his daughter, Isabel; and his niece, Tacha Chaparo. The horses bolt and overturn the wagon. Thirteen-year-old Nacho jumps clear and takes a bullet through his hand and one in his hip, but he is able to hide in the deep pool in the nearby stream, which is overhung with thick brush. He watches as one of the two men pick up Nacho's baby cousin, José Corral, by the legs and swing him through the air so as to strike his head with fatal force against the wagon wheel. The sentinel woman comes down from above. They strip the bodies, take the rifle, horses, harness, and destroy the contents of the wagon. They all have long black hair and wear red headbands. Nacho escapes discovery and runs home when the Apaches have left.

A posse is mounted, and the Apaches are trailed to a campsite across the Carretas Plains in the Espuelas. The two men vanish, and the Mexicans catch the woman. The only reason she is not killed on the spot is that she is pregnant, and the *presidente* of Casas Grandes is present and does not permit it. The camp contains toys: dolls, a small clay whistle, a small rattle, a toy saddle. The woman wears rubber-soled sandals with a heel and a toe strap.

The Mexicans let the woman go, and she vanishes into the mountains. She eventually joins the two men, and they are tracked north to a point where they cross the border. Although the people of Altamirano have caught disquieting glimpses of the Apaches, until now no blood has been shed. The next day another man is killed on the same road. The people of the village are terrified. This is the first real trouble with Apaches the people of Altamirano have experienced, and it opens a decade of regionwide conflict that will not end until well after the death of Apache Juan in 1930.

### Grenville's Diary, cont'd.

*—An interesting thing happened near Chuhuichupa some three or four years ago. One of Machichi's men, a character in the revolution of 1928,[2] while riding through the woods, suddenly came up on an Apache man, taking him completely unaware. The Mexican drew his gun immediately so that the Apache was afraid to run. The Mexican went up to him, and not knowing who or what he was, tried to get him to talk, but without success. The Indian would do nothing but lie on the ground, in spite of shakings, etc. Finally the Mexican rode off and left him there.*

### Neil's Diary, Apache Camp, Sierra las Espuelas

Like that Apache, inert on the ground, this camp, abandoned and harmless, has been left alone by everything but the elements. By now we are used to being where Grennie and Bill and Art stood, slept, camped, and swapped stories, but it is always with a start that I recognize an exact scene or object. Like the skyline above the site of the camp, the first stone house, when I see it, delivers a shock of recognition.

It is U-shaped, built very close to the arroyo, and one wall has collapsed because of frequent flash flooding. Moving quickly, Seth spots the big round house, in very good condition, and not far from that, house number thirteen, a dugout with a stone retaining wall and a chimney. We find one very old scrap of deer antler that Barney thinks was once worked with a knife. All the original wood from the structures is gone, except for one of the doorjambs in the entrance to the round stone house.

There are two rectangular houses here. One has straight walls with laid up, right-angle corners of interlocking rock, but the other has rounded corners. It's as if the mason did not know how to make sharp right-angle corners, or else had found an easier, better way. All of the stone houses appear to have been chinked with adobe.

The Mexican ranchers have installed a concrete spring box and a concrete stock tank, and there are the remains of plastic pipe—once buried, now exposed and snarled by the force of runoff water. The houses have not been disturbed at all. We spend the rest of the day locating all the structures of the lower camp, and scouting up the streambed and along the rim of the opposite bank until it gets too dark to work.

That night, having spent the day at the camp, rereading the diary is a completely different experience from what it had been the day before. All the details about vegetation, construction, the inventory of every fence and gate and corral, the exhaustive cross-indexing that once seemed obsessive, now have meaning. I can reconstruct the camp in my mind by placing in it all the things my father lists but that are no longer there. I look at the drawings and the faded photographs, the maps and the careful handwriting, and the place comes to life.

I can imagine shafts of light slicing through the smoke from campfires. I see the corrals, the animals: horses and mules shod with rawhide. The mules' ears droop because the Apaches have cut the tendons that keep them erect. The nostrils of some of the burros, horses, and mules are slit to keep them from braying and neighing. There is meat hanging on drying racks, a curing hide is pegged to the ground, and the rank smell of slaughter hangs still in the air. Scraps of sheet metal, wire, flesh, bone, and hide litter the ground. Suspended from a tree in the middle of the group of dwellings is a tin can. It's upside down, like a bell, and there's a stone clapper in its mouth. A line is tied to the clapper, and the sunlight catches it as it goes across the clearing and disappears into the trees at the base of the long ridge.

By a brush shelter there are two dolls, each a foot high: a man and a woman dressed in beautifully made buckskin clothes. She has a long skirt, long black hair. He has on knee-high moccasins decorated with tiny metal bells. They have no facial features. Next to them is a small toy saddle, some rattles made of dried gourds, and a pile of small round stones. There are small footprints in a level area in a circle drawn in the dust. It is as if a game has been interrupted, everything abandoned in alarm.

On the ground there is a rusty bucket full of acorns next to a pile of agave hearts. A pit for roasting the agave is half dug. There is a scattering of torn fabric, glass bottles, tin cans, and coils of barbed wire.

Up the arroyo, two children dart in and out of the sunlight, not making a sound. No one else is in sight. There is a feeling of being watched.

### Oct. 29, 1931, Apache Camp, S. Espuela, Chihuahua, Grenville's Diary

*Spent today in taking photographs, making drawings and plans. Went up canyon to caves in the morning, and up on top of mountain to corrals and over on other side of there to the small corrals which we were unable to find yesterday. On the general plan, page 108, the whole outlay of the rancheria is shown.*

*Coming up this side canyon from Las Piedras Canyon on trail (no. 20) for about 3 miles, you strike a brush fence across the bottom of the canyon (no. 1), and from here on you are within the rancheria. The approach up the canyon is very rough, and difficult to get over on account of the thick brush and rocks. The trail never was good, and when we went over it, it was almost entirely grown up. About 1/4 mile above this first brush fence the canyon forks, a small canyon taking off to the left. Just in the right fork of the canyon here, is the main camp. (no. 3). On the ridge between the forks of the canyon, at no. 11, is a brush shelter, used for a look out house, and so placed that the whole canyon, for more than a mile below, can be easily watched.*

*In this same picture can be seen the high, dark ridge to the right, from whose top Bill and Moroni Fenn first saw the main Apache camp. They lay here and watched for an hour with field glasses before descending the slope to the canyon and camp. On the way down this slope they suddenly heard a mule bray loudly, and soon saw him. He was side hobbled, and had both ears cut so they hung down on the sides of his head.[3] Further back on this same ridge, are two other brush shelters, which appear to have been used as temporary camps. (no. 12). Just above the main camp is another brush fence—across the bottom of the canyon. (no. 5).*

*A short distance below this fence, a trail turns off and goes up the side of the canyon. And out on the rim to a stone house, and small brush corral (no. 6). This stone house, (no. 7), appears to never have been finished. It was just being built when the camp was raided in 1926. The walls are well set up, and there are two doorways. The logs for the roof are there, peeled and ready to put in place. (The Apache that Bill and Fenn had run on to had probably been working on this house, and was just coming from there.) Bill and Fenn were in the canyon right where the trail came in, when they looked up on the side of the canyon, and saw this Apache riding down towards them, mounted on a buckskin horse, and leading a gray, entirely unaware of the two white intruders. Bill and Fenn let him get almost to them, at a place which you can see in the upper right hand picture just at the foot of a little rocky cliff on the side of the ridge, indicated by mark, then they made a noise. The Apache saw him immediately and Bill says he can still remember that Indian's face, very broad and shiny, with black staring eyes. The Indian was a big man, but active. He whirled his horse around and still leading the gray, rode off around the little rocky cliff as fast as he could go. . . .[4] [See appendix 3 for a detailed description of the camp layout.]*

*—On the general plan all mescal pits are shown as nos. 4. These pits were all small and none over 5 ft. in diam. The main trails are all shown, though most of them are barely traceable now. Bill says when he first came here in 1926, they were all plain, and that the brush which has grown up so thickly in the camp now, was then cleared away, and then surrounding ground tramped clear of grass, etc.*

## Neil's Diary, Apache Camp

When Grennie, Art, and Bill arrived, they went directly to the top of a long ridge where a satellite camp was—about a mile and a half north and a thousand feet higher. We have put this off until our second day—we're going to need all the time we can get.

It's cold and clear. We drive up the arroyo as we did yesterday—six bone-jarring miles. Parking, we follow the route of the trail my father must have taken in 1931, past the lower camp we saw yesterday, up the bottom of a long ravine, through patches of snow and thick brush, coming out on a flat savanna of oak and juniper. We spread out and begin to sweep east toward more open country. The first sign that we are close is a big pothole worn into a granite boulder— full of water, just as it was in 1931, when my father photographed it.

Seth sees something ahead.

Several hundred yards away, almost hidden in the shade of a big oak tree, is a low stone wall. Almost right away Barney sees the roof structure of another one.

The one Seth spotted is round, but smaller than the one in the lower camp. It is the one my father photographed with Art and Bill posed in front. The two doorjambs are still there. One of them has brands carved into it: we can make out "RC," and then what looks like two lazy "O"s. The Apaches knew the local ranch brands and carved them into a saddle found in one of these camps. They evidently had also carved them into this doorframe. "RC" was not the Rancho Carretas brand. That brand was "JC," with the "J" backwards, but there is no mistaking the "R" for a reversed "J." Nor do I know what the lazy "O" brand is, though an "O," possibly from the Palomas Ranch, was the brand carried by one of the steers the Apaches brought into the Bootheel in 1923.[5]

The wall is constructed of closely fitting cobbles and is about a foot and a half thick by about four feet high. The stones were once chinked with adobe. Inside, half-covered with snow, is a rusty, square, two-gallon lard tin with a piece of wire through the rim to make a handle. The Apaches used it as a bucket. Margot is behind the camera again today, and I tell her that I think this very bucket is one my father saw and inventoried.

Soon everyone is finding things. The ground is, in places, littered with bits of rusty metal, scraps of tin cans, barbed wire, and glass. We find many obsidian nodules called Apache Tears. Barney says he has seen them nowhere else on the way up or on any other part of the ridge, only in the vicinity of the houses. So they were almost certainly brought here — perhaps as gaming pieces or for ceremonial use. They could have been used in a children's game similar to jacks that both Western Apaches and Chiricahuas played.[6]

Not far from the round house with the carved door frame is a rectangular one with the same kind of rounded corners we found in the lower camp. This house still has part of its wooden roof structure: a support pole at each end supporting a ridgepole and one rafter. Seeing these weathered, sagging poles, just where the Apaches placed them at least seventy years ago, and just as my father saw them, is profoundly moving, because, though perishable, they have endured, just like the stone.

There is an unexpected find: a perfect deer skull. I am at once reminded of the only photograph of my father in the entire diary: one simply labeled "My first Deer." My father shot his first deer, a whitetail buck, and I sometimes think this may have been his proudest moment of the trip. He and Bill and Art lived off what they could hunt. Here he was proving himself as a hunter in the company of a couple of leathery veterans whose very living often depended on bagging wild game.

I tell this story to the others, and the skull takes on meaning—one of those bridges that we construct between events when it seems that certain things were meant to be, were preordained. As has happened so many times before on this quest, we have a talisman that seems to have been waiting, utterly undisturbed, like the perfect little stone houses.

This was an unimagined place we were looking for until we found it, and now, as we see it, the place slowly takes on the power of hallowed ground. Not because of my father and what he did here, but because of the Apaches and what they did. As we walk through the camp that afternoon, examining the houses, touching the stones, picking up artifacts, wondering how they were used, what it was like to live here, what the people were like, the camp takes on a life, a presence, a history of its own. It becomes for us a place rich in human history. It is hardly a lost city, but because we know some of what happened here, that which we do *not* know takes on the urgency of a half-remembered dream.

When the camp was discovered in 1926 those who found it came back more than once, looted the place, and fired some of the houses. The Apaches then returned and removed virtually everything in the camp. It appears to us that, after my father left the place in 1931, no non-Apache ever returned to disturb it—an act of omission that almost seems to have the weight of reverence. Neither Alfonso nor the owner of the ranch had any idea who built these houses or what went on here. It dawns on me that, possibly, we are the only ones left who know what this place is.

From up here the Apaches could have seen forever. They could have seen almost all the way to Janos, some fifty miles away; they could have seen clear to the south end of the Carretas Plains and to the mouth of the Carretas Pass. Up here they would never have had their backs to the wall; they could have disappeared in a flash into a dozen ravines and been unfindable in the maze of canyons and ridges to the west.

No one knows how long people had been living in this campsite. The people had to have been ingenious, industrious, and, above all, bold enough to have built an elaborate, permanent establishment in the backyard of their enemies. They had invested all they had into making the stone buildings, the corrals, the shelters. They felt safe; they had homes. But when Bill and Moroni found this place, the Apaches vanished in an instant, leaving everything behind: their food caches, their hides, their dried meat, weapons, and clothing, just as they had been doing for centuries when surprised or attacked. They left with only the clothes they wore and what they could grab and carry.

When these people left, my father assumes that they moved south and set up camp, though a much smaller one, in the Chita Huecas. Did the camp in the Espuelas house a large number of people, only some of whom went to the Chita Huecas? Francisco Zozaya thinks many of them went farther south, into the Sierra Tasahuinora. Others in Mexico think that some of them went back to San Carlos. Could some of them have gone beyond the Tasahuinora into the really wild country east of Nácori Chico? If so, does this bring us full circle? It was, after all, in October 1927, the year following Bill's discovery of this camp, that Francisco Fimbres and his family were attacked only ninety miles to the south.

This little site of human habitation is full of history, full of violence, full of secrecy and the determination to survive, but beyond the obvious, we are mostly guessing at what went on here, or at what these people's lives were like, where they came from or where they went after they left. Now we've been here, we know the place is real, but the people who lived here are no more real than they were before—in fact, even less so. The houses they built, the bits of rusty metal they saved and shaped, are so concrete, but the people themselves remain ghosts.

There are no recent signs of human activity, except for a truck tire—brought up as a feed container, the top of a fifty-gallon oil drum and a tin can or two. These might have been packed up here by cowboys a year—or many years—ago.

There are no signs of cattle, but there are many game trails leading in and out of the camp—probably bear trails, as there is a great deal of bear sign. How fitting, I think: this is the form in which the Apaches have returned—as their uncles, the bears. We feel that this is a secret place, with meaning only for us. For other visitors, the infrequent cowboy, the border-bound immigrant, the *narco-traficante*, the place means nothing, but it speaks to us, seeming to say: what took you so long.

**Grenville's Diary, cont'd.**

—*I have waited to describe in detail the main camp, the big corrals on the ridge, and the small corrals and calf pens, as these three places have more to them than do the other camps.*

—*The main camp consisted of 8 houses, and two brush shelters (nos. 14).*

—*The main corrals were extremely well made of posts and barbed wire, the fence being one of five strands, and the gates regular pull shut ones, the most common kind in this country. There were two of these corrals, side by side (no. 2 on plan). One had a large snubbing post in its center (no. 3). Their length and width would be about 30 paces by 20 paces. On the south and west sides of the corrals were two brush enclosures, in which houses stood.*

*No. 6 was of the circular kind, type 1.*

*No. 8 house was of type 6, and was completely in ruins.*

*No. 7 house was type 3. It was the best made house in the whole rancheria, and still in excellent condition. It was in this house that Bill found the reloading outfit. . . .*

*At no. 1, near the edge of the ridge and to southeast, are some pot holes in a group of large boulders there. These pot holes the Indians had used for tanning hides in, when they contained enough rainwater, and they still had a quantity of pounded oak bark in them.*

*Right north of the corrals was a mescal pit, near the edge of the ridge, (no. 11). Near this was a large pile of the bones of cattle, horses and mules apparently slaughtered there by the Apaches, for food. (no. 10).*

—*An excellent view could be had from the top of the ridge, in all directions, and this, strange to say, was the only camp which commanded such a position. . . .*

*It might be well to add here that the brush fences in this rancheria are exactly like those in the Chita Hueca rancheria. The house types both here and at the Chita Hueca rancheria are hard to account for, they not being of the true Apache type, with the exception of the temporary brush shelters, which are probably Apache. House type no. 1 is the nearest approach to the true Apache dwelling that I have yet seen. It is an interesting thing that the stone walls these Apaches have built, are very well laid up, in adobe usually, and are quite thick, being from two to two and a half feet through. All top layers of roofs here are of bear grass thatching, with a covering of adobe at times.*

—*The Apaches have not been back to this camp for at least two years or even three. They did come back after the raid in 1926 at some time or another, but never to stay, merely to clean up, and this they did thoroughly. Not a thing was left in the houses, or about the camps which was moveable. Every scrap of stuff, whether useful or not, was taken away, It seems as though the Apaches had made a point of doing this, maybe to give the idea that they had moved away, never to return. That they still come back to the S. Espuela is known though, and they certainly must have other camps in the mountains, not so far away to the south, west, or north.*

### Neil's Diary, Rancho las Piedras

The Apache have well-documented lifeways that they followed before and after the establishment of reservations. These two camps might be said to represent an undescribed lifeway—a post-surrender, Old Mexico way, adapted to an existence dependent on hideouts, stealing, raiding, and building occasional ties with non-Indian collaborators. I wonder if they could have been doing this all along, somehow unknown to the rest of the world. As much as my experience of being here adds to the information in the diary, many questions remain, and many new ones emerge.

Cautious to a fault, my father makes no interpretation of this remarkable rancheria, but to summarize and speculate is irresistible to me. This is a substantial rancheria—over two miles from end to end, with eight houses and two separate, elaborate corral-and-pen complexes built using five-strand barbed wire fences, slide-bar gates, even a snubbing post in one of the corrals, to be used for roping and training saddle horses. A number of people must have lived here, and it must have taken a great deal of cooperative effort to build all of this.

This camp resembles the other one, in the Chita Hueca, as my father notes, in building technique for houses as well as fences. Both camps, but this one especially, seem clearly designed as a livestock-handling facility, designed for butchering and for drying beef and tanning hides.

This camp could have been just a permanent rancheria where ten or fifteen people subsisted on other people's meat and a little hunting and gathering, hoping not to be discovered. It could have been a temporary base of operations for some group only when they wanted to steal livestock and butcher meat in some quantity to be carried away and used in another location where they could then live without having to steal, thereby not betraying their presence.

There apparently were calf pens, but used how? Perhaps the inhabitants were actually breeding and raising livestock. They must have had some way to feed animals for a length of time. Perhaps they were even letting them out to graze, unless they only used the pens to hold stock while they were preparing to butcher them. This could have been a volume operation: there was a sledge for hauling meat, and there were many drying racks.

The place is not far from the U.S. border and from the remote, sparsely populated New Mexico Bootheel. As noted before, Las Piedras Canyon feeds right into one of the two valleys the Apaches always favored for travel when raiding. This camp certainly does not prove that butchered meat was being smuggled across the border, but if the Apaches were going to do that, this is an ideal location.

What the camp seems to imply about the way it was used fits well with the Mexican oral history I have been hearing for years: that this was a rustling operation run by Apaches and others for smuggling dried meat and hides across the border. According to many, there was collusion between the Apaches here and those from San Carlos. In the 1930s Stewart Hunt saw what he was certain were heavily used Apache trails in the Espuelas above his ranch, El Tapila. Francisco Zozaya's old cowboy friend Agustin González, who was in on the discovery of the other Apache camp, was certain of this trafficking and even saw an American man and woman who were involved with the Apaches. The eminent archaeologist, Dr. Charles Di Peso, told me in 1978 that the Mexican cowboys he met during the course of excavations in the area thought that camps like this one north of the Carretas Pass were used by Apaches from San Carlos, who would drive pickups to remote border locations where they would meet Sierra Madre Apaches and trade with them.

From the historical record it is clear that for ten or fifteen years after the surrender of Geronimo, Apaches moved across the border: renegades leaving San Carlos, the Apache Kid, Apaches from Mexico making visits to San Carlos and Fort Apache. The camp was established by the 1890s, if not long before, and it remained in use until at least 1926, when it was discovered. Remote and sparsely populated today, the country between the Espuelas and San Carlos was much more so in the 1920s and 1930s. The roads were few, and it would not have been a difficult thing for a group of mounted men with pack animals to have moved between the Espuelas and the Apache reservations. It is a straight-line trip of about one hundred and seventy-five miles, and they could have done it in three or four days at the very most. Of course they would have had to travel without being detected or caught as they crossed the big ranches of the Bootheel.

Having said that, other questions remain. Was there a market for hides and dried meat, and would smuggling it have been worth the trouble and the danger?

There might well have been a market in Chihuahua and Sonora for jerky. Drying was the only way to preserve meat, but doing it took time and skill. There might have been an illicit market for well-tanned leather, too. Lloyd Davis, the saddlemaker I met in Tucson who grew up in Chuhuichupa during the 1930s, said that it was very difficult to get good tanned leather in local settlements.

There could easily have been a barter market on the reservations. San Carlos did not have much good agricultural land, and government rations had ended following the cessation of hostilities. Following 1886, Apaches had hardly any cattle of their own, and neighboring white ranchers grazed their cattle heavily on reservation land, with devastating effect. The economic depression that hit the entire country in the 1890s must have severely affected the reservations.

Between 1910 and 1920 the few cattle allocated to the Apaches by the government were usually killed for badly needed food, so the herds grew slowly, if at all.[7] The only real employment was off-reservation wage labor, and by the end of World War I this is how many Apaches made a living. At the same time, almost a decade earlier than the Great Depression of the 1930s struck the rest of the country, the economic crisis seized San Carlos. The superintendent of the reservation wrote, "It is impossible to picture to you the hard times these people have passed through since the late war." The mines closed, there was no road building, ranchers stopped hiring Indian labor, and "many Indians, heretofore independent, have returned penniless to the reservation and have to be fed from the storehouse here [at San Carlos]."[8] The employment situation at Fort Apache may have been worse.

Poverty, unemployment, a shortage of food, a demand for dried meat and good leather.

Need — opportunity — market.

Possibly, but worth the risk on the part of reservation Apaches? There were easier ways of getting food and making a living, but in certain quarters, status and glory may have been associated with such daring exploits. The risk may not even have been that great, if, as Di Peso suggested, collaborators drove to an isolated part of the border in pickup trucks and waited to meet people with pack animals from the other side. Other smugglers did it all the time.

## 20

# The Smugglers

**Oct. 30, 1931, Las Piedras Canyon, S. Espuela, Chihuahua,**
**Grenville's Diary**

*We packed up and came on out this morning. At the mouth of the canyon, where it enters Las Piedras Can., we ran on two Americans, friends of Bill's. Their outfit consisted of four pack animals, and two mounts. We gave them a bad scare, they having guilty minds, and being in the smuggling game. They had come south over the mountains from near the line, just got in that very morning, and were waiting for a load of illegal goods being brought to them from Casas Grandes.*

**Neil's Diary, Rancho las Piedras**

The border is like a third nation and always has been. These men had either followed the old smuggler's route down the Animas Valley or, even more likely, the spine of the Peloncillo Mountains, and had then gone up the Cajon Bonito, to connect with the canyons leading over to Chihuahua. In all the world this border is the longest between a "developed" and a "developing" nation. It created its own economy, and Bill Curtis may well have been a part of it. Prohibition was still in effect, so Bill's friends were most likely waiting for liquor, but the contraband could have been raw gold, silver, jewelry—anything in demand in one country and in supply in the other. It could also have been marijuana. Long grown in Mexico and used by Mexicans on both sides of the border, demand for it had been growing as the Roaring Twenties and the Jazz Age swept the United States.[1]

**Grenville's Diary, cont'd.**

*We all sat down in the sun to talk for a while. Right across the canyon from us was a rocky point, and in among the rocks there we heard a mountain lion scream. He soon came into view. Art went after him, but had no luck. All of us came on up Las Piedras Canyon about two miles, to water and make camp for tonight. The two Americans were pretty good biscuit makers. One of them says that the Mexicans of the Aros*

*River district, claim that these Apaches have their headquarters some-*
*where in the vicinity of the junction of the Aros and Bonita Rivers, on the*
*other side of the Aros Riv. from here. This place must be over 200 miles to*
*the south.*[2]

## Neil's Diary, Chuhuichupa

Barney, Nelda, Seth, Kathy, and I are talking with Juan Portillo. His
father grew up on a ranch called La Nopalera, south of Nácori Chico,
not far from the junction of the Aros and the Bonito Rivers.

Almost casually, Portillo has just told us something that we have
never heard: that his grandfather personally knew Apache Juan, that
Juan used to come to the Portillo Ranch. When we hear something
like this, that we have never heard before, it's like a glint of gold in the
quartz.

It's 1908, and Juan Portillo's grandfather homesteads a ranch on the
Rio Bonito, south of Nácori Chico. Not long after he has settled in,
Apache Juan pays a visit with a party of six people—two young
women and four men. Portillo is the first settler on this part of the
Rio Bonito, so of course the minute he appears the Apaches know it.

Portillo figures it might be a good idea to feed the Apaches and
help them out, to get on their good side. It seems to have worked.
Apache Juan comes back two to four times over the course of one
year, and he never bothers the Portillo Ranch.

Juan Portillo delivers a detailed description of these people. They
have bows, and their arrows are made from pitch pine with fire-
hardened wood points and feathers stuck on with pitch. They wear
gee-strings only, and have sandals or bare feet. They wear their hair
long and with a headband with "little things" hanging down. As a
present they give a beautifully tanned buckskin to his grandfather—
so soft you could fold it like cloth. The grandfather gives these people
denim clothes on later visits. Apache Juan speaks some Spanish.
When the Apaches do kill a cow, they leave behind a figure in the
shape of a cow, complete with the brand. There was never any trouble
with the Apaches in this area, Juan Portillo says—only up near Tres
Rios, where "they killed that lady."

This snatch of folklore may be entirely true. It was not at all unusual for Apaches to put in an appearance like this when someone

new settled in the mountains. As intriguing as the story is, it also tells us how little we know about Apache Juan. Nearly every Apache man encountered in Mexico after 1900 is called Apache Juan. Apache Juan is many men: the Apache Robin Hood.

### Grenville's Diary, cont'd.

*He [the American smuggler] also says that some three or four years ago, a white boy came down to Douglas with two Chiricahua Apaches from Mescalero. One of these was an old man, the other was a young fellow. They tried at Douglas to get passports to go to Fronteras, Sonora, but were refused by the Mexican authorities. Finally the white boy drove them out to San Bernardino, and the two Apaches crossed the line just above Slaughters,[3] after dark, and on foot. They headed for Fronteras, and stole two Mexican ponies in the Fronteras district, which they rode bareback. Some Mexican ranchers got after them to see what they were doing, and the two Apaches made a run for the U.S. line. The young fellow split off from the old man, and got back in a day and night. The old man did not make it back till three days and nights later. The white boy who picked them both up at the line again, took them back to Mescalero. They never got what they were after apparently.*

### Nov. 1, 1931, Las Cuevas, Pulpit Canyon, Sonora

*Left Las Piedras Canyon in morning, and came back by way of MacNeil's ranch. The two Americans loaded up their contraband, and went back over the mountains, to the U.S. line.*

### Nov. 2, 1931, Colonia Oaxaca, Sonora

*Left the Caves this morning, and came on down to the adobe house. Bill has 118 kids there now. Bill, Art and I went on down to Col. Oaxaca from there, I stopping on the way down to copy off the pictures in the cave at the foot of Pulpit Rock, before mentioned.*

### Nov. 3–Nov. 7, 1931, Colonia Oaxaca, Sonora

*Dug some more over at the ruins near here, but without finding anything beyond further house structures. Caught another big otter and also a large coon, both on the river bank. We also caught a skunk, but he was too little to skin. The skunks are very numerous and bold here, coming right in the house at night, if you leave the doors open. The dogs* had a fight with one which they had cornered behind some shovels on the back porch. They finally got him, but not before everything was pretty well perfumed.

### Nov. 8, 1931, Douglas, Ariz.

Left Col. Oaxaca this morning, and got in here about eight o'clock. It drizzled most of the way out, and the road got pretty slick, with the result that we were stuck two or three times, and well plastered with mud.

### Nov. 9, 1931, Douglas, Ariz.

Traded a couple of saddle blankets to Bill for a tanned cowhide which he had taken from the S. Espuela rancheria, during his raid, in 1926, and which he still had, although part of it is cut out. This along with the other articles he gave me, from the Espuela rancheria, are shown on pages 138, 140 [of the diary].[4]

—Leave for Tucson, and home now, by way of San Carlos.

—This ends the second trip to the Sierra Madre Apache country.

13. Top: The Apache Kid, center. Courtesy Arizona Historical Society. Negative #14335

14. Below: Guadalupe Quesada, Sierra Chita Hueca, 1976.

15. Above: Margot at the upper Apache camp, Sierra las Espuelas, 1997.

16. Top right: Chita Hueca Apache camp—group of dwellings.

17. Bottom right: First house, main camp, Sierra Chita Hueca, 1931.

APACHE CAMP ON SIERRA CHITA HUECA

←N
10 FT.

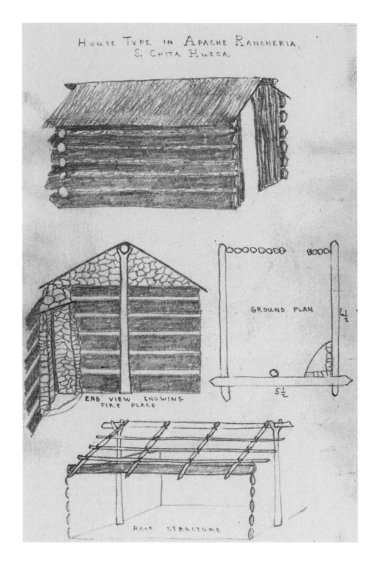

18. Above: House types, Apache Rancheria, Chita Hueca.

19. Top right: Circular piece of iron used by the Apaches as an alarm gong at the Chita Hueca camp, 1931.

20. Bottom right: Articles found at the Chita Hueca camp in 1931: 1. pack saddle; 2. worked stick of unknown use; 3. cantle of Gabilondo's saddle; 4. horn and pommel of Gabilondo's saddle; 5, 7. rawhide strips used in lashing fencing together; 6. rope twister.

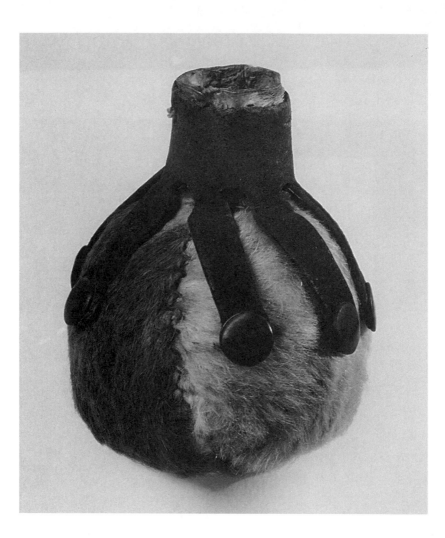

21. Small leather bottle
found by Bill Curtis at
an Apache camp in 1926
and given to Grenville
Goodwin. Now at the
Arizona State Museum.
Courtesy Arizona State
Museum.

22. Above: Neil approaching the Sierra las Espuelas Apache Rancheria, 1997. He is holding a photograph taken from the same spot by Grenville Goodwin in 1931. Photo by Seth Goodwin.

23. Right: Seth and Kathy, Rancho la Cabaña, 1995.

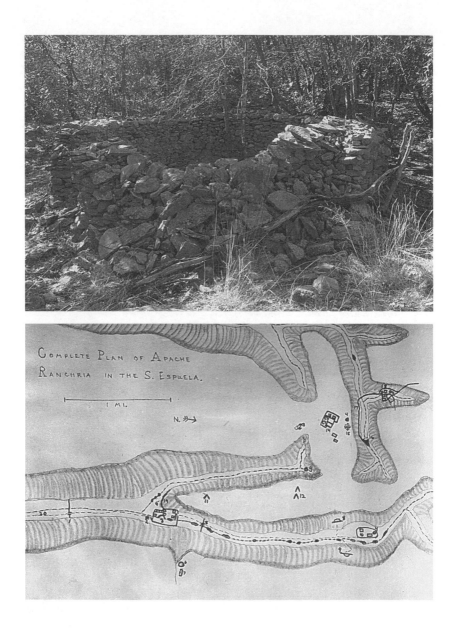

24. Top: Main Apache camp at Sierra las Espuelas,
house number 8, 1997. Photo by Seth Goodwin.

25. Below: Sierra las Espuelas Apache Rancheria —
complete plan.

26. Top: House number 8 near corrals on ridge, Sierra
las Espuelas, 1997. Photo by Seth Goodwin.

27. Below: Bill Curtis at the Apache camp, Sierra las
Espuelas, 1931.

MAIN CAMP OF APACHE RANCHERIA, S. ESPUELA

N.

10 FT.

28. Top: House number 7 at Apache camp on top of ridge in the Sierra las Espuelas, 1931.

29. Below: Sierra las Espuelas Apache Rancheria— main camp.

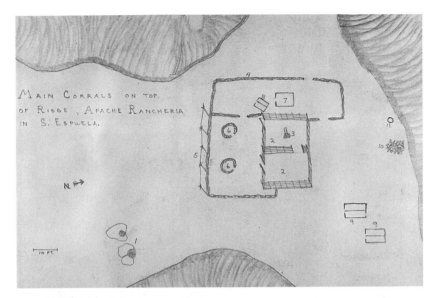

30. Top: Sierra las Espuelas Rancheria — main
corrals on ridge.

31. Below: Neil at Sierra las Espuelas Apache
camp, 1997. Photo by Seth Goodwin.

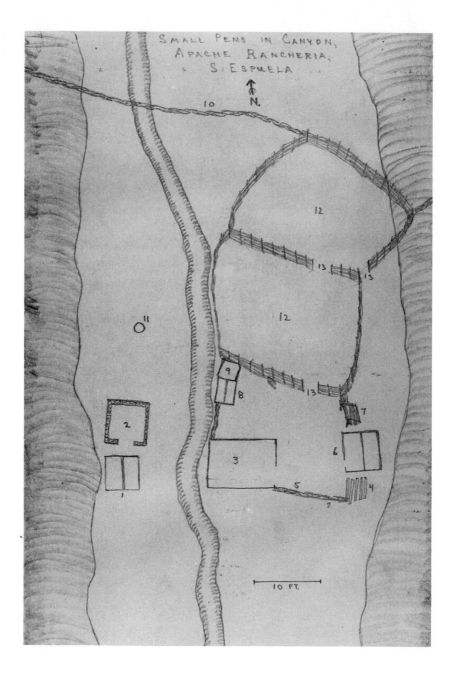

32. Above: Sierra las Espuelas Rancheria — small pens in canyon below ridge.

33a. Right: Stone house types, Apache camps, Sierra las Espuelas.

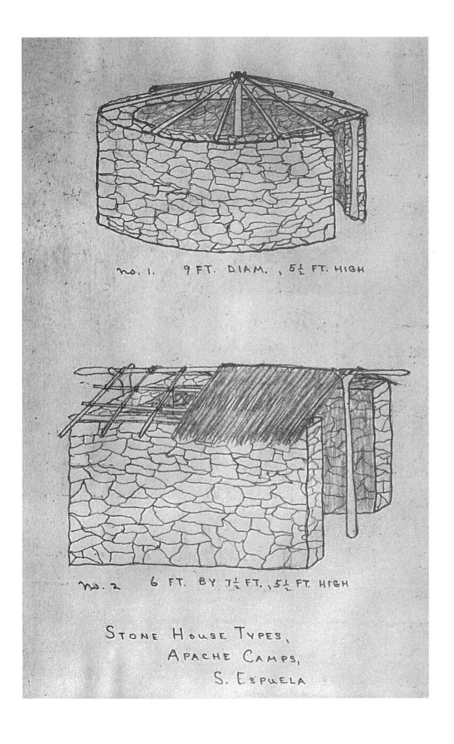

no. 1.    9 FT. DIAM. , 5½ FT. HIGH

no. 2    6 FT. BY 7½ FT. ,5½ FT. HIGH

STONE HOUSE TYPES,
APACHE CAMPS,
S. ESPUELA

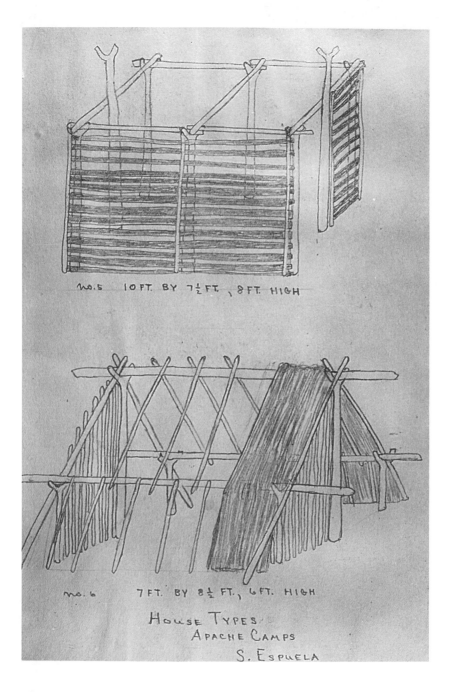

NO.5    10 FT. BY 7½ FT. , 8 FT. HIGH

NO.6    7 FT. BY 8½ FT., 6 FT. HIGH

HOUSE TYPES
APACHE CAMPS
S. ESPUELA

33b. House types, Apache camps, Sierra las Espuelas.

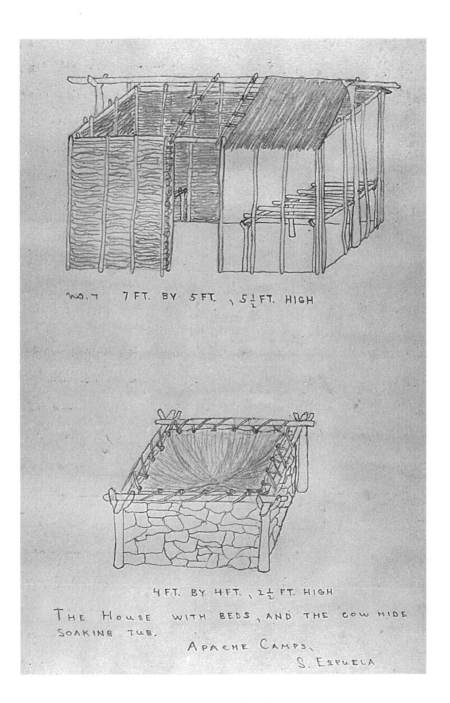

NO.7 7 FT. BY 5 FT. , 5½ FT. HIGH

4 FT. BY 4 FT. , 2½ FT. HIGH

THE HOUSE WITH BEDS, AND THE COW HIDE
SOAKING TUB.

APACHE CAMPS,
S. ESPUELA

33c. House type, soaking tub, Apache camps, Sierra las Espuelas.

7 FT. BY 9 FT., 6 FT. HIGH INSIDE,
SUNK 14 IN.

no. 3

8 FT. BY 8 FT., 7 FT. HIGH

no. 4

HOUSE TYPES,
APACHE CAMPS,
S. ESPUELA

33d. House types, Apache camps, Sierra las Espuelas.

# Part Four

## 21
# Echoes of Mexico at San Carlos

**Neil's Diary, 1962, Mount Kisco, New York**

I finish the diary, and I look up, look around. It's the same room at home north of New York City, it's still raining, still November, and only a few hours have passed since I began the diary. For the first time, I feel I have entered my father's world.

No one's here. Not my father, not the Apaches. Just the view out the window. The story might as well have ended in midsentence. It's almost like a death, where nothing happens next. But, as it turns out, it's not a death: plenty happens next. It's just that discovering and telling the rest of the story is more or less up to me. Grennie's travels to Mexico are over.

In the late fall of 1931, at the age of twenty-three and a half, my father resists what must have been a powerful impulse. He decides not to return for another trip to Mexico with Bill Curtis—or on his own for that matter. He also decides once and for all not to return to the University of Arizona. He has formulated a plan, and it is the beginning of a clearly visualized lifelong trajectory.

Years later he wrote a letter to describe this watershed decision:

**Oct. 10, 1937, Santa Fe, Grenville's Diary**

*. . . My interest in the Sierra Madre Apache is a personal one. I became interested in the southern Athabascan peoples some years ago. The Sierra Madre Apache offered intriguing possibilities and so I started there. I made two trips in the Sierra Madre country: in the fall of 1930 and again in the fall of 1931.*

*After completion of the second trip, the wisest course seemed to become intimately acquainted with an Apache culture and learn as much of the language as possible, before attempting to further investigate the Sierra Madre Apache, which at best would be very difficult. Accordingly I went to the San Carlos and Fort Apache reservations, commenced a study of the Apache located there, which has lasted over a period of seven years.*

*It was my fond hope to someday tackle the Sierra Madre Apache, taking only two or three Chiricahua Apache along, men who talked the language, had relatives among the Sierra Madre group and knew the country.*[1]

### Neil's Diary, San Carlos

So, biding his time, Grennie begins his seven years of study, with one eye on Mexico—just like the reservation Apaches themselves, as he is soon to find out. The Sierra Madre Apaches are still in the back of peoples' minds, still part of their lives, still to be reckoned with.

### 1932, Bylas, Grenville's Diary

*During ethnological field work on the San Carlos Reservation, March to July, of 1932, several instances of contacts with the Sierra Madre Apache from Old Mexico after 1886 came to light. They are set forth below.*

*Anna Price:*

*"This happened three years ago in the fall. I went across the river from Bylas and started back into the hills. I had gone about three miles when I heard some people coming, so I got in under a mesquite tree where I could hide. They were hai-aha and I knew this because I could hear them talking together plainly.[2] They must have seen me, because I could hear one of the men saying, 'do-da, do-da, don't kill that poor old woman.'[3] I guess some of them wanted to kill me, but they didn't bother me. I do not know where these hai-aha went from there or why they had come up from Old Mexico. I guess maybe they were going to Cibecue to try and catch some girls there while they were out gathering berries."*

### Neil's Diary, San Carlos

Anna Price, nearly one hundred years old, the daughter of the great White Mountain chief, Diablo, was one of my father's closest friends and one of his most knowledgeable and reliable sources of cultural and historical information. He spent hours listening to her, and it was like browsing through a great library. She called my father *Chi-cho*, my grandson.

When Anna saw this mounted party of men near Bylas in 1929 speaking the unmistakable Chiricahua dialect, she rightly feared them as marauders, maybe murderers. And she was not the only one;

the police at Cibecue saw them too, as Grennie learned back in 1930.[4] It was also in 1929 that the Apache camp on the Sierra Chita Hueca was discovered. In Mexico, opinion is divided on where the Apaches went from there. The people Anna Price speaks of could very well have come from the Chita Hueca camp, and they could have been constantly on the move, trying to avoid detection and find a safe haven.

Neil Buck, my father's closest Apache friend, had heard that the Sierra Madre Apache could have been hiding in the Huachuca Mountains, in Arizona, just north of the Mexican border west of Douglas.

### Dec. 17, 1932, Payson, Arizona, Grenville's Diary

*On a trip with Neil Buck, was telling him about the renegade Chiricahua in Mexico. He knew of them all right, and said that he had heard from Apache scouts stationed at Fort Huachuca that not long ago one of the scouts had been off in the Huachuca mountains and had heard a Chiricahua girl singing there.[5] He had known what she was, and so left her alone. Later on, quite often, they saw tracks which they knew to be of the renegade Chiricahua in the mountains, but they never had wanted to bother each other.*

### Neil's Diary, San Carlos

As always, these stories, so compounded of poignancy and menace, deliver a jolt of fear and mystery to the Apaches who recount them. Grennie makes no private comment on the credibility of the reports, but, perhaps convinced, accepts them at face value, knowing that the Sierra Madre Apache can cover great distances with equal measures of stealth and recklessness. It's not until later that year, when he goes to the Mescalero Reservation in New Mexico for the first time, that he meets some people who think of the Sierra Madre Apaches as kindred spirits, instead of as "enemy people."

### Nov. 16, 1932, Mescalero Agency, Grenville's Diary

*Visiting here, I met Sam Kenoi, a Ndéndaa'i Apache. I told him about hearing about there still being some Chiricahua in the Sierra Madre and he was very anxious to know if I knew the names of any of them. He knew of them apparently and from what can be gathered, the renegades now in the Sierra Madre must all be Ndéndaa'i.*

## Neil's Diary, the Bavispe Valley

If it is known anywhere what happened to the Apaches after 1930, it is in the villages of this valley and of the mountains to the east and south.

Like most other Chiricahuas, Sam Kenoi knew that there were some who remained in Mexico and never surrendered, and what he asks my father suggests that their names would still be recognized by family or friends now on the reservation. For Sam Kenoi and the other Chiricahuas, solid information from Grennie about long-lost relatives in Mexico might mean hope for the end to a separation long thought to be permanent. But even as my father and Sam are talking, that hope is growing dimmer, for the final act in the drama of the Sierra Madre Apaches is already under way in Mexico.

Since the fateful battle of April 1930 that claimed the lives of three Apaches and, ultimately, of Gerardo Fimbres, no sighting has been reported in Mexico. That surviving Apaches remain, hidden in the mountains, there is no doubt: they killed Gerardo, and some of them left their tracks in the Chita Hueca and Espuelas Mountains.

Following the death of Gerardo, the most hard-bitten of the Mexicans commit themselves to a campaign against all Apaches. The Mexican state and federal governments have washed their hands of the matter. The Sierra Madre, as always, is outside the law, and it is open season on Apaches.

In April 1932, only four months after Grennie left Mexico, an Apache camp near Nácori Chico is discovered and attacked, blood is shed, and a child is captured by the Mexicans. A brief mention of it is published in the Douglas paper a week later. I don't think Grennie ever saw the clipping; in any case, it appears nowhere in his papers. I will return to this story in detail later.

This act of violence revives the blood feud, which had been dormant for two years. According to another article in the Douglas paper, a few weeks after this attack Apaches come upon a Mexican cowboy in the mountains above Nácori Chico, catch him, and kill him with stones in revenge.[6]

Vengeful Nácori Chico ranchers determine once and for all to wipe out the Apaches. On what is described as "an errand of extermination," in late June 1932 a posse of fifteen forms, made up of men from Nácori Chico and Bacadéhuachi and led by Ramon Hurtado and Manuel Madrid.[7] On July 1, after combing the Sierra Madre for two weeks, the group comes upon an Apache camp with eight people—mostly women and children. The Apaches try to flee, but it's too late; the Mexicans are everywhere. The camp is a killing ground. One woman, about forty years old, one about thirty, and a girl about twelve are killed outright. At least two get away.

The dust settles. Amid the blood, the lifeless forms, the scattered possessions and the ringing silence, are three stunned and terrified Apache children: one boy, and a three-year-old girl and her twin brother. The twins are taken in by Ramon Hurtado and his family and are baptized as Rosa and Geronimo Hurtado.[8] They contract dysentery or some other disease and are unable to eat what the Mexicans feed them. They do not survive the year. According to one version I hear of, the boy deliberately bites through one of his own blood vessels, severing it and thereby bleeding to death.[9] What a deep river this stream of folklore is. This act of terrible determination by a child is equally remarkable whether imagined or factual.

If true—and the child would have to have been older than three—if true, what a ferocious imperative to be embedded in a being so young and so unformed. Or rather, the boy may have been young, but he was by no means unformed. I wonder, could this have been something he was trained to do: elect death before Mexican captivity? Or was it simply a last instinctive act, desperate and defiant, beyond reason or choice? An act of utter, final, abandoned hopelessness.

If not true, the story is an intriguing act of Mexican imagination, fully resonant with the Mexican view of Apache ferocity. Even if recognized as apocryphal, this story would transmit a fundamental, accepted truth in the villages of the Sierra Madre: that there is something in the Apache being that is simply beyond the experience of the Mexicans. But in their folklore, Mexicans find the humanity of the Apaches as compelling as their "savagery," as if, like the seventeenth-century Jesuit and Franciscan missionaries before them, the Mexicans see a human soul locked inside every Apache.

As other Apache captives before them, the twins are baptized at once. A lot has changed in a hundred years. In 1832 there was a bounty on Apaches in Mexico, and a child's scalp would have fetched twenty-five pesos in Chihuahua City, while his soul would have gone ignored. Now the soul goes to God. It must have been devoutly hoped that taking in the children, caring for them, and bringing them to Christ after murdering their families would gain some collective moral ground. When the children die, they are duly buried in the old cemetery of Nácori Chico.

Of the three children, the only survivor is a boy of perhaps two years old, who was unharmed in the bloodbath. He somehow survives what the other two could not and begins life with the family of Manuel Madrid, one of the leaders of the attack. He is given the name Julio, for the month of his capture.[10]

### Neil's Diary, Tucson, Arizona

Tom Hinton, an anthropologist who spent time in the Sierra Madre in the 1950s, met Julio, who was, at this time, working as a bookkeeper in a large pharmacy in Hermosillo. Fully acculturated twenty years after his capture, Julio was ever mindful of who he really was. Tom describes his conversation with a mutual acquaintance:

A school teacher from Bacadéhuachi, Lorenzo Robles, said that Julio is an intimate friend of his. He described him as very intelligent and of good character. He said that on one occasion Julio, who was a little drunk said, "You all tell me how grateful I should be for being raised like a civilized Mexican. *Pues no me agradacio nada.* [I can't feel grateful for anything.] If I had my way I would be up there in the Sierra fighting right now." (Robles says there was real malice in his voice.) Robles told him he did not really think he would want to be up there with the broncos living like an animal. Julio answered that he would rather be there. "I have one great desire—that would be to put a knife between the ribs of all those who killed my mother and my people there in the Sierra and I would start with Manuel Madrid.[11]

Julio agreed to talk to Tom under one condition: Tom was never to publicize his Apache identity or his whereabouts. Julio had already been burned once. He had loved a Mexican girl whose family, when they learned of his Apache blood, instantly forbade contact between the boy and their daughter. To be an Apache in Sonora is to be an untouchable, and Julio did not want anyone to know who he was ever again.

### Neil's Diary, Cumpas, Sonora

After a few years with the Madrid family, Julio was taken in by another family, the Medinas of Cumpas. It is ironic that we have nowhere to turn in trying to reconstruct the lives of the Sierra Madre Apaches but to the descendants of the people who swore to exterminate them. As we stand in front of the house that used to belong to the Medina family, people talk with us and summon fragmentary memories of Julio: he was different from Mexicans, his face was different. We meet a man who went to school with Julio for several years, but remembers only that he was very brown and he talked "muy mocho"—with a heavy accent.

I had heard that Julio was once a bookkeeper at a large pharmacy in Hermosillo. Now we hear that he was also a lawyer, a teacher, and a mechanic. The consensus here is that he was a schoolteacher—a very good one—and that while he was on a trip to Mexico City in 1962 with his students, there was a traffic accident in which he perished.[12] But we also hear of other ways in which he was thought to have died, even that he went to live among his fellow Indians, the Yaquis, along the coast of Sonora.

Reinvented in the Mexican rumor mill, taking on a new life as his story was told and retold, Julio seems more and more a phantom. He was real once, but has become a wisp of folklore. It's only because of Tom Hinton's brief encounter with Julio that I have much more than a name—and it wasn't even his real name.

I don't believe my father ever heard of Julio. If he had, the story would have appeared somewhere in his papers, where he faithfully reported even the most fragmentary stories, as in this letter to his colleague, Morris Opler.

### Jan. 8, 1934, Grenville's Diary

... *Last summer or spring, a little girl about eight years old was caught by two Mexicans. They kept her tied on the end of a rope that was fastened to a tree. A friend of mine down in Mexico offered a hundred pesos for her, but before be could get in touch with the Mexicans who had her, she had died. It is hard to imagine how wild these people are.*[13]

### Neil's Diary, Bavispe

In the Bavispe Valley I have heard of no captive girl taken in the spring or summer of 1933. Is this a lost story that somehow fell through the net of local folklore so that no one alive today knows anything of her? If so, it hints of the many secrets the Sierra must hide: Apaches encountered, captured, killed, and never spoken of.

I know of only one possible way this story could be tied to a known captive. When we were in Nácori Chico we were told of a beautiful fifteen-year-old Apache girl who came to Bavispe, badly wounded and desperate for help. The people of Bavispe did what they could for her. She refused to eat and died from her wound. That was all anyone knew in Nácori Chico.

However, when we ask about this story in the streets of Bavispe, the people tell us that there was an Apache girl, a much younger one — brought here uninjured a year earlier, in 1932. We turn to Francisco Zozaya, and soon we are joined by his cousin, Amiglia Samaniego. Together they tell us the story of the little Apache girl and Bil Bao, whose name was really Bill Bye. He was a Norwegian who came to Mexico via the United States.

As Francisco has already told us, Bye lived alone with a pack of dogs in the Sierra Tasahuinora, a wild mountain range east of Bavispe. He made regular visits to the village to see pretty Maria Rascón, who lived there, and to take her to the dances during festival days. But when he appeared in Bavispe one day in late July 1932 with a nine-year-old captive Apache girl he had caught in the mountains, it caused a sensation.

Bill had been hunting, as was his custom, with his dogs. They were following a scent, and he heard them ahead, out of sight, barking the way they always did when they had something treed. He came upon them and found they had driven a small girl into the lower branches of a tree. He called them off, tied them up and coaxed the girl out of the tree. She was alone and very thin, probably starving, so Bill decided to bring her into town. He named her for the month and place of her capture: Julia Tasahuinora.

The little Apache boy, similarly named Julio, had been captured above Bacadéhuachi, some seventy miles to the south and about two weeks earlier. The scene of his capture had been a massacre: women and children killed, though perhaps not all. Could nine-year-old Julia have been a survivor of this carnage, and could she have managed to cover those seventy Sierra Madre miles in a couple of weeks? Possibly, but Francisco Zozaya believes that there was already at that time a large group of Apaches in the Tasahuinora and that Julia was of this group.

Throughout Julia's first night in Bavispe she made owl calls and other kinds of animal cries. Amiglia Samaniego was nine, the same age as Julia. Remembering the very house where Bill and the girl stayed, Amiglia closes her eyes, and the summoned memory still has the power to move her. She talks through waves of emotion, remembering that Julia's hair was straight and long and shiny when it was washed by one of the village women. Her arms were very thin, and there was nothing she would eat. When we asked her what Julia's face was like, Amiglia put her hands up to the side of her face and drew back on the corners of her eyes. Oriental eyes. The epicanthic fold, so common to Apaches.

Bill wanted to adopt Julia, but had no way to tell her so. Amiglia remembers that Bill had devised a plan for communication, but she did not know what it was — only that he was going to take Julia somewhere else. Bill and Julia left town, and she was never seen again in Bavispe. But in Mesa Blanca, a remote mountain settlement, we hear the rest of the story from a remarkable woman whose grandfather played a part in it himself.

### Neil's Diary, Mesa Blanca, Chihuahua

Manuela Chafino is a handsome woman of sixty-five with a short, stylish haircut. Her face is dark and lean and knowing. Trained as a kind of nurse, she has also taught in the local elementary school. She is the most knowledgeable person about her village history. Back in Bavispe, they think that Bill's only home was in the mountains, but in fact Bill Bye had lived in Mesa Blanca since 1918, making regular visits to his farm in the Tasahuinora. Manuela repeats the familiar details of the capture of *la Apachita*, and she knows her by the same name as they do in Bavispe.

What they do not know down in Bavispe is that Bill brought Julia here to Mesa Blanca because of Manuela's grandfather, Jesús Chafino. Jesús was Bill's plan for communicating with Julia, for it was common knowledge in Mesa Blanca that Jesús was an Apache himself. Manuela tells us that he was a captive from the 1880s who had been adopted by a Mexican family in Chihuahua City.[14] In those days Apaches were often taken captive, but for us this is astonishing news — the first time we have ever come across a known descendant of an Apache in Mexico. My eyes are riveted to her face, knowing now that she is at least one quarter Apache. We are sitting in the shade of a big willow tree in her yard, which is, ironically, on the site of Bill Bye's first log house. She chain-smokes and speaks with a slight speech impediment that gives her an oracular authority.

Her grandfather and Julia communicated easily in the Apache language, but the girl revealed little about her way of life and the circumstances of her capture. She said that there were others in her group, though not how many. Just before she was captured, she said, when she heard Bill Bye coming, she thought it might have been some more of her own people, but then the dogs ran at her and she was so afraid, and she went up the tree. By then the others she was with had run off.

She had been gathering wild onions of some kind and had on a buckskin dress and moccasins. When Bill brought her to Mesa Blanca she would eat nothing but marrow from bones she would break with a rock. Bill wanted to adopt her, but the mayor said that Chihuahua state law required that he bring the orphaned Indian to the authorities in Casas Grandes.

He did so, hoping for the best, but in town Julia was taken from Bill Bye, and he returned to Mesa Blanca certain he would never see the girl again. Officials in Casas Grandes placed Julia in the jail, for lack of other housing, while the disposition of her case was under consideration. After the initial terror of her capture by Bill, it might have been reassuring to speak to the old Apache, Jesús Chafino, who told her that Bill would take good care of her. But in Casas Grandes she found an unimaginable betrayal. They say she snarled at people and would scratch, bite if she could, and hide in the corner, allowing no one to see her face. She would not, or could not, eat the food she was offered, and she did not live to leave the Casas Grandes jail. They say she was buried in the city cemetery, but no one knows where anymore, and there is neither a death certificate nor a baptismal record to be found.

The Apache holocaust of 1932 ended in midsummer with the capture and death of Julia. But, as noted earlier, it began in April, with the capture of another child, whose story I have saved until now because it is so much more complete and because it covers a much longer period of time. Although my father had heard about this other little Apache girl from Bill Curtis's wife soon after she was captured, it was not until 1935 that he recorded anything about her.

### Oct. 1935, Tucson, Ariz., Grenville's Diary

*Saw Art Schrader in Tucson, on his way back to Douglas.*

*He said of the little Sierra Madre Apache girl who was captured by an American Rancher near Nácori Chico, that it happened in this way.*

*The rancher was riding through a canyon in the mountains. He was quite high up on the side of the hill and as he happened to look down hill he saw a wickiup standing some ways below him. Wondering if anyone was in it he dislodged a stone and rolled it down hill so that it went right through the wickiup. Out ran a woman and the little girl. The rancher with his high powered rifle shot at the woman as she ran, hitting her in the shoulder and knocking her down. But she got up and ran on. The second shot killed her. The little girl ran up to her and cried over her. The rancher rode up to her and took the little girl home with him. Art claimed that he shot the woman to get the fifty dollar bounty on these Apaches offered either by the State government or Federal government, I don't know which.*

### Neil's Diary, Nácori Chico

Although there is no evidence for a state bounty on Apaches, the governor of Sonora had made it official: in the Sierra Madre, Apaches could be shot on sight in order to right the wrong of the murder of Maria and Gerardo Fimbres.[15]

The man brought the little girl here to Nácori Chico, and Barney, Nelda, Seth, Don Metz, and I have come to pick up the old, cold trail. Rodolfo Rascon, the journalist who lives here, has followed this story himself for years. He settles us in the plaza to listen to the old men who remember what happened. It was only a few miles west of Nácori Chico, on a ranch called Los Laureles by the locals, that the little Apache girl was captured. It was owned by two Americans, Jack Harris and Jack Rowe. They called it The 31 Ranch, because in 1931 they had spotted an Apache in the distance while out riding fence line.

Aristeo García, the foreman of the 31, was the cowboy—Mexican, not American—who killed the woman with the Apache girl. He brought the girl to Jack Harris and his wife Dixie, who adopted her and named her Carmela. She was about three years old. The details of her capture that were written down by my father correspond with the other versions told and retold to us today in Nácori Chico. They also say that García was trailing stolen livestock when he came upon the camp, and that he shot the woman because he was alone and afraid that he himself would be in danger of ambush if she got away to spread the alarm. In written and oral history there are different versions, different justifications, some designed to make a folk hero out of García. Context aside, about one thing there is no debate: he gunned the woman down in cold blood, as if she were an animal.

### June 1936, Geronimo, Ariz., Grenville's Diary

*Bill Curtis and his wife stopped in to see me here. They spoke of the little girl who was captured from the Apache, the one whose mother was shot, described above.*

*They said that she was now in California, with the man and his wife. They, wishing to bring her into the US from Mexico, had some trouble and had to legally adopt her before they could bring her over at Naco. She is beginning to talk English now. When first caught she just cowered in the room at the ranch house and would not talk, eat or do anything. She was dressed in tanned cowhide and they took these clothes from her, giving her cloth clothes.*

*When they later brought them out and showed them to her again, she was evidently pleased and glad to see the clothes again. They could do nothing with her, and so sent for Lupe, the Apache girl in Nácori Chico. She came and tried to talk in Apache to the little girl, but could get no response whatever, and the little girl seemed more afraid of her than the others. However, she finally started to eat a little and after a bit seemed to be getting used to things.*

### Neil's Diary, Nácori Chico

In Nácori Chico the old men show us where the Harrises lived and where, for a year, they made a home for Carmela. The family and the Apache child are vividly remembered, but no one seems to have any idea what became of them once they left for California.

In fact, many years ago one person—the anthropologist Helge Ingstad—did look for her and find her, after he made a 1938 trip to the Sierra Madre in search of the Apaches. He heard about Carmela in Nácori Chico and after returning to the United States tracked down the Harrises in California, where he conducted the only known interview with her:

"They called me Bui (Owl Eyes). There were only women and children in the camp—four young women and three children besides me. Nana decided everything, and she was very strict. We lived in caves and small huts made of grass. We were always afraid that someone would come, so we moved often from mountain to mountain. One time Nana took me on her horse and we rode through a dark forest where I was hit in the face by a branch. I began to cry and Nana hid me in the mountains for a whole day, until she finally came back to get me."

Ingstad: "I asked if there were other Apaches in the mountains, and she said, 'We visited Indians who lived elsewhere. Once in a while some men would visit us, and one of them had great feathers on his head.'"

Ingstad: "When I asked if she only saw Indians, she answered that, 'There was often talk about a white man who lived with the others in the mountain.'"

Ingstad: "What did you live off? 'We ate mescal and dried meat, sometimes grass. We didn't have much—some skins, a knife, nails, a cup, that's about it.'"

Ingstad: "How were you dressed? 'We made clothes from leather and also wore moccasins.'"

Ingstad: "She then ran off and fetched the leather dress and moccasins that she was wearing when they caught her. 'Nana had just sewn a nice new dress for me out of leather, but then I was captured.'"

Ingstad: "I inquired whether there was any singing or dancing, and she said that they dared not make any noise, but that sometimes a woman sang her to sleep. 'It was definitely not my mother though. I don't think that I had either a mother or a father.'"

Ingstad: "Did you like it in the mountains with the Indians? 'I was often afraid. Nana was so strict, and I wasn't allowed to do anything. Once a little child cried very loudly and she held its mouth so that it died.'"

Ingstad: "Did you believe in a God? 'Every evening we got down on our knees and reached our hands to the heavens. All was quiet, no one said anything. But I don't know what God we prayed to.'"[16]

## Neil's Diary, Nácori Chico

Except for Ingstad's interview with Lupe and Tom Hinton's with Julio, this is the only other time I know of that something said by one of these Apaches has survived for us to read. Carmela's words describe a life so severe and isolated that it is beyond my comprehension. From that, she is snatched abruptly into the world of the people who have killed all her family, where she must learn a new language, eat strange food, wear strange clothes. Somehow she adjusts; the scar tissue forms. After all, Apache children — and for that matter Mexican children — have been doing so for three centuries of bitter warfare.

Of all the things that Bui speaks of, one of the most fascinating is her name. A careful analysis of the word "bui" indicates that, if the name refers to "owl," it appears to derive uniquely from the Western Apache dialect, as there is no corresponding word in Chiricahua or Mescalero Apache dialects. This would suggest a significant admixture of Western Apache among "Bui's" people.[17]

Carmela's memory that men came sometimes, one with a feather headdress, is intriguing; the image is reminiscent of distinctive Apache turkey-feather headpieces. The isolation she speaks of is not the Apache way: they depend profoundly on one another's company, but perhaps there is a precarious safety in this apartness. Misfortune befalling one small group might leave others undiscovered and therefore unharmed.

While we are in the Nácori Chico Plaza talking with Jesús Fuentes, the little boy in the "victory photograph," Rodolfo Rascón, the reporter we have met, remembers something Jack Harris told to Fuentes's father years ago: Carmela married a man that she had met in Los Angeles, who may have been an engineer and was of Apache descent. Then they moved to Texas. Carmela would be about sixty-five now, and it's possible that she is still alive. It's an electrifying thought.

She is, perhaps, that exquisitely unique being: a sole survivor, and she appears to have vanished without a trace — which may be exactly what she wants, so that she can remain undiscovered.

At other times I have heard that she and her adoptive mother, Mrs. Harris, went to Italy for a period of time to visit another Harris daughter, and, as time goes by and the idea of Carmela takes up residence in my mind, I have this powerful waking dream.

It is so real that I can hear the cicadas and smell the burnt, ancient Italian earth. I am sitting in a deeply shaded grape arbor with a flagstone floor. There is dense planting all around, a large stone house to the left. Beyond the arbor, the land drops steeply into a valley, and I am looking out across it to the other side, which is almost blindingly bright in the sunlight. In the foreground, seen only in silhouette, is Carmela, and she is telling me the story of her life, and all I seem to be able to think, as I absorb her story, is that she has somehow triumphed. Not only did she survive capture and wrenching displacement, but the trajectory of her life has achieved escape velocity from Mexico and the American Southwest and has taken her from the New World to the Old: new language, customs, food, friends, perhaps even a little local distinction as the most unusual new arrival in some ancient Italian hill town.

# 22

# Carmela

**Neil's Diary, Agua Prieta, Sonora**

While high in the Sierra Madre, Barney heard a scrap of information that has lodged in a crevice of his mind. It was told to him only as someone's vague memory, but it may be our last chance at picking up the trail of the Apache named Carmela Harris. Someone who once knew Jack Harris told us that he had sown some wild oats south of the border and that he had sired a son, named Enrique Harris. Enrique married a Mexican woman from Agua Prieta, and she now owns and operates a certain store in that town. We think that if we can find her, we might be able to learn something about Carmela.

We find the store and in it a perfectly round woman with a pleasant face. She knows exactly what we are talking about: *la Apachita*, Carmela. She herself is Jack Harris's great granddaughter, and insists on taking us at once to her mother, once the wife of Jack's son, Enrique. From Magdalena de Harris we hear a great deal about the Harris family and the descendants of Jack, though there are no direct leads to Carmela. Both Jack and Dixie have died, but Dixie had a daughter, Anna, who used to live in Italy and France, and who was apparently married to a well-known artist from Bloomington, Indiana.

After months of searching and following many false leads, it is through the Bloomington Hall of Public Records that I find the needle in the haystack. The names are on a property deed, and a suggested call to the Office of Alumni Records at Indiana University yields a current address and phone number for Anna Harris and her husband in Newbury, Vermont — only thirty miles from a farm I have owned for many years.

I've probably been by their house once or twice. We may even have friends in common. In fatalistic Mexico, they might just nod gravely, understanding that such things happen when they are meant to be, and that they are to be expected. I cannot summon such equanimity.

I stare at the phone, pick it up, and call. There's a soft, complex, cultivated voice answering.

"I'm not sure if I have the right number," I say. "I'm doing some historical research. Is your name Anna?"

A pause, almost like a held breath, as if she had been waiting a long time for this call. . . . "Yes. . . . Ann, actually."

I begin: "My father . . . Mexico . . . Apaches. . . ."

Her voice: "Oh yes, you mean my sister, Carmie. Carmela."

It pours out. Their childhood together, the years in California, and finally Carmela's death in Italy in 1976, the same year Barney and Tom and Misse and I found the Apache camp in the Chita Huecas.

I tell Ann about my "waking dream," talking with Carmela in Italy. "Under a grape arbor, I say. . . ."

"Yes," says Ann. "It was a pergola covered with clematis and wisteria."

"It was very shady."

"Yes."

"We could look out across a valley where the sun on the hills was very bright."

"Yes. It was the other side of the valley of the Upper Tiber River."

"There was a cool, comfortable stone house nearby."

"Yes. Our old farmhouse. I am so moved by this. . . . This is so moving. . . . When she died it was horrible."

"There's so much. Can I come and talk with you about Carmela? Can Margot come? Can Seth and Kathy come? They are all part of this."

"Yes. Yes. Of course."

### Neil's Diary, Newbury, Vermont

"I was dreading this," says Ann, surrounded with family photographs and papers. "Mother kept all this stuff with her in Italy and then in the nursing home after that. I haven't looked at any of this since Mother died."

Ann crosses some inner threshold and begins traveling back through time, hovering first over one picture then another, encountering faces, voices, smells, and banished memories for the first time in years. Mama—Dixie—slender, almost frail, in jodhpurs and boots under a palm tree.

"She was part Cherokee and part Mandan, you know."

Papa—Jack. He's roguish, solid, capable looking. An adventurer.

"Oh here's Carmela. Her high school graduation picture. The fountain at our house, at the beach. Oh. And these are pictures she made living in Italy. She liked to take pictures of things that didn't look like what they really were."

"There's one album that's gone — the one you'd want the most to see. Oh, the pictures in it. I don't know who took them. The camp after Carmela was caught — burnt houses, a dead woman, things scattered everywhere. Carmie never forgot the gunshots and the fire. She remembered the fire, couldn't forget it. It was her grandmother, the dead woman was, she thought. But she didn't really know who it was. It was the one who took care of her."

Ann closes her eyes and summons up the memory of the photographs.

"I see burned things. There is a brush hut, sort of a lean-to that is mostly burned, but there is enough left to see how it was done. Poles leaning together, a lean-to, covered with branches, but all burnt. The wood is charred. There are trees in the background. The ground is rough. There's a body. Carmie's grandmother, I guess. She's lying on the ground in a fetal position, like this.

"The old woman has long straight hair, almost completely black. She's lying down, so it's all to one side. She's wearing something dark. A dark dress or something. Her face is old. It's all lined and old looking. There are things scattered on the ground — maybe artifacts, but I can't tell."

"What happened then?" I ask. "How did Carmela come from that burnt-out camp into your family?"

Ann tells us the whole story, as she heard it from her mother and her grandmother.

Jack was away, leaving Dixie alone in the village of Nácori Chico. There were several men in on the attack, and they had liquor. After killing the old woman and burning the camp, they came back to town, drunk, with three children.

"This," I say, "is the first I have heard of other children being taken along with Carmela."

"Oh yes. There were three."

Dixie was convinced, right or wrong, that the children were in grave danger. She thought the men might actually kill them — and these were men she knew. Dixie, who was a seemingly demure southern belle from West Virginia, took over. When the raiding party came into town with the children, Dixie faced them down in the plaza. She was determined, and she commanded a certain unassailable respect. People often came to her with an illness, thinking she might have medicine, knowledge of a cure. She told the men that she was going to take charge of the children. They needed medical attention. She and her housemaid, Chu, carried and bustled them into the house and barred the door. Dixie armed herself with a loaded rifle and made sure the men knew she had a weapon.

Now what? She couldn't keep the children like this indefinitely. Jack was not due to return for several days.

There was another American in town who had a truck. She got a message to him, and he came to her house. She convinced him that he must hide two of the children in his truck and drive them to Hermosillo, the state capital. Once there, he must take them to a convent whose name she gave him. He was to tell the nuns who the children were and that they were the children's last hope, that they would be doing God's work if they saved these orphans.

While trying to protect the children Dixie had also been soulsearching. Before summoning the man with the truck, she had reached a decision. The third little girl was older than the others, and her fear and hostility tore at Dixie. Dixie and Jack had been married several years, and Dixie, who was childless, thought she might be barren—forever unable to have children. So she decided to adopt this terrified Apache waif.

Dixie summoned a local official, very likely Dolores Fuentes, the town's mayor, dictated a statement, and had him sign it. The statement said that Dixie and her husband, Jack, had legally adopted the Apache orphan. She hoped the paper would give her determined act of motherhood an official seal of approval and that it would be good enough to get her across the border when the time came to leave Mexico. Once in the United States, they could disappear.

Saving Carmela from death was as powerful an experience for Dixie as giving birth. She loved Carmela fiercely, and it brought about a sea change in Dixie. Within the year, she was pregnant. Dixie and Jack and Carmela left Mexico so that Ann could be born in the Douglas hospital.

They moved back to California, where Carmela and Ann grew up together in Tujunga, a Los Angeles suburb. Ann remembers that Carmela was the only Indian kid in their white-bread school, so when other kids tamed the West in make-believe, Carmela was always on the losing side. Only she knew what it was really like.

Photographs. Carmela, twelve, posed in the garden at home by an ornate fountain, in stylish slacks and blouse, a wavy, grown-up hairdo, her concentrated gaze skewering the camera. Carmela, fifteen, perched on the railing of a beach house in bobby socks and skirt—a regular teenager. Carmela, eighteen, her beautiful, exquisitely Apache face grave, deadpan, betraying nothing, but there's no repose there.

Carmela remembered a few things, says Ann, from the old days, and she used to tell Ann about them. Her Apache name was Bui, and she remembered a few Apache words, written down and preserved by Dixie. The old Apache woman who took care of her used to take her out at night when it was clear and they could see the stars, and she would tell Bui stories about the stars.

When Bui was caught she was wearing a tanned leather skirt and moccasins, and she had a little bag around her neck in which there was a deck of leather cards, like tarot cards, says Ann.[1] There was also a string of small wooden beads and a drum recovered from the campsite. Jack gave the drum to a friend in California, but the other things were all given to a museum in Los Angeles. A careful search has failed to reveal the whereabouts of all but one of these articles. Carmela's dress was recently found in the attic of the Harris's Tujunga house and, after being deposited at the Mary Hill Museum in Washington State, has been turned over to an individual of the San Carlos tribe. As of this writing the future of the dress and anything else found with it is uncertain.

Ann got married and, with her husband, lived for long periods of time in France and Italy. Carmela went to college and became a nurse, but she never left Dixie and her magical childhood home in Tujunga. For about twenty quiet years Carmela lived this way, working as a nurse. From time to time she made brief contact with Native American groups, especially while she was in school, but she apparently was hesitant to develop relationships with such groups. She could have sought out some way to contact Apaches on American reservations, but she didn't.

Ann says that Carmela never knew what she was. "I'm not Indian," she would say. "I'm not American. I'm not Mexican. Maybe I'm all of them."

Maybe she was none of them.

In 1972 Carmela and Dixie decided to leave California and join Ann and her husband in Italy. The Apache orphan, born in the Sierra Madre wilderness, captured by the killers of her family, and by this time, as far as I know, the sole survivor of her people, emigrated to Perugia, where she lived in a stone farmhouse and watched the Umbrian countryside bake in the sun, where she could explore the towns and cities, find refuge and solace in the history of a people not her own. She loved it all, as much as anything in her life. She was in her mid-forties, having an adventure, when it ended quite suddenly. An accident. For no apparent reason, she simply fainted one day at home. She passed out while standing up, and then fell like a tree, striking her head with a fatal blow. It was over in a second.

"I think," says Ann, "that my mother took Carmela's death harder than any other death: harder than her own mother's, harder than Papa's."

Ann talks through welling tears.

"She was her daughter. She had saved her life, she had brought her all this way, against all odds. Carmie was still young. Her life was incomplete. There could have been so much more. She could still be alive."

# 23
# Are There Any Left?

**Neil's Diary, Tucson, Arizona**

Throughout 1932 and most of 1933 Grennie is conducting fieldwork at San Carlos and Fort Apache. He spends many hours each day deep in conversation with Apaches. He understands and speaks the language, but always has an interpreter and companion as a double check on subtleties and for advice on lines of inquiry: where to tread and where not to. At night he spends more hours writing up the day's notes.

He is mastering the language and the culture and is busy writing what is by October of 1933 a 490-page first draft of *The Social Organization of the Western Apache*. Perhaps weakened by the grueling pace, perhaps reexposed to some vector of contagion, Grennie has a relapse of tuberculosis in the fall of 1933. He will spend the next year convalescing in Colorado Springs at his mother's house.

He begins to correspond with another anthropologist, Morris Opler, on the subject of the Sierra Madre Apaches. Opler is conducting parallel studies of other Apache groups in New Mexico: the Chiricahua, the Mescalero, the Jicarilla, the Kiowa-Apache, and the Lipan. Grennie clearly thinks that there is a viable group of Sierra Madre Apache but that their days may be numbered. He is itching to put them back on his agenda.

**Jan. 8, 1934**

*Dear Morrie,*

*. . . there is one thing in particular that I wanted very much to talk over with you. This was concerning the remnant of the Apache people who are still running wild in Mexico. You might know some of their relatives there among the Chiricahua at Mescalero, and if so, you might know of their attitude toward them, etc.*

*The reason that I say this to you is that, as you know, I have been twice into Mexico to get information on them and am much interested in them. Do you think that the Chiricahua at Mescalero would want to get* into touch with these people and that they would like them to come back to the States and live with them on the reservation?

As far as I can find out, there are only about thirty men, women, and children left, roughly. They are fighting a losing battle in Mexico, and it seems only a question of time till they will be exterminated. In the last few years about five of them have been killed in fights with the Mexicans, and two of their girls have been captured by the Mexicans also.[1] One of these girls is now grown and living at a town in Mexico. I heard that she wants to come back to her people on the reservation, if they are still alive.[2]

... if you want to help me on this, it would be a fine thing if you could keep track of anything that you hear concerning these people. I would like to see something done about it, but just how it is to be done is the question. It is needless to add that anything concerning this subject that I tell you is in strict confidence.[3]

### Neil's Diary, Tucson, Arizona

Grennie is hatching a scheme to rescue the Sierra Madre Apaches and is enlisting Opler's help. There are tremendous obstacles and difficulties, but Opler is going to test the waters among the Chiricahuas at Mescalero on the subject of the return of the Sierra Madre Apaches. Grennie is playing his cards close to the chest. Although he is willing to share his discoveries with Opler, he doesn't want anyone else to know what he knows. He doesn't want to be scooped by another anthropologist, and he doesn't want to see some thoughtless adventurer blundering into the mountains.

Opler writes back:

### Spring 1934

*Dear Goodwin,*

*Just a note to let you know that I'm getting a list of people who are still in Old Mexico, that is their descendants probably are.*

*One of these men came up this far once and captured a Mescalero woman. He took her back to those people. She and her children finally got back to the reservation. One of the girls born out in the wilds is still living today. The woman herself died recently. She claims to have seen the Apache Kid killed by that bunch down there, shot while drunk after he had shot a member of the group. She claimed that the story of Apache Kid being killed by white cowboys is a lie.[4]*

**Neil's Diary, Tucson, Arizona**

The name of the captured woman was Mrs. Jacinto Ramirez, and her daughter, of whom Opler speaks, is Alberta Begay.[5] Her captor, referred to by Opler, is Massai, a Chiricahua who was captured in 1886 and put on the train to Florida with Geronimo and the others. Massai escaped from the train as it was passing through Missouri, and in an epic journey of endurance and resolve made his way back to the Southwest—a trek of at least six hundred miles. He remained in hiding on both sides of the border until he was killed by a posse in the Black Range of New Mexico in 1907. Often referred to as New Mexico's Apache Kid, Massai is frequently confused with the "real" Apache Kid, the Western Apache outlaw referred to throughout Grennie's Diary.[6] If the "real" Apache Kid died in the way Mrs. Ramirez describes in the Opler letter, this is the first time such a version appears in print, as far as I know.

**Opler's letter, cont'd.**

*Now, have you got someone down there who could get in touch with these people and assure them that they will not be harmed? Can the girl [Lupe] who has been working in the Mexican village communicate with them? From the stories I have heard they are terribly wild and even "sleep with one eye open."*

*If they cannot be reached by any other way, perhaps we could take some old fellow who has relatives down there, go down with him and use him as a go-between for communication. At the same time we could make observations upon the material culture they have and mode of life they lead.*

*As soon as I have the list of the families involved and am assured that they want their relatives back, I will get in touch with you and we can decide on the next move.*

**Neil's Diary, Tucson, Arizona**

Opler may have the impression that this is going to be easy. He is gathering a list of people thought to be in Mexico, and he wonders if Lupe, or perhaps an older man who knows the country and the people, could help with making contact. He is already thinking ahead about practicing some ethnology on material culture and way of life.

Grennie writes back, sounding almost as if he has had a change of heart: Slow down Morrie!

Jan. 1934

*Dear Morrie,*

*About the Apache in Old Mexico we can talk later. Can only say here that at present it would be utterly impossible to get anyone to represent them, as you suggest. In view of this, I wouldn't approach the Mescalero agent, would you (at least, not at present)?*

*Your letter has just come telling about the old Mexico Apache, and I was very interested to get it. It almost makes me wild to have to sit at home like I do, [recovering from tuberculosis] but never mind. I'll be on the way soon. The stories you give about the Old Mexico Apache are very interesting to me, and the list of people will be no end of help. But don't get the expectations of your friends up for a safe return of these people, at least so far as I will be of any help.*

*If it ever goes through, it will be a process of several years, don't you think? So don't lead your friends to expect anything, will you? There is too much of the wild goose chase about the whole thing to put any dependence on results.*

*Will say here that it would be utterly impossible to get any white man or Mexican who could get in touch with these people. They are too wild, and it would be like trying to get into touch with a pack of wolves. They have absolutely no contact with any people outside themselves that I know of. My own friends, the W. Apache, are scared to death of them and have no contact. It may be possible to act through the girl in the Mexican village, though I don't know. She has been so long away that it may be impossible to get her to help. These people are only rarely seen by Mexicans and whites, and then only by accident. They live back in the Sierra Madre, and if you had been down there, you would understand how inaccessible they are. I have thought about it a lot, and what you say about taking an old timer down there seems to me the only way of getting any results, even if this is possible. But we can talk it over later, and I want you to see some of the material that I have which was taken from a camp of these people. The only thing is that I won't be able to help in any way for a year or so, and there is not a soul in Mexico whom I know that could help. It may be possible to get in touch with the Apache girl [Lupe] by mail, and I will try it sometime. But I just wanted to let you know that it will all take a long time, a very long time, so don't get your friends steamed up for immediate action, will you? When we get together this summer, we can put all the odds and ends that we have on the subject together and see what they come to. Will let you know when I will be in Santa Fe, and in the meantime if I can give you any information about the Old Mexico Apache or W. Apache (comparisons with Mes. and Chir.), let me know.*[7]

### Neil's Diary, Tucson, Arizona

Grennie wants to go back to Mexico, but, incapacitated by tuberculosis, "it makes me wild to have to sit at home like I do, but never mind. I'll be on the way soon."

He wants this one to himself, not only because of his personal connection with the story, but also because he knows it will be so easy for someone else to ruin all chances for contact. Opler has probably written another letter or two (which are now lost) to give the impression that there may be a movement already afoot among the Ndéndaa'i at Mescalero to repatriate their cousins. Grennie, unable to do anything himself, enumerates the obstacles in an effort to discourage Opler: (1) there is no one to speak for the Sierra Madre Apache; (2) don't speak to the agent at Mescalero—(he'll interfere and intimidate); (3) don't get the Apaches "all steamed up"; (4) bringing them home will take a very long time; (5) it sounds like a wild-goose chase; (6) they're as wild as wolves; (7) there's no contact; (8) Grennie's friends are afraid; (9) no one in Mexico will be of any help; (10) Grennie will "sometime" write to Lupe; (11) again, it will take a long time. He wants everyone's hands off, because, judging from a line in his next letter to Opler on the subject, it is clear that he and Opler may not be the only ones with their minds on the Sierra Madre Apaches.

### Feb. 2, 1934

*Dear Morrie,*

*Was interested to hear what you had to say in connection with the Apache in Mexico, and even if someone else does do something before we get a chance to, it won't stop our interest in the matter, do you think? I am looking forward greatly to talking it all over with you.*[8]

### Neil's Diary, Tucson, Arizona

He does not give any clue as to who else might be making plans along similar lines — perhaps it is other anthropologists or reporters or adventure seekers, not to mention the Apaches themselves. As he heard from the American smugglers in the Espuelas, reservation Apaches slip across the border from time to time. In fact, as my father will find out later, as he and Opler are corresponding, a small group of men are in the process of planning to do just that.

### July 4, 1938, Mescalero Reservation, Grenville's Diary

*Sam Kenoi (a Chiricahua at Mescalero) says that about 4 years ago three Chiricahuas from Mescalero made an expedition into the Sierra Madre in quest of an old treasure which they thought they knew the location of. One of these was a young man who spoke fluent Spanish, another was Perico, an old man since dead and the third was Ya-no-zha. The three were also accompanied by a white man, now a salesman for a motor company in Tularosa. This white man has an unsavory reputation for being crooked and an outlaw.*

### Neil's Diary, Tucson, Arizona

Perhaps by coincidence, or even possibly stimulated by what Opler has been telling the Chiricahuas at Mescalero about the Sierra Madre Apache, this party plans an illegal border crossing. Yanozha and Perico did their share of raiding in Mexico in the old days, and they think they can find a fifty-year old cache of plunder somewhere in the Sierra Madre.

Accompanied by the "unsavory character" from Tularosa, New Mexico, they cross the border at El Paso, whereupon Yanozha gets drunk and lands in the Ciudad Juárez jail. Minus Yanozha, the party makes a rendezvous with some Mexicans, but Perico decides that they are plotting to kill him once he has found the treasure, so he walks out of camp one night and disappears into the bush. After two months he ends up in Casa Grande, Arizona, and writes a letter to his family, who come and get him.[9] Perico is glad to get out of Mexico and come home alive, but Yanozha, as Grennie soon discovers, is not through with Mexico yet.

By mid-1934 Grennie's convalescence in Colorado Springs is over, and he moves to Santa Fe to regain strength and work on his manuscript. At the same time he subscribes to Tucson and Douglas newspapers, or perhaps people in those towns keep an eye on articles with Mexican datelines for him. In September 1934 he receives this brief clipping.

### Apaches Raid Ranch in Sonora; Two are Killed

TUCSON, SEPT. 28, 1934 (AP)

Reports that two Indians were killed near Nácori Chico, Sonora, Mexico in a raid upon a ranch several days ago were brought to Tucson, today by John E. Burrule, American mining engineer of that district.

The Indians, Apaches, swooped down from a mountain retreat where members of the tribe have lived since the capture of Geronimo in 1886, in an attempt to rustle cattle.[10]

### Neil's Diary, Bavispe

A ranch attacked, blood shed. No more. Another skirmish, now long forgotten. Nevertheless, if true, it confirms Grennie's belief that there are still a few Apaches left in the Sierra Madre. Their numbers are now further reduced, and the prospects of making contact with them are ever more daunting and dangerous with each such report.

Mexican folklore contains ghostly echoes of reports such as these. Amiglia Samaniego, Francisco Zozaya's cousin, remembers one January 14 night in 1934 that she spent at the Carrera Ranch, just east of Bavispe. The family of the ranch hosted a festivity in honor of Santo Niño de Atocha, and after the fires were put out there were animal calls all through the night. They were strange, memorable cries, utterly unlike the commonplace night sounds. The people were certain that all these calls were made by Apaches lurking in the nearby shadows.

I hear a similar story in 1976 from Walter Ramsey, the old cowboy who once worked for Stewart Hunt. In early 1933, while hunting in the mountains up the Bavispe River two days' ride beyond Huachinera, he saw a single fresh sandal print in a sandbar in a place where no Mexican ever went. That night in camp rocks mysteriously flew through the air, his animals were utterly spooked, and all night long there were bird calls of a kind he had never heard before. Now in his seventies, he tells me the story with a light touch, calling the episode the night he was "surrounded by Apaches," but at the time it made his blood run cold with naked fear.

By late 1934 Grennie returns to San Carlos for a solid year and a half of fieldwork. Not until 1936 is there further word of the Sierra Madre Apaches: a brief contact in Mexico reported in *The Douglas Daily Dispatch* by Arizona Deputy Game Warden Ralph Morrow, who has spoken with a man named Martineau in the Mormon mountain colony of Pacheco.

DOUGLAS, NOV. 1937

Deputy Morrow spent several days with J. H. Martineau, postmaster at Colonia Pacheco and a noted hunter and trapper there since 1887. The deputy warden said yesterday that Martineau told him a band of the Apaches had come in to a trading post near Pacheco about a year ago, but that none of them had been heard of since.

Morrow said he gathered from what Martineau told him there was no doubt the Apaches are still somewhere in the Sierras. The deputy game warden said he did not believe there was a stretch of country on the face of the earth as rugged and wild as the Sierras and that a thousand Indians could live out their lives there without anyone ever finding them.[11]

## Neil's Diary, Tucson, Arizona

It was not far from Pacheco that Apaches had briefly kidnapped a young Mexican boy in about 1928, so they would not have been able to count on a warm reception there. But that might have depended upon whom they encountered. There may have been, according to one story I have heard, friendly contact between at least one Mexican family in Pacheco and the Apaches. In about 1915 an Apache family, "in desperation," sent a very young daughter to live with some people in Pacheco, and they raised her as their own. Barney was told this story by a close acquaintance, a Mormon man who grew up near Pacheco and remembers hearing his mother speak often of the Apaches. In 1932 this Apache girl married a Mexican and had a family of her own in one of the hill towns.[12] Could this twenty-year-old connection have been known among the Apaches in 1936, and could it have drawn them to the settlement? They were normally so wary; a visit to Pacheco only makes sense if they knew how they would be received. On the other hand, by 1938 Pacheco was nearly abandoned, most of the Mormons having moved out of the mountains, so a bold and well-armed, well-mounted group of Apaches might have had little to fear.

In 1938, while Grennie is visiting the Mescalero Reservation, he hears of another, more reliable sighting. In a series of conversations, the old Chiricahua, Sam Kenoi, tells him two stories about four "wild" Indians who came to the Mescalero Reservation in the fall or summer of 1937. They were seen by two separate witnesses, and the visiting Apaches spoke Spanish.

### July 4, 1938, Mescalero, Grenville's Diary

*Sam says that the authorities at the Mescalero Agency will not believe that there are any wild Apaches in Mexico. But he says that he knows there are. He says that last fall or summer a young man was out with a labor camp in the vicinity of Snake Tanks. This is a wild part of the reservation. He looked across a little valley not far off and on the opposite hillside, he saw what he says were wild Indians. I think one man and a woman. The woman seemed to be doing something with her hands, either digging something up, or a similar action. They had not seen him yet, but they did almost immediately and were gone like a flash in the underbrush. The Navajo said that he got out of there as fast as he could also, as he was badly scared and thought he was lucky to get out of there alive.*

*Another similar report came through a quiet young Apache who lives on the reservation. He never says much, and he would not be one to make things up. He had been talking with a cowboy, a white man, who owns a small ranch up near Cloudcroft. This white man has not been living there long. He asked the young Apache if he knew anything about some Indians who had been up there living about Cloudcroft last summer. The Apache replied that he did not, and the white man told him the following story:*

Last summer, along towards fall, four Indians, two men and two women, came to my farm. They stood there, not far from the field, where they could see me. They talked in Spanish to me. They talked good Spanish. They said that they wanted some food. They wanted some flour and other things, so I gave it to them, as they looked hungry. Then they told me they had been living about here all summer. That they had often seen reservation Indians, but had done no harm as they were tame Indians living in a good way. They said that they had been close to the Agency and seen the white people there. But they had troubled no one and had let no one see them. They wished to do no one any harm. They said they were not from the reservation, but from another place, far off, and they pointed to the southwest. They said that it was getting cold now, and soon they would be moving back to their own country, where it was warmer. They were going in three more days. They pointed to a long ridge to the southwest and said that they had made it their headquarters for a long time and would be camping there tonight. That if I wanted to I could come and see where they stayed. But I did not know how I would find them, so they said they would cut a limb off every so often from the base of the ridge up to their camp, so I could follow it. They told me to come at night, but not to bring a gun of any kind. I told them I would come.

It was moonlight that night, and I started out to where they told me. Sure enough, I found the branches marked for me and I made my way to their camp. There was no indication of any kind where the camp was till you got to it right in the brush. It was very small and in thick brush and they had a tiny fire about which they were sitting.

I got off my horse, and talked in Spanish there with them for quite a while. But I had tucked a six-shooter in my belt before leaving, inside my shirt. They told me that they had decided to leave for home that very next day, instead of waiting three days. Then after we had talked I got on my horse and came home. I have not seen them since then. I did not want to harm them because they had done no harm to anyone.

Whether these people who are evidently "wild" Apache had contacted reservation Apache or not, Sam did not say. What they had come for also remains a mystery.

### Neil's Diary, Tucson, Arizona

The echoes of these events and others like them reverberate to this day at Mescalero. From several Chiricahua elders I have heard stories that are unmistakable versions of what Grennie heard in 1938. When I took up the trail in 1976, among the first people I spoke with was Russell Taylor at the B and P Palace Bar in Douglas. He assured me gravely that he could take me out that day and show me moccasin tracks in the Peloncillo Mountains, east of town. I must have looked like an easy mark to him, but, all the same, I think he half believed it himself, feeling that, as long as there was a chance of finding moccasin tracks in the Peloncillos, there was hope that the West would never be tamed.

In 1937 my father, too, believed there were some Sierra Madre Apaches left. As a scientist with discipline and rational method, he relied on what evidence he had, but, by now, I think of him as a closet romantic as well, hoping, like Russell, that there were a few left. He has seen at first hand the Apaches' uncanny skill at stealth and survival, and if there were only one or two chance sightings a year, Grennie would not have been surprised, given that the Sierra Madre Apaches were such masters of concealment. In the absence of conclusive proof that there were none left, my father saw no reason not to believe that a few were still there. And he was not alone.

# 24
# Fugitives and Descendants

**Neil's Diary, Tucson, Arizona**

In a letter to Morris Opler in 1934, Grennie mentioned unnamed others who might have been wanting to make contact with the Sierra Madre Apaches. He gave no hint of whom he was referring to, but it could have been Helge Ingstad, the Norwegian anthropologist who was, perhaps as early as 1934, planning an expedition to find them. Ingstad had already spent several years in Canada among the northern Athabascans, and having come south to study their linguistic cousins, the Apaches, he has heard about Fimbres and the Sierra Madre Apaches. By 1937 he has determined to mount an expedition into the Sierra Madre himself to solve the mystery of the so-called lost tribe. On the eve of his departure for Mexico, he writes to my father asking for advice and for information about the Sierra Madre Apache.

My father's reply to Ingstad's letter is arresting because it points up the difference between the two anthropologists' operating styles, and, more important, because it is the fullest synthesis of my father's view of these people.

But it is even more than that.

By 1937 the underlying human mystery and tragedy of the Sierra Madre Apaches have deeply penetrated Grennie's imagination. As he writes about them to Opler, and now to Ingstad, it is, I think, in a voice very different from what it was in 1931. He is more mature and assured. He now has deep friendships with people at San Carlos and Fort Apache, and this intimacy with reservation Apaches must be bringing those isolated in the Sierra Madre vividly to life for him.

**Oct. 10, 1937**

*401 Delgado Street, Santa Fe, New Mexico*
*Dear Mr. Ingstad,*

*. . . I read your book, "The Land of Feast and Famine" some years ago and enjoyed it tremendously.[1] While in Tucson recently, I noticed a*

piece in the paper mentioning your proposed trip to Mexico in search of the Apaches and this is my first knowledge of your plans. . . .

With the idea of learning the lay of the land and finding out what possibilities there might be of actually contacting these people, I made two trips in the Sierra Madre country.

You will understand that it was not my intention to attempt contact with the Apache at that time, but merely to visit some of their old camp-sites and learn something of the terrain and of the attitude of Mexicans and Americans in the region concerning these people. It was possible to obtain considerable data on all these points.

It was my fond hope to someday tackle the Sierra Madre Apache, attempting it in the same manner as you apparently are. However you seem to have gotten there ahead of me and I can only wish you the best of luck and offer what help I can. There is so much to do in the southern Athapascan field that one cannot hope to do it alone and in the long run the best method is for those doing the work to cooperate. . . .

You asked for suggestions and information I might have to offer, so here they are.

1. The Sierra Madre Apache are actually Chiricahua Apache who failed to come in when Geronimo surrendered to the Government in 1886.[2] At that time, a few families slipped off into the mountains in Mexico and were never taken. As I understand it they belonged to the southern-most of the three Chiricahua bands, whose old territory lay mainly in the northern end of the Sierra Madre. . . .

2. Since 1886 to the present time the Sierra Madre Apache have led a precarious existence and several of them have been killed in skirmishes with Mexicans and Americans. These Apaches keep following their old pattern of raiding ranches for horses and butchering range cattle when they needed them, just as they had done before the surrender. They also exist by wild plant foods and game. Being such a small group, they could not carry on the daring raids of old times, but had to drive off the ranch stock secretly, taking it out of pastures, etc., without the knowledge of the owners. The number of horses and cattle that fall to their lot in this manner are becoming increasingly few due to the growing pressure and danger of attack from American and Mexican ranchers.

As you know, these Indians have been shot on sight, regardless of age or sex and I understand the Mexican government has had a bounty on their heads, though whether this still continues at present I do not know.

Naturally blame falls on both sides, but recently some needless brutalities have been reportedly perpetrated by Americans and Mexicans. These hostilities, lasting over many years have, as far as I know, absolutely cut off all outside contact of these Apaches with Americans, Mexicans and other Indians. They are not able to trade and obtain outside supplies in any way, except to steal them. Thus they cannot be well equipped with firearms or ammunition, though there is a possibility they may have some firearms.

When they are seen by Americans, Mexicans or other Indians, it is due to accident, not an intentional meeting (at least as far as Mexicans, Americans and other Indians are concerned). Due to their small number, it seems to be only a question of time before they are wiped out. I have also heard that they have very few women among them. It is impossible to say for certain how many in all are in the group, but probably, all told, there are not more than forty, not less than fifteen.[3]

3. If these people are to be saved from their present fate, the most logical step would be their removal to some place where they can settle down to a safe life. The majority of their kinfolk are now on the Mescalero reservation. It would be worthwhile to know how these people would feel about their wild relatives being settled with them. How the Apaches in the Sierra Madre would feel is another question, only possible to answer by contacting them.

However it is quite possible that they might desire such a move if they were granted a complete amnesty from any misdeeds they might have committed in the eyes of the Mexican or United States Government or citizens of these countries. Reprisal or treachery from their enemies they would fear most of all, and it would take a great deal to convince them of their safety should removal be possible. Purely from a humanitarian standpoint, the most important accomplishment in connection with these wild Apaches would be some sort of arrangement for their future benefit. Therefore if it is at all possible, it would be of tremendous value for anyone attempting to contact them to have the authority to act for the United States government and possibly the Mexican government.

4. You have probably chosen your Apache companions by now and so any remarks that I might make would be superfluous. However I would say that it is important to have at least one older man along who knows the country and favorite camp locations prior to 1886. Also, if

possible, to obtain Apaches who actually may have blood relatives among those in the Sierra Madre should prove of tremendous advantage.

It has been my experience that it is better to travel with more than one Apache, as two or more keep each other company and converse among themselves. I think you should be careful of what Americans or Mexicans you take with you, if any, for many of them would like nothing better than to get a shot at the wild Apaches. This would not help you, particularly if you managed to contact them.

Some years ago a girl twelve years of age was captured by Mexicans from these Apaches. She was living in Nácori Chico with a Mexican family by the name of Fimbres, when last I heard of her. Her name is Lupe and she must be some twenty-five years old at present.[4] It might prove of value to you to contact her. At least she could tell the Apaches with you just what individuals were in the band when she left it.

6. The Apache camps which I have seen were only two. One was located on the east side of the Sierra Chita Hueca, high up on a shoulder of the mountain. This mountain lies just north of a line between Janos, Chihuahua, and Bavispe, Sonora. The other camp is near the head of Las Piedras Canyon, on the east side of the Sierra Espuela in Chihuahua. Both of these were old camps, and long in use, and I visited them to see what might be determined concerning the culture of the Apache using them.

They were very interesting and I have complete photographic records of them, together with maps and specimens picked up on the sites and some procured from Americans who had visited the camps previously. Both camps were abandoned at the time of my visit. The chief point of interest was the very evident acculturation they exhibited. The dwellings were still standing at the time. None of them were the wickiup type which we know as the old Apache houses. Several varieties of houses were present, among them structures made with logs and stones. They resembled far more those recorded for Mexican Indians further south, such as the Tarahumara, etc.

One hears wild tales of renegade Americans and Mexicans being with these Apaches. If this be true, it may account for such a wide departure from the old wickiup. Again, the change may have been instigated by the Apache themselves. Possibly the two camps I saw were exceptions and those which you may find further south will be more along the aboriginal type.

*Another interesting point is the extensive use of cowhide for different articles and in dress. I have seen no buckskin from these people, though it may exist.[5] There are other things which I will not list here.*

*From the size of the camps, I would say that the one on the Sierra Chita Hueca with its seven dwellings, probably contained twenty people at the most. The second camp was divided into three parts, separated by a mile or two, and altogether with some eighteen dwellings may have housed more, though here it was difficult to tell whether all had been occupied at the same time. One may have been abandoned at the time the other was built, and some of the houses were undoubtedly used for storage. The Chita Hueca camp was built and used after that in Las Piedras Canyon was abandoned.*

*7. As to the possibility of making an ethnographic study of these Apaches, it will be extremely difficult. If it is at all possible to contact them, they will be very suspicious and at best only observations on the material culture and economic life could be made. As to social customs and religion, it is hard enough to get data on these aspects of the cultures on reservations where the Apaches are friendly and speak English. Judging from the campsites I have seen, certain aspects of the material culture are somewhat changed from the original of fifty years ago and you would not be studying Apaches as they were before the era of reservations. The main study value of these people it seems to me would be their position as an isolated group who have in certain ways retained their old culture and in others changed it under other stress than that encountered on the reservations. If complete study could be made of a group like this, it should prove a considerable contribution to Anthropology.*

*I hope you will pardon my writing you so fully on points which you probably have carefully considered. The reason I have gone into detail on certain points is merely to give you all the assistance I possibly can. If I can be of further help at any time during the course of your undertaking, do not hesitate to call on me as I am deeply interested in what you are doing and in the Apache themselves. . . .*

*Sincerely,*
*Grenville Goodwin*

## Neil's Diary, Tucson, Arizona

Grennie is working out the details of his own return trip to Mexico when Ingstad appears on the scene. My father is gracious to this unknown colleague and generous with his own time and information. He never hints at what he thinks Ingstad's chances are, or whether his true feelings about being beaten to the punch are any different from what his letter indicates.

Whatever Grennie thinks, he clearly believes that he should tell Ingstad everything he knows in the belief that the better prepared Ingstad is, the more likely he is to avoid grave mistakes. A serious blunder on Ingstad's part would not make Grennie's future trips any easier.

Ingstad's three-month expedition in the fall of 1937 makes headlines. As my father and others suggested, he chooses two Apaches to accompany him — one of them is Yanozha, a warrior who had held out with Geronimo until the 1886 surrender, and who was involved in the 1934 border crossing described to Grennie by Sam Kenoi. Ingstad finds these two men at the Mescalero Reservation in New Mexico, where most of the Chiricahuas are living. As Ingstad soon discovers, these two are not dependable, to say the least, and they may be more focused on recovering buried treasure than on helping Ingstad find the Apaches.

Once in Mexico, Ingstad makes a disastrous choice of guide. Isidro Mora is a villainous, vainglorious semi-bandit. He had been one of the party that wiped out the Apache camp and captured Julio in July 1932, and he will be well known to the Apaches. Mora himself would like nothing better than to get a shot at a few more of them.

Because of his inexperience and impatience, Ingstad does not have a chance of making contact, peaceful or otherwise. He might as well be marching into the Sierra Madre with a brass band. The Apaches, on the other hand, are going to know every move he makes and might even amuse themselves by playing cat and mouse with him. In any case, they will keep their distance. To the Sierra Madre Apaches, Ingstad's party will be puzzling in its makeup: one white man who gives the orders, one known enemy, and two unknown reservation Apaches who might very well intend to betray the Sierra Madre Apaches.

Ingstad goes to Bavispe, Bacerac, Bacadéhuachi, Huachinera, and Nácori Chico. He rides into the mountains, where he finds Mora. He has plenty of adventures, including a near-mutiny that he has to put down at the point of a gun. He crisscrosses the Sierra Madre, gathers much information, and encounters many of the main characters in the epic, including the three Apache captives, Lupe, Julio, Carmela, as well as a number of Mormons, but he never sees any Apaches, though, as my father is to find out, the Apaches see him.

## July 4, 1938, Mescalero, New Mexico, Grenville's Diary

*While down at Mescalero for the celebration of the 4th, I had a chance to speak with Sam Kenoi and Allan Houser's father about the wild Chiricahua in Mexico.*

*Sam said that he had known Ingstad had come to Mescalero last fall, but he had not talked with him. He considered the expedition to the Sierra Madre to have been a failure. Ingstad took Yanozha with him, whom Sam thinks was unfit to go, as he seems to disapprove of the old man, hinting that he is unreliable.*

*He tried to dissuade him from going, saying, "You know what happened the time you went before.[6] Besides you are an old man. You know you cannot see far, you can't run all day, you might fall over a cliff and kill yourself. No one would do anything about that. This white man is not related to you. He is not going to feel bad if anything like that should happen. You will just be out of luck. Besides, how do you think you are going to catch these wild people. You know it took a lot of Apache scouts and five companies or more of soldiers to do it when Geronimo was caught. How in the world do you think you three men are going to what it took so many to do?"*

*But the old man was determined to go, and said that if he saw these people on the side of a hill at a distance, it would be enough, for then he would holler at them and they would come to him. He said he would not have to walk, but could ride a horse. He was going to go anyway. So they went. The younger man who also went along spoke fluent Mexican, but from Sam's talk I think he is not trusted by the people, and there was some hint of his interpreting things to suit himself with Ingstad.[7] I don't know if he was the same one who went four years ago or not.*

*When they got down to Mexico, they came to one ranch where a number of cattle had been butchered by someone. This was near the place called dzilda na- goul.[8] The cowboys on the ranch had set out some days before to find out who had been killing their cattle. They determined that it was the Sierra Madre Apache. They were thought to be camped on a high mountain, not far from there. Ingstad and the two Chiricahuas hearing this came to the ranch, and with the cowboys made up a party* to try and contact the Apaches. They set off in the early morning, about 3 AM. They reached the mountain and made their way carefully up it on foot, to where they thought the Apache camp was. When they got there the Apaches had just left. They were gone like a flash. They had tracked them to their camp. There they found meat still boiling over the fire and other things, but they left them just where they were. The Apaches had known they intended to come the night before, and they had been ready to go. Yanozha saw the tracks and verified them to be of his people. They could not follow the tracks on from there, so turned about and came home. That was the closest that the party came to the wild Apache while the two Chiricahuas were with Ingstad. They never saw them at all, as far as Sam knew. If Ingstad did see seven at a distance it was after the two Chiricahuas had left him.*

### Neil's Diary, Tucson, Arizona

It was only in newspaper articles that Ingstad is quoted as having made this claim. In his book he does not say that he saw wild Apaches, only "some shy people who I thought were Apaches."[9] Curiously, Ingstad does not mention the campsite Yanozha described to Sam Kenoi. This could mean that Yanozha did not tell him about his discovery and kept it to himself, telling only other Chiricahuas at Mescalero.

Ingstad describes the certainty of his two Apache companions that other Apaches are near. At this point Ingstad and the two Apaches separate for several days, during which time Yanozha and Andrew Little come upon the unoccupied camp. I can only think that Yanozha may have decided to protect the Sierra Madre Apaches by concealing the existence of the camp from Ingstad.[10]

### Grenville's Diary, cont'd.

*When I asked Sam how the people at Mescalero felt about having the Sierra Madre Apache brought to live at Mescalero, he said, "Why yes, the people would like to have them here, but there is no way to keep them here. They might take it into their heads to run off at any time."*

### Neil's Diary, Tucson

In the following notation made by Grennie after a meeting with Morris Opler, it is clear that the people at Mescalero have mixed feelings about being joined by the Sierra Madre Apaches. The latter are closely associated with Geronimo, whose defiant escapades provoked the wrath of the U.S. government in 1886. The result was a brutal injustice: all Chiricahuas including those living peacefully on reservations and even those serving as Army scouts were exiled to prison in Florida. All of them were prisoners of war for the next twenty-five years.

Even though it is 1938, the Chiricahuas have not forgotten the U.S. government's treachery, and they fear the same thing might happen again.

### Grenville's Diary Notes

*Opler told me that he had obtained a complete list of the people who remained behind in Mexico after 1886. He said he had difficulty in getting it from their relatives at Mescalero because they feared that they might become involved with their wild relatives and stand in danger from reprisals by the government and Whites because of what their relatives had done.*[11]

### Neil's Diary, Tucson, Arizona

And, of course, the Sierra Madre Apaches themselves would have even greater reason to fear such reprisals.

In his letter to Ingstad, Grennie as much as says that if he were in Ingstad's place, he would be making the trip with official credentials from the federal governments of both countries to guarantee safe passage and amnesty.

Beyond scientific enterprise, I believe the Sierra Madre Apaches represent to Grennie a chance to right an ancient wrong. As much as he knows that an attempt to rescue them is more likely to be a wild-goose chase than a heroic humanitarian achievement, it is irresistible to contemplate. In his letters to Opler the suggestion of an attempt to bring them out and settle them on the reservation is a dominant theme. In his letter to Ingstad, four years later, the idea is even more strongly framed.

These people are the last holdouts, the survivors of the longest war waged against an indigenous people by either the U.S. or the Mexican government. In reaching these people and persuading them to leave the mountains for the safety of the reservation, however problematic that might be, my father saw a way to end the killing before the killing ended the Sierra Madre Apaches.

What appears to have happened, though, is what usually happens: by the end of the 1930s the Apaches had simply disappeared. When I began working on this project I assumed their disappearance simply meant extinction—from bloodshed, starvation, capture, or misadventure. Although there is a small but persistent countercurrent, Mexican folklore on the fate of the Sierra Madre Apaches is fairly consistent in supporting the assumption that any surviving Apaches eventually fled north across the line and back to the reservation.

Mexican and Apache oral history are, I find, mirror images of each other. At Fort Apache and Mescalero and especially at San Carlos they say no Apaches ever returned for good, but that somewhere south of the border they survive in secret enclaves, some still speaking the language and wearing traditional clothing. It is a persistent oral tradition, and over the years I have heard it from a variety of sources.

Two Western Apache men, the father and uncle of a woman I know, went to Ciudad Juárez in the 1940s. While speaking to each other in Apache in the street they were accosted by a man who spoke to them in their own language. They turned around and replied to the man in Apache, and they spoke for a long time that way. With the man were two women. He said that there were other Apaches living in Mexico, that they lived in certain places, that they had fields and planted crops and were more or less integrated into Mexican society, but that they stayed out of the way and tried not to attract attention to themselves.

There is more: I know of a young woman who was born and raised in Colorado by parents who were immigrants from Mexico. In due course her paternal grandmother moved up from Mexico to join the family. When the grandmother arrived, she spoke in a strange language with her son, the young woman's father. This language was Apache, and she learned it by hearing it spoken at home. Her Apache-speaking father and grandmother were born in a settlement in the mountains west of Chihuahua City where "everyone is related to each other." This was a household, perhaps even a village, where the Apache language was spoken as recently as the 1950s.[12]

Another man, from Ascensión, Chihuahua, who refers to himself as a Mexican Chiricahua, told me vividly of his own grandfather, once a warrior himself, who migrated south after the fighting ended in the 1880s. He went "almost all the way to Tarahumara country" and was taken in by a family in the mountains who gave him a home and ultimately their name, Gonzalez. Slowly he became Mexican-ized—marrying, raising a family, earning a living on the railroad, moving out of the mountains into Chihuahua City.

The families of both of these Mexican Apaches seem to have orig-inated in a region of the Sierra Madre west of Chihuahua City, well south of Nácori Chico. It is a place so vast and wild that even today there are virtually no roads. The people who live there are for the most part Mountain Pimas, Indians who have for centuries shared the Sierra Madre with the Apaches.

It wasn't until I reread material gathered by the anthropologist Tom Hinton that enough of a pattern emerged to suggest this area as a possibility for at least one of the Apache escape hatches. While Hin-ton was traveling through this part of the Sierra Madre on horseback in 1955 he met a mining engineer named Neil Parker who told him about an extended exploratory pack trip, taken in 1948, during which he found Indians who described themselves as Apaches. Parker spoke with one of them at length. The man wore buckskin clothing, a gee-string, and moccasins; he had long hair and spoke some Span-ish. He said there were about thirty families living in isolated camps and that they were partly descended from Chiricahuas, who were led by the old chief Nana who broke out of American reservations in the 1880s, and partly from renegades who left the reservation at later dates. They lived in groups of three or four families, planting small patches of corn and living in wickiups of grass.

Tom heard a similar story from another American named Gor-don MacMurray who said that, in the Sierra Madre in about 1920, he had seen some people who told him they were Chiricahuas. They had broad faces, large features, and long hair tied with red sashes. They were mining for gold, and there were Mexicans among them. Most interesting of all, MacMurray said these people called them-selves "O-o-pas," which is the Pima word for Apache.

How often a snatch of someone's language can tell us who they may be. The Pima word for Apache is "ohbi", with the "i" silently as-pirated. More than one Apache is "Oh'ohbi." In fact the term is a general one that means "enemy," but since Apaches were the most common enemy, it usually refers to them.[13] I was told a story by a man who met a self-described Apache in the Guyanopa country, close to Mountain Pima territory, in the 1970s. The Apache said that "Apache" meant "enemy" and that he was no one's enemy, but just wanted to live in peace.[14]

These stories give added meaning to the claims of the two smugglers Bill and Grennie encountered after leaving the Apache camp in the Sierra Espuelas. According to those men, the Mexicans of the Aros River say that the Apaches have their headquarters in this district. The Aros River flows though the heart of Mountain Pima country.

None of these stories should be taken at face value, but considered in light of what I have heard firsthand about Apache descendants emerging from the vast wilderness east of Sahuaripa, they suggest a possible hypothesis. Not only could Apaches lose themselves in Mountain Pima country, they could lose themselves among the Pima people—and they could have been doing so since the final days of the Apache Wars in the 1880s.

The grandfather of my friend from Ascensión, mentioned above, drifted south as the fighting died down in the 1880s. As he did so he would necessarily have entered Mountain Pima country, and the Pima people might very well have taken him in. The same circumstance could account for the family of the young Apache woman from Colorado. It is conceivable that, instead of being a unique occurrence, this was a pattern: as military, vigilante, and development pressure in the northern Sierra Madre drove the Apaches farther south, they simply settled anonymously among the Pimas.

As I spin out this hypothesis, other Mexican adventures are taking shape in my imagination, because the only way to advance this scenario beyond a hypothesis is to go there and pick up this trail where Tom Hinton left it some forty years ago, writing in his field diary: "Parker pointed out on the map where he had seen them. He said that they would know about them at Rancho Malanoche." And that's where we'll start.

Whether or not this hypothesis is supportable with more investigation, one thing can be said with certainty: there is by now, after all these years of warfare, captivity, assimilation, and survival instinct, a good deal of Apache blood in these parts of Sonora and Chihuahua.

In fact, there are probably four different strains of Apache descent in northern Mexico. The best known comprises the descendants of Apache Mansos who have lived in peace at towns such as Janos, Casas Grandes, Bavispe, and others since the eighteenth century. Another comprises the descendants of Apaches captured by Mexicans during the warfare of the nineteenth century. Others are descended from people who remained in Mexico after Geronimo surrendered, but settled peacefully in remote locations, such as the one described above. And the fourth group, if it exists at all, would be descended from the mountain people, the Sierra Madre Apaches. Even after all these years Apache lineage is something few in Mexico are eager to acknowledge. As a result, any contact between Mexican Apache descendants and Apaches in the United States has been only of the most private, even clandestine kind.

Even so, knowing that there may be a potential rendezvous with distant kin, present-day Apaches feel a powerful gravitational pull from northern Mexico. It is for them a kind of holy land. But there is an almost equally strong anti-force as well. Until recently the Apache memory of Mexican enmity was so palpable that to cross the border now would be as harrowing for an Apache as dreaming of the dead. To be outnumbered in Mexico and at the mercy of Mexican authority is to be cornered in a position of unthinkable vulnerability.

It wasn't until 1987 and 1988 that Chiricahuas entered Mexico openly as a large group. Margot and I and our nephew Billy McCullough and other historians accompanied them on a commemorative visit to the location of Geronimo's 1886 near-surrender to General Crook. Among the group were Berle and Aryliss Kanseah, brothers whose grandfather, Jasper, was one of Geronimo's youngest warriors. We had with us photographs showing this selfsame grandfather, then a boy of twelve or thirteen, standing by big rocks with other members of Geronimo's band, holding a carbine as long as he was tall. We found these very rocks, and when the two brothers stood where their grandfather had stood, and touched the rocks their grandfather had touched, there was for them the beginning of a kind of closure and an understanding that it might at long last be safe for an Apache to return openly to Mexico.

The two spoke to each other in their own language as they stood by the rocks. It was a place at which they entered the history of their own people. It was a moment that was as compelling as time travel. Aryliss walked away from the rest of us, and I remember he stood there for a long time, saying nothing, just looking up the canyon. This was for Aryliss and Berle a place unlike any other place: here Chiricahua Apaches had camped, been born, died, and held religious ceremonials for centuries. But being here was also like returning to the scene of a holocaust, and therefore it was doubly powerful.

Later during that trip the Chiricahuas conducted their holiest of rituals, the spellbinding crown dance. It begins with an immense leaping bonfire. There is a line of drummers and chanters. Shockingly, out of the darkness, come the dancers. They circle the fire wearing masks with high, antlerlike crowns, short kilts, painted bodies, a thousand tiny bells, a sword in each hand—they reel, hover, sway, and as they do, they become the mountain gods. The assembled Apaches are witnessing the first crown dance held in these mountains for a very long time. It is at long last a dance for the peaceless dead, and it is overdue by a hundred years or more.

Mildred Cleghorn, the beautiful, regal seventy-four-year-old chairwoman of the Fort Sill, Oklahoma Chiricahua/Warm Springs Apache Tribe, speaks to me about the "wild Apaches" as if they were still there—as powerful in myth as in reality.

She's also mischievous: "When we were kids, we were always in trouble, especially me and my cousin. Once my mother got so mad at us that she put us both in a gunny sack and hung it from a tree until she thought we'd had enough to stay quiet. But when nothing else would work, my grandmother or my aunt could make us behave by saying they'd call in those "wild ones" from Mexico. Oh, we'd heard all about them. We were more scared of them than anything. They'd tell us stories about them. Those people, when we were kids, they still lived the way my great grandparents once lived."

Go where they want.

Do what they want.

34. Above, from left to right:
Yanozha; Chappo, Geronimo's
son; Fun, Yanozha's half
brother; Geronimo. Cañon de
los Embudos, March 1886.
Yanozha returned to Mexico
with Helge Ingstad in 1937 in
search of the Sierra Madre
Apaches. Photo by Camillus S.
Fly. Courtesy Arizona Historical
Society. Negative #71014.

35. Right: The Apache captive
boy named Julio Medina,
Hermosillo, Sonora, about 1950.
Courtesy Arizona State
Museum.

36. The Apache captive girl Bui in 1932. She was later adopted by the Harris family and named Carmela.

37. Carmela, the Apache captive girl
adopted by the Harris family, Los Angeles,
about 1935. Courtesy Ann McGarrell.

38. Left: Carmela's high school graduation
picture, Los Angeles, about 1948. Courtesy
Ann McGarrell.

39. Above: Jan and Grennie, Santa Fe, 1937.

40. Above: Grennie with Neil Buck and his family, Santa Fe,
1938. Barbara is in the front seat.

41. Right: Neil Buck, my father's best friend, San Carlos, about
1951. Photo by Charles Kaut.

42. Barbara Buck King, the daughter
of Neil Buck, San Carlos, 1997.

# Epilogue

**Neil's Diary, Vermont**

Eventually my father would have gone back to Mexico with Bill Curtis and Art Schrader, and then he would have realized his "fond hope" of tackling the Sierra Madre Apaches. If he had, they would not be the mystery that they are today. Whether or not there were any left, he was superbly prepared to tell their story by continuing with what he had begun in 1930 and 1931. He had since then had plenty of practice.

At San Carlos he was learning how to enter an alien culture—almost like learning to breathe underwater, so he knew how important the discipline of total immersion was. He was doing the pick and shovel work of learning language and customs, of gaining trust. Strong friendships developed, but he had a finely tuned sense of balance. My mother wrote me this in a letter in 1980: "He never lived among the Apaches, as he knew that a certain distance always had to be kept because of his work and its demands, but he was accepted more than any white man had ever been."

His observations of daily life became so acute, his awareness so finely tuned that, in time, he would be able to harmonize his behavior with that of the Apaches with a kind of perfect pitch—not to become one of them so much as to become invisible. Soon he would be able to detect deep rhythms in their culture by glimpsing only nuances. He would come to know what taboo, belief, or kinship bond was embedded in each small gesture, expression, or turn of phrase. It required a kind of suspension of self, almost a suspension of identity while among the Apaches, but it gave him a unique identity among his own kind.

Back East, I suspect he relished being the quintessential outsider: a young man at ease among the infamously hostile Apaches, able to speak their language, not to mention fluent Spanish.

When my mother, Jan, met him at his brother's wedding in 1929, he must have been quite the most exotic being she had ever seen.

Anne Stockton, one of her closest friends from New York, became engaged to my father's older brother, Henry Sage Goodwin. My father was best man, my mother maid of honor—it was a storybook constellation.

Their paths crossed only twice in the next seven years, but in early 1936, after the second of these meetings, he returned to Arizona, and they commenced a correspondence. His letters have an ingenuous, boyish quality. They are full of sweet, vivid, simple descriptions of his days, Apache life, and the dramatic Arizona landscape. They were planning to meet back East later that year so they could travel around New England together: see the coast of Maine, Cape Cod, swim in the ocean.

The New England odyssey materialized and fostered a whirlwind romance, as they both must have hoped. They eloped in his jalopy, a 1934 Ford coupe, drove across the country, and were married by a justice of the peace in Holbrook, Arizona. They got a stranger off the street for a witness. Her parents were appalled at this flouting of convention; I suppose his were too, but they had come to expect it from him.

My mother told me a story about a camping trip they took together on the Navajo Reservation after they were married. Their car became stuck in deep sand, and some passing Navajos pushed it onto firm footing. Grennie gave them a silver dollar. After they left, Jan asked if he shouldn't have given them more. He said that more than that would have been too much, impolite—a gratuitous reminder of wealth to people who have very little.

Although my mother never forgot the simple dignity and respect expressed in this transaction, she sometimes saw another side to my father's "Indian code"—a moral superiority, even a rigidity. When I pressed her on this, she wrote to me:

*While we were on the reservation, G. instructed me how to behave:*

> *Women must never shout or run. (I had run to greet him back after a trip and was severely reprimanded by him).*

> *Women must wear skirts at all times.*

> *Women gather the firewood and do all the cooking.*

> *Whites should never stand around, but should sit or squat on the ground while conversing, and never stand when eating.*

*Apache men never dance with their wives at social dances, so G. refused to dance with me at the fiesta dances in Santa Fe, even though this was not the reservation and our married friends danced with their spouses.*

*Married couples never show any kind of affection towards each other.*

For my mother, this was more than culture shock; this was a man she hardly recognized. Something had changed in the months following their marriage. My mother says he became disappointed in her. She saw a dark and moody side. One picture taken of them together in Santa Fe betrays a jarring disharmony.

As I was growing up my mother talked about him to keep his image strong for me. She was as frank about their difficulties as she was about the things she admired most in him. Her admiration, love, and loyalty transcended, and at the same time coexisted with, their grave differences. She may have been one of the few who saw the best and worst of him.

As well as Jan knew Grennie, I think there was a great deal in his life among the Apaches that he never revealed to her. Just as it must have felt to Jan, Grennie's experience among the Apaches has always felt inaccessible to me: a secret within the secret of who he was. This inaccessibility had kept me from paying a visit to the descendants of his Apache friends for years.

It wasn't until 1997, after beginning the intensive research and reflection needed to write this book, that I went to San Carlos and Fort Apache. With a better picture of my father and a point of departure for myself, I first visited Barbara King, the daughter of Grennie's best friend, Neil Buck, after whom I was named. We talked about our fathers and the things they did together and the ways in which the lives of our two families would have been intertwined, had Grennie lived.

### Neil's Diary, San Carlos

Barbara is sedate and quiet, but moved by my unexpected visit.

"I had always hoped," she says, "that you would come to visit me. I remember holding you when you were just a baby."

Her whole family must have come for a visit while we were living in Tucson—just as they had come for a visit to Santa Fe. If my father had lived, she would have been my Apache sister; our fathers were that close. I feel the residual power of the nexus that bound Grennie and Neil to one another and through that, our two families across space and time.

"You look like your father. He could talk Apache real well," she says.

"The Apaches had names for him: Indaa yalti'í—'talking white man'—because he was always talking with the Apaches; and Gotah nagháhá—'walks among homes' because he was always visiting people."

She remembers my mother well. Fragments come to the surface of her memory: the two-week trip the Bucks made to Santa Fe, and a funny joke about Navajos that my father made, the dress her mother made for mine.

Then she tells me something I have never heard. Before my father died, Neil Buck and his family were planning to move to Tucson, probably near our ranch in the Rincon foothills east of town. Grennie had found a piece of land, and the Bucks were going to live there. She didn't know exactly where the land was, or who was going to buy it, but for Barbara and her family it was for a while a reality.

It was another plan, made, but soon undone, that might have determined the trajectory of my life. Had it been realized, would I have grown up in some way among this Apache family and become from birth what my father may always have wished for himself? The plan must have been that the Bucks were to live near or even with us and that we would have made a life together.

"Us."

My mother, my father and me. A family. So hypothetical, this "us" is the family that never was, or, rather, it was so embryonic that it almost never was, except for two anguished months in early 1940. Still, to say "us" this way opens the door on a life, a me that might have been. And it has taken this long-delayed meeting with my "Apache sister" to give life and form to the landscape along this road not taken.

We come to forks in the road so often that we rarely look back to wonder how different it all might have been, if only. . . . But this fork is a momentous juncture for me, because I can so vividly imagine the elements and structure of my world if my father had lived, if there had been this "us": the desert, a father, parents—as a couple so different from an individual father and mother. I might be fluent in the Apache language. I might be, what—a Republican, a Vietnam casualty—the list goes on and on, and I contemplate with near despair the prospects of the survival of my parents' marriage, given what I now know about Jan and Grennie.

By late 1938 *Myths and Tales of the White Mountain Apache* had been published, and the manuscript for *Social Organization of the Western Apache* was nearing completion.[1] But there were already signs of trouble with Grennie's health, and he told my mother that he was beginning to worry about strange feelings in his head.

"It is as if," he said, "the top of my head is coming off."

He went to a neurologist in Colorado Springs who could neither diagnose the problem nor offer any useful advice. The problem persisted. Jan saw disquieting changes: an oppressive and temperamental moodiness as distressing to him as it was to her. As stoic as he was baffled, Grennie moved back to Tucson with Jan for the summer of 1939 when he was given an appointment at the University of Arizona as research associate. Then, even though my father's headaches were worsening and there was still no diagnosis, he decided it was time for a new and demanding undertaking.

Grennie had had no formal training in anthropology, so, putting aside his immense body of fieldwork for consideration later, he enrolled at the University of Chicago for postgraduate courses. Jan and Grennie spent the winter there while his head condition grew worse, affecting his eyesight and causing headaches. "He carried on with his studies just the same," my mother told me, "and did remarkably well."

I was born in Chicago on March 29, 1940, and was named after Neil Buck. My mother had told me many times how much my father loved me and how well his work was going, but within two weeks of my birth his brain tumor was discovered, and he underwent surgery, thought at first to be successful. From then on a nightmare had control of our lives, and my mother was the last to find out the worst of it.

She is gone now. I know she died, but I just think of her as gone. I wasn't there when she took her own life at the age of eighty-six in a final defiant, desperate act of independence. Just as she held the key to her own life and took it with her, so she may have held and kept a key to Grennie's life.

I can only imagine why she was not told that Grennie would never recover, but none of it makes any sense. Perhaps my father persuaded his own mother and doctors to keep it from her. His mother was autocratic and used to taking control: perhaps she decided that with a newborn, my mother was in no condition to absorb such news, and that, for her own good, or for my good, she was not to know. My mother was tougher than any of them realized, but she was also intimidated by Grennie's formidable mother and family and must have felt she had no choice but to trust them and the doctors, though in fact they were depriving her of the one crucial piece of information she needed in order to decide what to do next.

Jan and Grennie had planned to spend the summer in California. The doctors, knowing now that there would be no recovery, advised my mother, without telling her the truth, to take the train to California, and what . . . ? Convalesce in the healing sun? It all seems like such a pointless lie. Does Grennie, in his stoicism, imagine that he is protecting my mother and me? Or has his mother taken over, cowing the doctors, Grennie, and Jan alike, imagining that by controlling the truth, she could somehow control the outcome of events? Did she believe that if Jan weren't told that Grennie was dying, somehow she wouldn't be aware of it until it was mercifully over? Was it all just well-meaning but poor judgment? The outcome of this deception was a descent into hell.

There were now three of us. Somehow my father must have appeared to be well enough for us all to board the Los Angeles train in Chicago. My mother had no idea what was in store for the next three days. There was a trained nurse traveling with us. En route my father's condition quickly deteriorated, and his postoperative pain became unbearable. The nurse refused to administer more painkiller, though my father and mother begged her to do so. By the time the situation had become extremely serious there was nowhere to get off the train. There were no adequate medical facilities along the way and none on the train crawling across the desert. When we got to Los Angeles he was taken off the train by stretcher, put in an ambulance, and driven to a hospital. Doctors could do nothing for him during the next four days. From Los Angeles, on July 30, 1940, his mother sent a telegram to his older brother Sage, saying simply, "Grennie died peacefully this morning."

I am always so affected by reading my mother's simple description of his burial on our ranch east of Tucson that I must let her describe it. She was there.

"The ceremony was held on the ranch on the highest piece of land facing west and opened to both mountain ranges—with mesquite trees and a giant cactus. Ned Spicer stood up and said a few words, beautifully simple and moving. My own great loss is subordinated by the relief that his suffering is over. Afterwards we had a fire and a little picnic supper and the sky was full of stars."[2]

Neil Buck wrote a letter to my mother in which he mentions a ceremonial dance to be held at Bylas in Grennie's honor. She told me, "I don't believe that any other white man had ever had such a tribute paid to him by the Apaches."

*Dear Friend Jan Goodwin,*

*Your letter of July 8 received about my brother G. Goodwin was died in Los Angeles. So I open it up right away and see my brother has died, and so we just drop our supper and cry with all of my family. I got no more friend than he. I been told all his friend whom a living at Bylas. They said they thinking that Mr. Goodwin was never going to die because he is a good man.*

*I heard the Indians said that some dance going to start next Friday night up about one mile above Bylas. You know where the dance ground is. They going to dance two night.*

*Say, Jan Goodwin, where did you buried him I like to know about where that is so I might go there see sometime.*

*This is all today so good bye from your truly friend Neil Buck.*

HORSE PRAYER
*Horse, his hair is made of Lightning, they say.*
*His ears move about separately with Small Whirlwinds, they say. . . .*

*If I ride him, pray to him, they say.*
*White Water makes you move with it, my brother. White*
*shell beads with holes in them; breathe hard through these.*
*Suck the air in; sweat will not appear. Pollen boy you ride*
*before me. Pollen girl you ride behind me. Between you two*

*I sit. Black dirt of Horses I move up and down on top of
you, since long ago.*[3]

    This is Grennie's translation from the Apache. A rider would sing
this to his horse while on a long trip so that the horse would not tire,
and as I read it I wonder: perhaps when he spoke Apache, he spoke
with passion.
    Like a wolf, he circles once, slowly, incandescent in the brush;
then he is gone. The search always ends by his graveside. No matter
how much I learn, no matter how much ground I cover, all I can do
is finally put him to rest.

## APPENDIX 1

# Historical Chronology

1882  Capture of Maria Samaniego at Arroyo los Alisos, Chihuahua.

1885  Arrival of Mormons in Colonia Diaz; settlement of colonies begins.

Founding of Colonia Juárez by Mormons.

1886  Surrender of Geronimo (Sept.).

1887  Founding of Colonia Dublan by Mormons.

1888  Founding of Colonia Pacheco by Mormons.

1889  Apache Kid escapes en route to Yuma Prison (Nov. 11).

1890  Outbreak from San Carlos of an undetermined but small number of people; many reports of violence throughout the year on both sides of the border.

French miners discover gold in the Espuelas (sometime during the 90s), most of them killed by Apaches.

1891  Lumholtz Sierra Madre expedition; reports Apache sign; meets Mexican soldiers in pursuit of Apaches.

1891–1896: Reciprocal Border Crossing Agreement between Mexico and United States for pursuit of Apaches.

1892  Thompson Massacre by Apaches in Cave Valley (Sept.).

Frequent reports of Apache robberies and attacks on both sides of the border.

1893  Founding of Colonia Garcia by Mormons.

Founding of Colonia Oaxaca by Mormons.

1894  Founding of Colonia Chuhuichupa by Mormons.

1895  Apache Kid kidnaps Dja'okin, a woman from Fort Apache.

H. H. Merrill and daughter killed by Apaches near Solomonville, just south of San Carlos (Dec. 6).

1896  Murder of Alfred Hands in Cave Creek Canyon by Apaches (Mar. 28).

Apache scout Sherman Curley identifies Adiɫnazi·d during attack on camp of Apache in Sierra Madre — the same Apaches who killed the Merrills and Alfred Hands (May 11).

Apache May captured at this camp and adopted by John Slaughter (May 11).

Railroad under construction from Colonia Dublán to Colonia Chuhuichupa.

1899 Apache Kid (probably) killed by Mormons near Cave Valley in the Sierra Madre.

1900 A man named J. D. Mack is shot by Apaches in the Chiricahua Mountains (Apr. 9).

Twelve Apaches and a number of Mormons killed in a battle near Pacheco, Chihuahua (Nov. 16).

Founding of Colonia Morelos by Mormons.

Col. William Greene begins large-scale mining at Cananea and gains control of timber rights in the Sierra Madre from Bavispe to Sahuaripa.

Lupe's mother and her cousin captured from Solomonville (approx. date).

1902 Eighty-five miles west of Casas Grandes in the Sierra Madre, an attack on some miners by Apaches (Apr.).

Arizona Apaches reported in Sonora (May 24).

1904 Altamirano, Chihuahua, settled.

Forty Lipan Apaches removed from Mexico to Mescalero (May 31).

Miners strike at Cananea, Sonora.

1907 Birth of Grenville Goodwin.

The Apache, Massai, killed in New Mexico.

1908 Murders near Moctezuma, Sonora, are credited to Apaches (Mar. 20).

Maria Gereque, six, captured by Apaches near Mineral de Dolores. She escaped two years later.

Apache Elias reported in attack on miners thirty miles east of Nacozari, Sonora. (June 18).

Apaches reported encamped between Ascensión and Janos, Chihuahua.

Kickapoos settle near Huachinera.

Sierra Madre Apaches appear near Willcox to steal women.

1909 Founding of Colonia San José (Rusvayo) by Mormons.

Uprisings in Chihuahua and Coahuila: Beginning of the Mexican Revolution.

1910 Portillo family homesteads on the Rio Bonito, and encounter Sierra Madre Apaches.

Policeman John Hoffman's encounter with Apaches (approximate date).

Revolution-related battle between San Miguel and Bavispe.

1912 Mormons forced out of Mexico.

1914 Gold miners return to Espuelas with French map.

1915 Fimbres family moves from Nácori Chico to Mesa Tres Rios.

Stewart Hunt catches old Apache woman in Sierra el Tigre.

1916 Pancho Villa attacks Columbus, New Mexico (Mar. 16).

Capture of Lupe, an Apache girl (Oct. 23, probable date).

1919 Sierra Madre Apaches come to San Carlos to steal women.

1920 Apaches kill men seventy-five miles south of Casas Grandes in the Guyanopa District (Oct. 12).

Mexican postcutters robbed in Las Piedras Canyon (approximate date).

American killed by Apaches at Tapila Ranch: see Stuart Hunt's story about his hired man (approximate date).

Gordon MacMurray encounters people who call themselves Chiricahuas mining in the Sierra Madre east of Nácori Chico.

Molina Massacre in the Tinaja; pursuit of Apaches.

Stewart Hunt sees many Apache signs in the Espuelas.

The MacNeils find an Apache camp at Las Varas (sometime before 1927).

1922 Grenville Goodwin goes to Mesa Ranch School.

1923 Murder of Olivas and Pedregón on the Carretas Pass, Chihuahua (Sept. 10).

John Swanson settles near Huachinera.

1924 Sierra Madre Apaches in the Animas Valley, New Mexico (Aug.).

1926 Bill Curtis finds Apache camp in Sierra Espuelas.

1927 Grenville Goodwin moves west permanently, following high school.

Apaches steal Vance horses from Chuhuichupa.

1927 Fimbres family ambushed by Apaches (Oct. 15).

Machichi's soldier encounters an Apache "playing 'possum" near Chuhuichupa.

1928 Grenville Goodwin living in Tucson, University of Arizona affiliation.

Capture of Dórame boy at Pacheco by Apaches.

1929   Cristero Rebellion in Mexico.

Manhunt for Apache kidnappers of Gerardo Fimbres planned (Jan.).

Gov. Topete of Sonora issues order for arms against Apaches (Feb. 9).

Chiricahuas seen in the Huachuca Mountains, southern Arizona, according to Neil Buck.

Grenville Goodwin at University of Arizona as freshman (Sept.).

Anna Price and the Cibecue police report sighting of Sierra Madre Apaches on the reservation (fall).

Stock market crash (Oct.).

Discovery of Chita Hueca Apache camp. (Dec.).

1930   Apaches seen near Miller Ranch in Chihuahua (spring).

Apache Juan, two Apache women, Gerardo Fimbres, killed (Apr.).

Gordy Boyd discovers an Apache camp on the Carretas Ranch.

Grenville Goodwin spends the summer on the Apache and Navajo Reservations.

Grenville Goodwin's first trip to Mexico (Nov–Dec.).

Apache tracks seen in Sierra Espuelas (Nov.).

1931   Grenville Goodwin's second trip to Mexico (Sept–Oct.).

Apache sign at the Chita Hueca campsite (Oct. 15).

1932   Attack on Apache camp near Nácori Chico; Carmela captured (Apr.).

Cowboy stoned to death near Nácori Chico (June).

Attack on Apache camp near Bacadéhuachi, Julio Medina and two other children captured. Only Julio survives (July).

Julia Tasahuinora captured near Bavispe. She dies in captivity (July).

1933   Walter Ramsey, a night on the Bavispe with Apaches (Mar., possibly 1932).

Apache girl caught by two Mexicans somewhere in the northern Sierra Madres; she dies in captivity.

1934   Amiglia Samaniego remembers owls calling all night on the feast day of Santa Niño de Atocha.

Yanozha, Perico, and a third Chiricahua cross the border at Ciudad Juárez to look for treasure.

Newspaper reports two Apaches killed near Nácori Chico (Sept.).

1936  Apaches seen near Pacheco (Nov.).

1937  Sierra Madre Apaches reported at Mescalero (summer).

1938  Helge Ingstad's trip. Yanozha finds Apache camp.

1940  Neil Goodwin's birth, Grenville Goodwin's death, publication of *The Social Organization of the Western Apache*.

Apache-speakers encountered in Ciudad Juárez by Apaches from San Carlos.

Neil Parker finds Apache descendants in Mountain Pima country.

# The Chita Hueca Camp Description

Oct. 17, 1931, Apache Camp, S. Chita Hueca, Chihuahua, Mexico, Grenville's Diary

(full text of this entry)

This morning we found a lump of beef tallow thrown under a bush near our camp at the springs. It had not been there very long, and was probably left over from the last time the Apaches traveled through here.

Marcos left for the caves in Paso Pulpito this morning.

This day I spent in taking pictures, following fence lines out, and plotting the rancheria in general. The whole thing lies on the east slope of the S. Chita Hueca, well up against the mountain. To the south end is the spring, reservoir, and little corral. The spring, (no. 12) is in a small draw, and fenced around to keep stock out. The water is very good, and always there. Right below this is the little reservoir (no. 13), held in by a small dam across the draw, about 6 feet wide. Right at the side of the spring is a lean-to shanty, open on sides and front, with stone wall in rear, and with a roof covered with pine bark (no. 11). A little below the reservoir, and in the bottom of the draw, is a small brush corral, with what looks to be the frame of a sort of small shelter, and this frame against the brush fence of corral, and itself fenced around (no. 15 and no. 16). There is a short drift fence connected with this corral which is shown on the map (no. 14).

On a little rocky knoll, below the little corral, the Apaches have camped, the remains of their temporary brush shelters still being there (no. 18). At this knoll there was a great quantity of cow, horse, and mule bones. Right off this knoll, in the draw, are two or three large rock tanks, full of water. At one of these was half a barrel, which had been used as a tub, and a dilapidated tin pan, which had a big patch of canvas on the bottom (no. 17).

Up the draw from the springs, on its left hand side and at about 3/4 of a mile distance, is a small cave (no. 10), located in a white sandstone ledge there. In this cave was found some salt. Right in front of this cave was a patch of soft ground, and at the time we were there, some horse tracks showed in it which must have been made within the last month. These tracks were most likely made by ridden Apache ponies, as they were flat bottomed, and left an impression as does a horse shod with rawhide in the Apache manner.

—About one mile from the springs, north along the edge of the mountain, is the main camp (the following numbers locate these points; no. 19 the piles of wood, no. 7 the stockade fence). Its plan is shown on page 82. This main camp is located on the point of a rocky shoulder, high up on the side of the mountain, and jutting out abruptly. The color of the rocks here is dull gray, they being of a sort of tufa formation. As the wood in the stockade of the camp has weathered to the same color almost, it is extremely difficult to distinguish the camp from any distance, unless you know right where to look for it. No one would ever suspect a camp there, looking from below, or even from above. Right on the edge of this point are some good sized yellow pine, and other trees, which completely conceal the camp from below.

There is a small level place where the houses rested. The whole place was in a tumble-down state, but enough was left to get a good idea of the arrangement. There was a good picket fence surrounding the place, well made of poles about 2 to 3 in. in diam., about 7 feet tall and set closely together, upright, in the ground where not too rocky. These upright poles were lashed together with horizontal poles running along in lines, and tied securely with strips of rawhide. This picket fence, or more truly stockade, guarded the camp on the downhill side, and ran up to the rocks, on the uphill side of the camp, thus forming a regular little fortified village of the place. The plan, it will be seen now, is made looking more from the uphill side of the enclosure, and looking off downhill. The stockade was entered, on the north side, by a swinging gate, strongly made, about 8 feet wide, the poles lashed together with rawhide, and the hinges, on which the gate swung, made of the same material also (see no. 1, also). Both gates on the south side were of the slip bar type, and well made (see nos. 6 and 7). No. 2 on the plan locates one of the wood piles, and the both of them are shown on the general plan. Just what the purpose of these wood piles was, is hard to say. They were composed of large logs of oak and pine, and stood some 4 feet high, by 6 feet in diam. The wood in them was not such as Apaches would gather for cooking purposes, there being too much work required to cut it up to the required size.

In the enclosure were seven houses originally, all of similar appearance, and structure, except for the largest cabin, the only one still retaining its roof (see no. 11). In these houses, three sides were of regular log cabin structure, the fourth side and front, in which the door was, was made by planting poles, vertically, and close together, which extended right to the peak of the roof. The doors were low and narrow. All the logs and poles in these houses were roughly peeled. The chinking was done with rocks and mud. The back end of the cabin had a double log structure where the log part of the wall ended; and on this rested a thin stone wall, which closed in that portion between the logs, and the V of the roof.

Six of the houses had a fire place and chimney, built in one of its corners, against the logs, and of rocks and mud, the enclosed chimney part not beginning till about 4 feet above the ground, and being very narrow at that. The chimney did not come vertically up out of the house, but came out through the end of the house passing through the side of the stone partition between log wall and roof.

The roofs were hipped, the ridge pole being held up by two crotched poles, one at each end of the house, sometimes inside, sometimes outside the walls. From the ridge poles the roof poles were laid, sloping down to the walls, and extending so as to form slight eaves. Across these other poles were laid, all lashed on with yucca strips. A good thatching of bear grass, with a layer of adobe on top of it, formed the top part of the roof.

These cabins must have been very snug in cold weather, but could not possibly have held more than 3 sleepers. The largest house appeared somewhat newer than the others, and had no fireplace or chimney, and no attempts had been made to close the ends of the house up, between logs and roof. This house had a small covered entrance.

Besides the houses in the enclosure were two structures made of poles laid across, and between four crotched sticks, probably used for storing things on and for shade in hot weather (see no. 9). Right next to the rocks, on the upper side of the enclosure, there was a short ditch dug, about 2.5 feet deep, and two feet wide. This was bridged by a piece of flat wood. It looked as though the mud used in chinking the cabins had been taken from this place, and that the ditch left was later used to hold water in, for drinking purposes, or for the soaking of hides, etc. (see no. 8).

Right beside the first house, mounted on a stout pole frame, was a large, flat circular piece of iron, about 2 feet in diam., a part of some machine I think (this was the cow-bell). Marcos said it had originally been at Las Varas, where the general called his troops together by beating on it, when the soldiers were there during the revolution of 1928. The Apaches had probably lain and watched this crude gong used, and when the troops left, had taken it away to their own camp for a similar purpose (see no. 4).

Between this gong and the first house was a gate (see no. 5). From here to gate no. 6 there was a natural rise of ground which formed a sort of fence. Between the first house and extending around past the north gate (no. 1) was a brush fence to keep stock out (see no. 12). Right above, on the same ridge as the main camp, were two beds of brush, laid flat on the ground, on which hides had been pegged out to dry. The pegs still remained in the ground, although the hides had been taken up (see no. 8, general plan). A little higher up this ridge still, and to the right, is the shallow cave (see no. 9, general plan).

Right below the main camp, at the bottom of a little cliff, were strewn many bones of animals. There must have been the remains of at least 150 head of horses, mules and cattle. There were very few deer bones, which may indicate a lack of ammunition or rifles, or the fear of making a noise by shooting.

About a quarter of a mile from the main camp, on the trail out, and right in the bottom of a small draw is a little mescal pit, not more than 5 feet in diam. (see general plan no. 5). Starting directly below the camp and continuing thence, as shown on map (no. 4) around the foot of the mountain, and north, is the brush fence that shuts in the other side. This fence is about 2 miles long and has two gates, both good slide-bar ones (see general plan, no. 6). One of these gates is right below main camp, the other is lower down. At its further end this brush fence terminates at a good brush corral, situated in a little saddle, on a ridge, jutting out from the mountain side. This corral is slightly larger than the one at the springs, and has a few logs in its walls (see general plan no. 2). Right at this corral were the remains of five temporary brush shelters which the Apaches had camped in. Here also I found part of a saddle, and some hair, braided, which appears to be human.

The remarkable thing about all the work done in this rancheria, is that all brush or timber which these Apaches have had to cut by ax for use in fences or houses, etc., has been cut so carefully as not to show any traces of the work on the slopes of the mountain. These brush fences are made of poles, brush, old logs, etc., laid up together, lengthwise, and horizontally, so as to originally have been about 3 feet, or more high.

—The main trails only are shown on the general plan (nos. 1), as these were the only ones still distinct. There is a good plain trail coming up from the llano to within a mile of the brush fence of the pasture where it plays out, and does not again become evident till within the pasture. This seems to have been the only precaution taken to conceal the entrance trail.

# The Espuelas Camp Description

Oct. 29, 1931, Apache Camp, S. Espuela, Chihuahua, Mexico,
Grenville's Diary

[A]

Another mile or so up the canyon, and on the right side going up, is a small
open cave which was used for storage. It is situated in a pink colored tufa
ledge. Across the mouth has been built a stout stockade fence about 9 feet
high. At one end of this cave was another small chamber entered by a door
which had been sealed with rocks and mud, but was now broken open. Inside this were some sticks and the remains of some prepared mescal (see
no. 13). This little chamber had been enterable from outside, as well as inside the larger cave, but a good stone and mud wall had been built across
this outside entrance to close it. Right outside this wall were the remains of
a pole structure of some sort, probably a cache of some sort. It was in this
cave that so much of the material was found by the raiders (see general plan
no. 9). A little way down the canyon, on the opposite slope, was a large, over-
hanging bluff, fairly high up, under which Apaches used to camp. (no. 8,
general plan). About 80 yards up the canyon from the storage cave, and on
a little pine flat to the left, were two houses, of the type no. 6. These were
surrounded by a brush fence, (see no. 10, general plan). In the canyon bottom here, were pools of water at intervals, and extending, less frequently
down to the main camp.

—The big corrals lay about two miles from the main camp, right square
on top of an open, level topped ridge (see no. 14, general plan). Right to the
North of here, is a deep, dry steep sided canyon, which is really the head of
Las Piedras Canyon, as it makes a big swing around to the north, and then
east, and ends up at this place. Right in the bottom of this canyon, across the
creek bed, is a rock dam, built to hold seepage water, which comes to the
surface at that place. This dam is made of rocks set in adobe, and is about
4-1/2 feet high, by 10 or 12 feet long, built directly on bed rock (see general
plan, no. 16). About half a mile below this dam, there is a little draw, going
up to the right, and a quarter of a mile up this draw are the small corrals and
calf pens (see general plan, no. 18). From the draw, running down the left

side of the creek bottom, and crossing over, and up the side can on to the small corrals, is a brush fence, part of a large pasture fence apparently (see general plan, no. 17). This fence also runs up the side of the ridge from the small corrals, and clear to the top of the high hill at that place.

—On this general plan all mescal pits are shown as nos. 4. These pits were all small and none over 5 ft. in diam. The main trails are all shown, though most of them are barely traceable now.

[B]

—I have waited to describe in detail the main camp, the big corrals on the ridge, and the small corrals and calf pens, as these three places have more to them than do the other camps.

—The main camp consisted of 8 houses, and two brush shelters (nos. 14).

Two of the houses had been burnt down by Bill's raiding party (nos. 9).

House no. 10 was of type 7, but had no beds.

House no. 11 is the one shown as type 7, and had two frame beds in each of its ends. These beds were naturally small and cramped on account of the size of the house.

House no. 12 had stone walls, and is of type 2. House no. 13 was built against the bank, half of upright poles, and half of rock and adobe walls. This house was about 7 feet high, flat roofed, and well built. It had a chimney which was blocked up, and was the only house which had one in the whole rancheria. This along with a house of similar dimensions in the little corral camp, were the largest structures which the Indians had built (see type 4).

House no. 8 was of type no. 1. The roof of this house was burnt off, but the walls still stood. On the top of the walls of this house were two tin, conical bells, such as the Apaches and other Indians attach to the end of buckskin fringes on dresses, etc., and which produce a jingling effect when in motion. There were also three pieces of hematite, paint rock.

House no. 15 is of type 2.

This main camp is enclosed by a brush fence, (no. 2). There are two entrances, no. 1 in the creek bed, and no. 3 in the brush fence, on the up canyon side of the camp. Right near the lower entrance is a pile of boards, all hand hewn from pine trees, and a frame with some peeled logs piled on it (no. 16). These boards were about 6 feet long, by 5 to 10 inches wide, in most instances, and some 1-1/2 to 3 inches thick. They, along with the logs, had apparently been placed there for future use in building houses, etc. In this camp was also a rigging for soaking hides, in the process of tanning (no. 6).

A cowhide was hung on a square frame of logs, and used as the water container. Under it was a foundation of rocks to hold up to the weight. The water was obtained from a pool in the creek bed, which appears to be permanent. In this pool in the bottom, is set a small wooden box, which must have been used as a spring box from all appearances (no. 4).

There was a small, brush walled corral in the camp (see no. 5). This had apparently been used for stock which was kept up for use. One of its sides was bounded by the steep bank of the arroyo, and thus was not fenced. Upon the other fork of the creek bed, around the hill, was a small mescal pit (no. 7). About from this mescal pit to the house no. 12, ran the remains of a brush fence, which originally went further on around the hill from the mescal pit (no. 17).

—These corrals were extremely well made of posts and barbed wire, the fence being one of five strands, and the gates regular pull shut ones, the most common kind in this country. There were two of these corrals, side by side (no. 2 on plan). One had a large snubbing post in its center (no. 3). Their length and width would be about 30 paces by 20 paces. On the south and west sides of the corrals were two brush enclosures, in which houses stood.

No. 6 was of the circular kind, type 1.

No. 8 house was of type 6, and was completely in ruins.

No. 7 house was type 3. It was the best made house in the whole rancheria, and still in excellent condition. It was in this house that Bill found the reloading outfit.

Houses nos. 9 were of type 6, and quite large. These last were a little ways to the northeast of the corrals.

At no. 1, near the edge of the ridge and to southeast, are some pot holes in a group of large boulders there. These pot holes the Indians had used for tanning hides in, when they contained enough rainwater, and they still had a quantity of pounded oak bark in them.

Right north of the corrals was a mescal pit, near the edge of the ridge (no. 11). Near this was a large pile of the bones of cattle, horses and mules apparently slaughtered there by the Apaches, for food (no. 10). Along the south side of the brush enclosure around the corrals, were some drying racks (no. 5) on which meat was hung, in the process of making jerky. Near house no. 7 was the sled Bill told me about last year, used in hauling meat out to the drying racks.

—An excellent view could be had from the top of the ridge, in all directions, and this, strange to say, was the only camp which commanded such a position.

—The plan of the encampment at the small corrals and calf pens is on page 136. There were two small, low fenced brush corrals, here about 20 paces by 18 paces roughly. The fencing was made mainly with poles and stood some 3-1/2 to 4 feet high (nos. 12), and had two outside gates and one inner gate (nos. 13). No. 9 was a small pen, apparently used for calves, and no. 8 was a structure for the same purpose, only with roof.

Four houses were in the camp, two of them on the west side of the arroyo. House no. 2 was of stone, and type no. 2. It was in this house that Bill found the bows and arrows he told me about, hung up under the roof.

House no. 1 was of type 6. It has completely fallen down. House no. 3 was of type no. 5. It was the largest house in the whole rancheria, and appeared never to have been entirely completed.

House no. 6 was of type 7. There were a pile of logs at no. 4, peeled, and put there for use in building most probably. At no. 7 was a kind of roofed over cache.

The houses, calf pens, etc. on the east of the arroyo, were linked together by two sections of brush fence, put there to keep stock out. There was a small mescal pit at no. 11. No. 10 is the brush fence going up to the mountain, already described. It might be well to add here that the brush fences in this rancheria are exactly like those in the Chita Hueca rancheria.

# Notes

PROLOGUE

1. Edward H. Spicer, "A Dedication to the Memory of Grenville Goodwin 1907–1940," *Arizona and the West* 3 (autumn 1961): 203.

2. Edward H. Spicer, biographical note to Grenville Goodwin, *Western Apache Raiding and Warfare*, ed. Keith H. Basso (Tucson: University of Arizona Press, 1971), 3.

3. Morris E. Opler, ed., *Grenville Goodwin Among the Western Apache: Letters from the Field* (Tucson: University of Arizona Press, 1973), 11.

4. John G. Bourke, *On the Border with Crook* (New York: Charles Scribner's Sons, 1891); Britton Davis, *The Truth About Geronimo* (New Haven CT: Yale University Press, 1929); Charles R. Lummis, *General Crook and the Apache Wars*, ed. Turbesé Lummis Fiske (Flagstaff AZ: Northland Press, 1985); John C. Cremony, *Life Among the Apaches* (Glorieta NM: Rio Grande Press, 1969).

5. Goddard held important curatorial positions with the American Museum of Natural History in New York from 1909 to 1928. He published widely on Athabascans of northern California and the Southwest.

6. See the bibliography in Alfonso Ortiz, ed., *Handbook of North American Indians*, vol. 10, *Southwest* (Washington DC: Smithsonian Institution, 1983), for Hoijer's many articles and papers published between 1938 and 1975.

7. Alfred L. Kroeber, *Cultural and Natural Areas of Native North America* (Berkeley: University of California Press, 1953), 35–36.

8. Edward H. Spicer, *Cycles of Conquest* (Tucson: University of Arizona Press, 1962), 229–45; Charles Di Peso, pers. comm. 1978.

9. Victor Orozco, *Historia General de Chihuahua III, Primera Parte, Tierra de libres: Los Pueblos Del Distrito de Guerrero en el Siglo XIX* (Chihuahua: Universidad Autónoma de Ciudad Juárez Gobierno del Estado de Chihuahua, 1995), 69, 71, 89.

10. William Griffen, *Apaches at War and Peace: The Janos Presidio, 1750–1858* (Albuquerque: University of New Mexico Press, 1988), 29–30. For a thorough treatment of Spanish policies toward the Apaches, see Max L. Moorhead, *The Apache Frontier: Jacobo Ugarte and Spanish-Indian Relations in Northern New Spain, 1769–1791* (Norman: University of Oklahoma Press, 1968).

11. Spicer, *Cycles*, 239.

12. Evelyn Breuninger, Elbys Hugar, and Ellen Ann Lathan, *Mescalero Apache Dictionary* (Mescalero: Mescalero Apache Tribe, 1982), 86.

13. Ruth McDonald Boyer and Narcissus Duffy Gayton, *Apache Mothers and Daughters* (Norman: University of Oklahoma Press, 1992), 4. See also *Handbook of North American Indians*, 10: 418; and Eve Ball, Nora Henn, and Lynda Sanchez, *Indeh, An Apache Odyssey* (Provo UT: Brigham Young University Press, 1980), 2.

14. *The Silent Enemy* was released as a feature film in 1930. Its production is described in *The War, The West and The Wilderness*, (New York: Alfred A Knopf, 1979) by Kevin Brownlow. Douglas Burden became a naturalist of some note and explored and collected specimens for New York's American Museum of Natural History.

15. Goodwin, *Western Apache Raiding*.


## 1. STOLEN CHILD

1. John B. Hoffman was bonded by the BIA as a special officer at large, mostly to control traffic in illicit liquor on the Navajo reservation. He apparently served on the reservation from 1927 to 1933. He was born in 1876, so was fifty-one at this time. United States Office of Personnel Management Records, St. Louis.

2. Because Hoffman said "just south of the border," this meeting almost certainly took place in a range of mountains directly south of the New Mexico "Bootheel." This was the Apaches' northernmost Mexican stronghold, and was used well into the twentieth century. The meeting probably happened some time between 1900 and 1920. The message for San Carlos Apaches indicates some sort of contact between these people and reservation Apaches.

3. This place, called Desperation Ranch, is on the eastern flank of the Chiricahua Mountains. John Hands was an Englishman who settled here in the 1880s. A miner and rancher, he worked with Dean Byron Cummings of the University of Arizona in excavating southwestern and Mexican archaeological sites. My father met Hands through Cummings.

4. *Douglas Daily Dispatch*, Jan. 2, 1929.


## 2. PHANTOM APACHES

1. Bert Rufkey and his family ran a trading post on the San Carlos Reservation for many years.

2. See Percy Brown, "Apaches In The New Mexico Bootheel: Geronimo's Ghosts," in *Geronimo's Ghosts: Old West*, reprinted in *The Cattleman* (fall 1967).

## 3. TO RESCUE HIS SON

1. For the most thorough discussion of the McComas attack see Marc Simmons, *Massacre on the Lordsburg Road: A Tragedy of the Apache Wars* (College Station: Texas A&M University Press, 1997). See also Ball, Henn, and Sanchez, *Indeh*, 51; and Jason Betzinez, *I Fought with Geronimo* (New York: Bonanza Books, 1959), 118.

2. *Arizona Daily Star*, Jan. 1, 1930.

3. Douglas Meed, *They Never Surrendered: Bronco Apaches of the Sierra Madres, 1890–1935* (Tucson AZ: Westernlore Press, 1993), 127–29.

4. Allen A. Erwin, *The Southwest of John H. Slaughter* (Glendale CA: Arthur H. Clark Company, 1997), 302; Grenville Goodwin, *The Life Story of Sherman Curley* (unpublished manuscript). For a full account of the death of Alfred Hands see Alden Hayes, *A Portal to Paradise* (Tucson: University of Arizona Press, 1999).

5. Jesús Fuentes Yánez, *Correrias Apaches en Nácori Chico* (Sonora, Mexico: Area de Publicaciones de Extension Universitaria, 1991), 45.


## 4. GERONIMO'S PEOPLE?

1. See Anna Price's sighting of the same party, chapter 21.

2. Grenville Goodwin, *The Social Organization of the Western Apache* (Tucson: University of Arizona Press, 1969), 6. "An interesting sidelight on the derivation of the word 'Tonto' (Spanish: 'fools') is that the Chiricahuas applied the name *bini-edine*, ('people without minds')—in other words, 'crazy' or 'foolish people'—to all Western Apaches. It is quite possible that the Spanish knew the meaning of this Chiricahua word and shaped their own after it. Escudero, in his *Noticias Esdtadisticas de Chihuahua*, published in Mexico in 1834, gives the names of various Apache tribes in Apache, together with their Spanish equivalents. He records 'Viniettinen-ne' as the Apache (Chiricahua division) name for the Tonto (Western Apaches)."

3. Apache land-claims case hearing held at Mescalero, May 13, 1950, 32. Furnished by Morris Opler to me, Oct. 6, 1974.

4. Grenville Goodwin, unpublished field notes, private papers.

5. This is Sam Haouzous, also the father of Ruey Darrow, the current chairwoman of the Fort Sill/Warm Springs Chiricahua tribe of Apache, Oklahoma.

6. This phonetic spelling is slightly different from John Rope's, but clearly refers to the same person.

7. Grenville Goodwin, unpublished field notes, Arizona State Museum, box 3, folder 37, biographies, Sherman Curley. I am indebted to the historian Edwin Sweeney for help in identifying Adiɬnadzi·d.

8. Edwin Sweeney, pers. comm., Oct. 7, 1998. This man may also have been known as José Maria Elias (not to be confused with Jesús Maria Elias, a Mexican involved in the 1871 Camp Grant Massacre).

9. Edwin Sweeney, pers. comm., Oct. 7, 1998.

10. One outbreak took place at the end of March 1890. See series of articles in the *Tombstone Daily Prospector* and *Epitaph* beginning Mar. 29, 1890. Another outbreak was noted in the *Solomonville Bulletin*, Dec. 12, 1895, quoted in Erwin's *The Southwest*, 298.


## 5. MENACE IN THE MOUNTAINS

1. According to an article in the *Douglas Daily Dispatch*, Jan. 10, 1929, Fimbres made a trip to San Carlos for information about the Sierra Madre Apaches and found the Western Apaches there terrified of the idea of contact with the Sierra Madre Apaches.

2. On March 9, 1916, Pancho Villa and 360 soldiers attacked Columbus, New Mexico, in retaliation for U.S. aid to the federal Mexican government during the Mexican Revolution. On March 17 a 6,000-man punitive expedition under General John Pershing entered Mexico from Columbus in pursuit of Villa. It withdrew after ten months.

3. My father later acquired the bottle, a rawhide rope, the saddlebag, and the calfhide bag from Curtis. They are in the Arizona State Museum in Tucson.

4. He is probably referring to one of the villages of the Bavispe River Valley.

5. Interview with Curtis's nephew, James Dowdle, Apr. 30, 1997.

6. Nelda Villa, pers. comm., Dec. 15, 1996.

7. Interview with Amiglia Samaniego, Jan. 9, 1997, Bavispe.

8. Interview, Mar. 20, 1996.

9. *Douglas Daily Dispatch*, Jan. 10, 1929.

10. Rodolfo Rascón, "El Famoso Apache Juan," *El Impartial* (May 1996).

11. Sherman Curley, a Western Apache scout interviewed by my father, served in these pursuits of the 1890s and confirms that they were often stopped at the border or forcibly detained in Mexico by Mexican troops. However, on June 25, 1890, a reciprocal agreement was negotiated between Mexico and the United States to permit pursuit of marauding Apaches across the border. It was renewed in 1896. These dates coincide with the outbreaks of 1890 and 1896. The document is in the Historical Archives of the State of Sonora, Hermosillo. For a thorough account of U.S. army activity in pursuit of Yaquis and Apaches in the 1890s see Shelley Bowen Hatfield, *Chasing Shadows: Apaches and Yaquis Along the United States-Mexico Border, 1876–1911* (Albuquerque: University of New Mexico Press, 1998).

12. *Douglas Daily Dispatch*, Sept. 16, 1924 (Hinton Files).

13. Beth Noland Willis, "The Apache Scare of 1924," *Cochise Quarterly* 14, no. 4 (spring 1984); Brown, *Apaches In The New Mexico Bootheel.*

14. Marjorie F. Lambert and J. Richard Ambler, *A Survey and Excavation of Caves in Hidalgo County, New Mexico* (Santa Fe NM: School of American Research, 1965).

## 6. DOUBLE REVENGE

1. Morris Opler wrote to me on Aug. 10, 1976: "The Chiricahua never braided their hair. Of Apacheans, the Lipan, Mescalero, Kiowa Apache and Jicarilla did. *If* the Indians killed were Apache, they were most likely to have been Lipan." It is entirely possible that Lipans, even Yaquis, Mountain Pimas, Mayos, or Tarahumara were mixed in with these people, or that they had been separated so long from other Apaches that they had changed their ways.

2. Charles Di Peso, interview with Cayetano Fimbres. From the unpublished notes of Tres Rios Survey 1958, Di Peso Papers, The Amerind Foundation.

3. For a discussion of Chiricahua caps, see Morris E. Opler, *An Apache Life-Way* (Chicago: University of Chicago Press, 1941; reprint, Lincoln: University of Nebraska Press, 1996), 310–11. For a discussion of Western Apache caps, See Alan Ferg, *Western Apache Material Culture* (Tucson: University of Arizona Press, 1987), 133–38. See pictures in Thomas Mails, *The People Called Apache* (Englewood Cliffs NJ: Prentice Hall, 1974), 111–14, 254. For comparison with the Navajo, see Clyde Kluckohn, *Navajo Material Culture* (Cambridge MA: Harvard University Press, 1971), 272–78.

## 7. CROSSINGS

1. *Arizona Daily Star,* Mar. 6 and 7, 1930. This fictitious fight was given lurid coverage in several newspaper articles.

2. There is a settlement of Kickapoo Indians, originally from the United States, near the village of Huachinera, fifty miles south of the border.

## 8. PULPIT ROCK

1. Pancho Villa's forces marched through the Pulpit Pass in 1915, prior to Villa's attack on Agua Prieta. The most recent military use of the pass was in early 1929 toward the end of the abortive three-year Cristero Rebellion.

2. There are two passes to the north, both named San Luis — one is about

three miles north of the border and the other is only a few hundred yards south of the border.

## 9. THE CAVES

1. Very little is known about the petroglyphs found in these caves. Some might well have been made by Apaches, while others were made by outlying communities of the Casas Grandes culture, or even by earlier peoples. See Linda Cordell, *Archaeology of the Southwest* (New York: Academic Press, 1984, 1997), 409–13.

## 10. APACHES AND THE BAVISPE

1. Reyes Arguayo was his full name. Interview with Aïda Desouches Gabilondo, Dec. 1997.

2. Chiricahuas rarely farmed. Opler, 1996, 372–75. Western Apaches did, so this could indicate some Western Apache connection or mixture.

3. At the time, the Carretas was owned by a non-Mormon American named Gordy Boyd in whose family it had been since 1886. It had been established in the 1870s and, in the spring of 1882, it was the site of a ferocious battle between the Mexican army under General Lorenzo García and a group of Warm Springs Chiricahua Apaches led by Loco.

4. Enrique Krauze, *Mexico: Biography of Power. A History of Modern Mexico 1810–1996* (New York: Harper Collins, 1998), 256–60. Florence Lister, *Chihuahua, Storehouse of Storms* (Albuquerque: University of New Mexico Press, 1966), 212. For a readable, very well illustrated history of the Mexican Revolution, see: Anita Brenner, and photographs by George R. Leighton, *The Wind That Swept Mexico: The History of the Mexican Revolution 1910–1942* (Austin: University of Texas Press, 1993).

5. Clarence F. Turley and Anna Tenney, *History of the Mormon Colonies in Mexico 1885–1980*, 2nd. ed. (Publisher's Press, 1996), 299–302.

6. Interview with Miguel Burquez Ramos; Barney Burns field notes, Oct. 1996.

7. Chy Chamberlain grew up in the Mormon town of Morelos, and returned to settle in Bavispe to open a flour mill, which was still operating in 1976 but is now in ruins.

8. There are cobblers/saddlemakers in the region who still make the local footwear, called *tejiras* or *tewas*.

9. Paul M. Roca, *Paths of the Padres Through Sonora: An Illustrated History & Guide to Its Spanish Churches* (Tucson: Arizona Pioneers' Historical Society, 1967), 225–28.

10. Spicer, *Cycles*, 233–36.

11. Spicer, *Cycles*, 240.

12. Spicer, *Cycles*, 241.

13. Dan Thrapp, *Encyclopedia of Frontier Biography*, vols. 1–4 (Lincoln: University of Nebraska Press, 1991), 788. Born in Belfast in 1792, James Kirker was in New York City by 1810. Finding his way via St. Louis to Santa Fe, he at first traded with the Apaches, and then, as hostilities escalated following 1837, became an Indian hunter for a few years. By 1849 he was in California, where he died in 1853.

14. Ralph A. Smith, "Scalp Hunting: A Mexican Experiment in Warfare," *Great Plains Journal* 23 (1984): 41–79.

15. Rodolfo Rascón, pers. comm., Mar. 1996, Mochopa.

16. Bourke, *On the Border*; Davis, *The Truth*.

17. See Goodwin, *Western Apache Raiding*, 56, for John Rope's account of the U.S. army's arrival in Bavispe; see also page 197 for David Longstreet's account of the same event.

18. Dan Thrapp, *The Conquest of Apacheria* (Norman: University of Oklahoma Press, 1967), 283.

19. J. Frank Dobie, *Apache Gold and Yaqui Silver* (Austin: University of Texas Press, 1996); Steve Wilson, "Tayopa, Guaynopa, and Guaynopita: Lost Silver Triangle of the Sierra Madre," *Great Plains Journal* (1987–88), 26–27.

20. See Linda Cordell, *Prehistory of the Southwest* (New York: Academic Press, 1984), 276.

21. See Felipe A. Latorre, *The Mexican Kickapoo Indians* (Mineola NY: Dover, 1976), 99; and Marcella Villegas Rodríguez, ed., *Ethnographía Contemporánea de los Pueblos Indígenes de México, Region Noroeste* (Mexico, D.F.: Instituto Nacional Indigenista, 1995), 64.

22. Dr. W. J. Spencer gave my father his card, which said Dr. Spencer was on the faculty of the University of Southern California.

23. He may mean Colonia Morelos. Colonia Juárez is a Mormon town seventy-five miles to the east across the Sierra Madre, and the people who lived there would have had little interest in this Apache camp.

24. Opatas were the dominant tribe in the Bavispe Valley when the Spanish came, and Opata place names abound. Even the name "Chiricahua" is Opata, meaning "People of Bird Mountain."

25. See Thrapp, *Conquest*, 341–42.

26. Edwin Sweeney, pers. comm.

27. Philip Greenfeld, pers. comm.

28. Interview with Francisco Zozaya, Jan. 1997.

29. Janos was one of the Establishments of Peace—places where, by treaty, Apaches could camp, come in, and trade unmolested. This was a

Spanish policy that had been instituted in an attempt to put an end to the debilitating cycle of raiding and warfare. The practice lasted from the late eighteenth century to shortly after Mexican independence from Spain in 1836, and was eventually abandoned by the Mexicans because of a lack of funds. The easterly route followed by southbound Apaches most likely took them through country much less settled than Sonora, with its many Bavispe Valley towns.

## 11. ENEMY PEOPLE

1. Hachita is in the New Mexico Bootheel. The route Gabilondo followed was from El Paso north to Las Cruces, New Mexico, then west to Hachita, then south to the border crossing at Antelope Wells. There were no passable roads directly across Chihuahua from El Paso to the Gabilondo Ranch.

2. Helge Ingstad, *Apache Indianerne: Jakten på den Tapte Stamme* (Oslo: Gyldendal Norsk Forlag, 1939), 309 (this passage appears on page 106 of an unpublished English translation by Liv Bjørnard, 1976).

3. Tom Hinton, unpublished notes, June 27, 1955, the archives of the Arizona State Museum at University of Arizona.

## 12. TAKING STOCK

1. In 1889, the Apache Kid, a scout for the army, was convicted of attempted murder, and with other Apache convicts escaped en route to the Yuma, Arizona prison. Two lawmen were killed in the escape, but, as it was determined later, not by the Apache Kid. For a biography of the Apache Kid, see Phylis de la Garza, *The Apache Kid* (Tucson AZ: Westernlore Press, 1995).

2. Ingstad, *Apache-Indianerne*, 38.

3. Di Peso, 1958 interview with Cayetano Fimbres. For a description of Chiricahua dolls see Opler, *An Apache Life-Way*, 47.

4. For a history of Col. Greene's empire, see C. L. Sonnichsen, *Colonel Greene and the Copper Skyrocket* (Tucson: University of Arizona Press, 1983). For an account of Lord Beresford's San Pedro Ojitos, see Colin Rickards, *Bowler Hats and Stetsons* (New York: Bonanza Books, 1966); and Lawrence Milton Woods, *British Gentlemen in the Wild West: The Era of the Intensely English Cowboy* (New York: Free Press, 1989). For descriptions of the San Pedro Ojitos and other great Chihuahua haciendas in 1886, see Britton Davis, *The Truth About Geronimo*.

## 13. SAN CARLOS CONNECTION

1. Carl Lumholtz, *Unknown Mexico*, 2 vols. (New York: Charles Scribner's Sons, 1902), 1: 26, 79.

2. Goodwin, *Social Organization*, 600. The tá(ha)gaidń, meaning "white water people," is one of the sixty western Apache clans. There is a reference to this raid in my father's field diary dated Nov. 7, 1934.

3. Unpublished field diary, Nov. 7, 1934.

4. Turley and Tenney, *History of the Mormon Colonies*, 226–28.

5. There are many written and oral sources for this story. Nelle Spillsbury Hatch and Carmen Hardy, eds., *Stalwarts South of the Border* (Colonia Juárez, Chihuahua, Mexico: Ernestine Hatch, 1976), 697–702, 719; Turley and Tenney, *History of the Mormon Colonies*, 226–28; *Hans Adolph Thompson, as told by Floyd L. Thompson, son of Elmer Thompson*, June 28, 1959, Elfrida, Arizona; interviews with Annie McNeil Thompson (1978), Lloyd Davis (1997), Chester Davis (1976), and Lavine Fenn and Mrs. Golden Fenn (1978).

6. Charles M. Cook, *A History of San Carlos and Fort Apache Reservations 1873–1950*, Defendant's Exhibit C-1, San Carlos et al. v. United States, Docket No. 22-H, Indian Claims Commission (Washington DC 1976), 173.

7. Grenville Goodwin, unpublished field diaries (May 20, 1936), 175.

## 14. CLOSE ENCOUNTERS

1. For a discussion of political scandals in Sonora, see Meed, *They Never Surrendered*.

2. James Dowdle, Curtis's nephew, pers. comm., Apr. 30, 1997.

3. See Nov. 14, 1930, diary entry, page 41, about a cowboy who was killed.

4. This is typical of the clothing my father describes in his unpublished diary notes, page 223, of old Western Apache women who are very poor or when they have nothing else to wear.

5. Moctezuma is forty to fifty miles southwest of Stewart Hunt's ranch in the Sierra el Tigre, and is administrative center for the district of Moctezuma, in which Hunt's ranch lay. The name of this ranch was Los Otates, according to Stewart's son, José.

6. For a very similar story with a different outcome, see John Rope's description of an Apache woman who successfully escaped from a Mexican jail. See Goodwin, *Western Apache Raiding*, 113.

7. Thrapp, *Encyclopedia*, 94.

8. Interview with Cliff Bowman, Oct. 30, 1997, Colonia Dublán, Chihuahua.

9. Ingstad, *Apache Indianerne* (page 50 of unpublished English translation).

10. Edwin Sweeney, pers. comm., May 1998.

11. Carl Lumholtz, *Unknown Mexico*, 1: 26.


## 15. APACHE CAMP

1. The *cordada* is a rural Mexican officer of the law, not unlike the American sheriff.

2. Yánez, *Correrías Apaches*, 42–46.

3. This is now at the Arizona State Museum at the University of Arizona in Tucson.

4. They are mentioned and described in some detail in Grenville Goodwin's unpublished diary notes on pages 198 and 216.

5. Francisco Zozaya said that the old cowboy Agustin González told him that the smoke was ducted out of the houses into nearby brush or thickets in order to disperse it so that it couldn't be seen. Interview with Francisco Zozaya, Oct. 3, 1996.

6. See appendix 2 for the full text of this diary entry.

7. Interview with Quinn Boyd, Apr. 9, 1998.


## 17. APACHE GOLD

1. Goodwin, *Western Apache Raiding*, 107–72.

2. The date was probably before 1927. The MacNeils were a Mormon family, and in 1927, Beula Fenn (b. 1911), daughter of Joe Fenn (Moroni's brother) married Wayne MacNeil who owned Las Varas. Wayne and Beula lived in Bavispe off and on between 1930 and 1938, approximately. After 1938 they moved to Colonia Dublán, at which point the ranch was sold to the Gabilondo family, who still own it. Beula MacNeil interview, Nov. 3, 1997, Colonia Dublán.

3. The Nogales Ranch is at the north end of the Sierra el Medio, and is one of the properties that made up the Palomas Land and Cattle Company.

4. Napoleon III had sent the French army to invade Mexico in 1864, hoping to add it to his empire. At the request of collaborating Mexican conservatives, Napoleon installed Maximilian, an Austrian archduke, as emperor of Mexico. This scheme failed in 1867 with the withdrawal of the French army and the assassination of Maximilian. In the meantime many Frenchmen had been attracted to Mexico, and a number of them stayed to seek

their fortunes. This may help to explain why there were many Frenchmen in Mexico at the time. In addition, in the late nineteenth century, under Porifirio Diaz, foreign capital was encouraged to invest in the development of Mexican natural resources, such as mining, cattle, and timber, attracting fortune seekers of all kinds, especially to Chihuahua. Mark Wasserman, *Caciques, Capitalists and Revolution* (Chapel Hill: University of North Carolina Press, 1984), 84–95.

5. Interview with Billy Martineau, June 10, 1987; interview with the Hatch brothers, June 14, 1987; interview with Marion Vance Jr., June 14, 1987; interview with Chester Davis, Apr. 1976.

6. This story probably refers to cowboys from the Nogales Ranch, part of the Palomas Land and Cattle Company, referred to above.


## 19. REFUGE IN THE ESPUELAS

1. Interviews with Manuela Chafino and Soccoro Molina, Oct. 31 and Nov. 1, 1997.

2. Born in Bavispe, Pablo Machichi was a Carranzista captain in the Revolution. He later became involved in the Cristero Rebellion and sided against the federal government. He commanded Cristero troops in a well-known battle east of Huachinera in the spring of 1929. Interview with Miguel Burquez Ramos, Oct. 11, 1996.

3. This must be a standard Apache trick: cutting the ear tendons so the ears hang down and can't be spotted so easily. Interview with Esquipulas Moreno Martinez, Sept. 9, 1995; interview with the Hatch brothers, June. 4, 1987; interview with Marion Vance Jr., June 14, 1987.

4. See *Douglas Daily Dispatch*, Feb. 1, 1929, for Moroni Fenn's description of finding the camp.

5. Interview with Russell Taylor and Ed Maddox, Mar. 1976.

6. Opler, *An Apache Life-Way*, 53; Grenville Goodwin, unpublished notes, University of Arizona, Section 12, Games, 146.

7. Keith H. Basso, Lori Davisson, Michael W. Graves, M. Priscilla Johnson, "Persistence and Change in Western Apache Culture," report for the San Carlos Apache Tribe, 1980.

8. Cook, *A History of San Carlos*, 164.


## 20. SMUGGLERS

1. Carl E. Prince and Mollie Leller, *U.S. Customs Service: A Bicentennial History* (Washington DC: U.S. Government Printing Office, 1989).

2. The *Bisbee Daily Review*, Mar. 20, 1908, quotes a recent article in the

*El Paso Herald* describing an attack near Moctezuma, Sonora, attributed to Apaches, who were chased by Mexican soldiers all the way to the Rio Bonito.

3. This is the San Bernardino Ranch, fifteen miles east of Douglas, Arizona, owned until 1937 by the John Slaughter family.

4. These are now in the collection of the Arizona State Museum in Tucson.

## 21. ECHOES OF MEXICO AT SAN CARLOS

1. From a letter to Helge Ingstad, Oct. 10, 1937.

2. "*Hai-aha*" is a Western Apache term for the Chiricahua, meaning, literally, "people of the east." Jeanette Cassa, pers. comm., 1998.

3. Translation of this Apache phrase: "*do . . . dah*" is the standard Apache discontiguous negative. The whole phrase in Apache might have been: "Dah dah sá doyizinyeedah"—literally: "No, no old woman no you kill her not." Philip Greenfeld, pers. comm.

4. See Grenville Goodwin's August 1930 diary entry, page 31.

5. The Indian Scouts units, in existence since 1866, were finally discontinued in 1922, and the few remaining Apache scouts were moved to Fort Huachuca to be carried on the Detached Enlisted Men's List. Their duties included patrolling the sixty miles of fort perimeter, which took them often into the backcountry of the Huachuca Mountains. "Study Guide—us Army Intelligence Center and Fort Huachuca."

6. *Douglas Daily Dispatch*, July 16, 1932.

7. *Douglas Daily Dispatch*, July 13, 1932.

8. Interviews in Nácori Chico, Mar. 19, 1996.

9. Tom Hinton, unpublished field notes, recorded June 16, 1955, Archives of the Arizona State Museum, University of Arizona.

10. Rodolfo Rascón, *El Imparcial*, Oct. 19, 1993.

11. Tom Hinton, unpublished field notes, recorded June 17, 1955, Archives of the Arizona State Museum, University of Arizona.

12. Rodolfo Rascón, *El Imparcial*, Oct. 19, 1993.

13. Opler, *Grenville Goodwin Among the Western Apache*, 47. Reprinted with permission of the University of Arizona Press.

14. He was captured as a young man, most likely during a fight such as the one at Sahuaripa in 1883, or the one at Casas Grandes in 1882. Only captive women were reported from the battle of Tres Castillos in 1880, so he was almost certainly not captured there. It is unlikely as well that he was taken at the battle of Alisos Canyon, as these captives were not distributed in Chihuahua City, according to material gathered by historian Edwin Sweeney. The Arizona Historical Society, microfilm collection: documents copied

from the Archivo Historico del Estado de Sonora, Hermosillo, Sonora, Mexico, roll 21.

15. Yánez, *Correrías Apaches*, 46. Extermination of the Apaches had Sonora state government sanction.

16. Ingstad, *Apache Indianerne*, 315–16 (page 112 of unpublished English translation).

17. Philip Greenfeld, pers. comm.


22. CARMELA

1. Virginia Wayland, *Apache Playing Cards*, Southwest Museum leaflets, no. 28, 1971; Ronald McCoy, "Apache Rawhide Playing Cards," *American Indian Art Magazine* (summer 1984): 52–59.


23. ARE THERE ANY LEFT?

1. The five deaths he refers to are: Juan and the two women killed in April of 1930, Carmela's grandmother in April of 1932, and one other referred to briefly on page 60 in his diary entry of February 1930 (which appears at the beginning of chapter 3 of this book). The two captives he refers to are Lupe and Carmela. In addition, I can account for seven more deaths: those of the two captive children and four adults killed in July of 1932, and that of Julia Tasahuinora, also in July 1932, for a minimum total of twelve killed between 1930 and 1934. There were two known surviving captives, Julio and Carmela, and perhaps two more, counting the children Dixie Harris sent to the Hermosillo convent.

2. This reference is to Lupe, but there is no way of telling to which reservation she is referring: San Carlos, Fort Apache, or Mescalero.

3. Opler, *Grenville Goodwin Among the Western Apache*, 47. Reprinted by permission of the University of Arizona Press.

4. Undated letter from Morris Opler to Grenville Goodwin, in the author's collection. Reprinted with the permission of Morris Opler.

5. A 1933 article cut out by my father from an unidentified newspaper with a Mescalero dateline tells the story of the life of Mrs. Jacinto Ramirez.

6. For a good biography of Massai, see Karl Laumbach, "Massai (New Mexico's Apache Kid)," a paper presented to the Historical Society of New Mexico, Apr. 23, 1993.

7. Opler, *Grenville Goodwin Among the Western Apache*, 50. Reprinted by permission of the University of Arizona Press.

8. Opler, *Grenville Goodwin Among the Western Apache*, 58. Reprinted by permission of the University of Arizona Press.

9. From conversation between Grenville Goodwin and Sam Kenoi, July 4, 1938, at Mescalero, New Mexico, unpublished notes.

10. Unidentified (probably the *Arizona Daily Star*) Tucson newspaper, Sept. 24, 1934.

11. *Douglas Daily Dispatch*, Nov. 1937.

12. Barney Burns, pers. comm., from a June 9, 1998, letter from Erv Wilson.

## 24. FUGITIVES AND DESCENDANTS

1. Helge Ingstad, *The Land of Feast and Famine*, trans. Eugene Gay-Tifft (New York: Alfred A. Knopf, 1933; reprint, Montreal: McGill-Queen's University Press, 1992); originally published as *Pelsjergerliv Blandt Nord-Kanadas Indianere* (Oslo: Gyldendal Norsk Forlag, 1931).

2. He clearly does not believe that there are Western Apaches among them, except for those who may have been kidnapped.

3. He seems to believe that the Sierra Madre Apaches are a single band, though both Lupe and Carmela stated that there were several small bands.

4. If Lupe was captured at the age of about twelve in 1915, she would have been at least thirty-four, not twenty-five.

5. There is ample oral history describing buckskin recovered from raided camps, including a buckskin pouch, which I saw in 1997 in Douglas, Arizona. It belongs to a man to whom it was given by Francisco Fimbres, who found it at the camp where Lupe was captured.

6. This is a reference to the border crossing made by Yanozha and Perico in 1934.

7. This younger man was Andrew Little.

8. Judging from Ingstad's description of his route (*Apache Indianerne*, 71–75), Dzilda na-goul (roughly meaning, according to Jeanette Cassa, pers. comm., July 1, 1998, "mountain floating with rising water around it," or possibly "mountain in a mirage") probably refers to a place somewhere between Pico de la India and Tres Rios along the Sonora-Chihuahua boundary.

9. Ingstad, *Apache Indianerne*, 87.

10. Ingstad, *Apache Indianerne*, 75.

11. Grenville Goodwin, diary notes, spring 1934. No such list survives in either the Opler or the Grenville Goodwin papers, but, as noted earlier, on Oct. 7, 1998, Ed Sweeney informed me that three of them were: Adiɬna·zid, Natcuɬba·ye (AKA José Maria Elias) and, possibly, Satsinistu, brother-in-law or nephew of Naiche.

12. Interviews at Fort Apache and Tucson, Oct. 1997.

13. Bernard Fontana, pers. comm., May 22, 1998. For a discussion of the Pimas and other Sonoran tribes, see Thomas B. Hinton, *A Survey of Indian Assimilation in Eastern Sonora* (Tucson: University of Arizona Anthropological Papers, 1959).

14. Interview with Billy Martineau, Oct. 6, 1987.

EPILOGUE

1. *Myths and Tales of the White Mountain Apache* was published by The American Folklore Society and republished by the University of Arizona Press in 1996.

2. Letter from my mother to her mother, Lillian Hastings Thompson, July 1940.

3. From a White Mountain prayer, translated from the Apache by Grenville Goodwin, published in *The New Mexico Sentinel*, June 5, 1938. This is part of a longer prayer used in a ceremonial context, which Anna Price taught my father. Recording and printing such prayer texts is a sensitive matter among Apaches, and I have sought guidance on the propriety of doing so here. Because of the context, the use does not appear to be inappropriate.

# Index

Adiłnadzi·d, 32, 33, 245, 272 n.11
adoption: of captives, 46, 209. *See also* kidnapping
Agua Prieta, 28, 61, 122–23, 132, 263 n.1
airplanes, 146–47
Alamo Hueco Mountains, 48
Alamos Canyon, 154
alarm systems, 143, 173
Alisos Canyon, Battle of, 93, 94, 95–96, 245, 270 n.14
Allen, Tom, 159
Altamirano, 112, 170–72, 246
Americans, 131, 140, 154, 201; attacks on, 41, 124, 247; with Sierra Madre Apaches, 100, 101, 103, 181; smuggling by, 184–85, 186. *See also* Mormons
Animas Valley, 25, 48, 141, 156, 247
Antelope Wells, 122, 131, 266 n.1
Apache Elias, 47, 246
Apache Juan, xiii, xiv, 45, 47, 52, 104, 121, 127, 185–86; killing of, 56, 158, 159, 248, 271 n.1
Apache Kid, 32, 110, 115–17, 120, 181, *plate 13*, 213, 245, 246, 266 n.1. *See also* Massai
Apache Mansos, 235
Apache May, 246
Apaches, 46, 70, 236; as captives, 6, 93, 94–95; as enemy, 3–4; "friendly," 96, 235; Mexican perceptions of, 72–73; with Pimas, 234–35; raids by, 39–40, 47, 48, 80–81; research on, 2–3. *See also* Sierra Madre Apaches
Apache scouts, 82, 83, 110, 116, 245, 262 n.11, 270 n.5
Apache Wars, xv, 3–4, 65, 82–83
archaeology, archaeological sites, 48, 86, 97, 102, 105, 186; at Las Piedras, 172–73, 175–76, 179, *plate 24, plate 25,*

*plate 26, plate 27, plate 28, plate 29, plate 30, plate 32, plate 33*; at Sierra Chita Hueca, 137, 138, 142–45, 150–51, 251–54
Arista family, 96
Aros River, 185
arrowheads, 74, 102
Arroyo de los Alisos. *See* Alisos Canyon, Battle of
Arroyo de los Jucoros, 128
Arroyo Taste, 127–28
artifacts, 111–12, 142, 150–51, 176, *plate 21,* 257, 262 n.3, 272 n.5; at Chita Hueca camp, *plate 19, plate 20,* 253
Ascensión, 232–33
Azules. *See* Sierra Chita Hueca

Bacadéhuachi, 77, 79, 81, 195, 198, 228, 248
Bácame, Antonio, 95
Bacerac, 78, 79, 81–82, 83, 88, 93, *plate 9, plate 10,* 228
B and P Palace Bar Billiard Hall (Douglas), 24–25, 48, 221
Bao, Bil. *See* Bye, Bill
baptism: of Apache captives, 195–96
Barela, Lola, 94, 95, *plate 11,* 128–29
Baviacora Valley, 112
Bavispe, 40, 79, 83, 97, 98, 99, *plate 12,* 131, 228, 235; Apache captives in, 197–98, 199; and San Miguel, 77, 78, 247
Bavispe, Rio, 40, 65, 76, 114, 218–19
Bavispe Valley, 79–81, 113, 197–98, 265 n.24
Bedonkohe, 5
Begay, Alberta, 214
Bennett, Frank P., 125, 127
Beresford, Delaval, 112, 146
Bonito canyon, 141

Bonito River, 113, 185, 247, 269–70 n.2
Bootheel, 48, 176, 181, 182, 266 n.1. *See also* Animas Valley
bounties, bounty hunters, 80–81, 196, 201, 224
Bourke, John, 2
Bowman, Cliff, 128
Boyd, Gordy, 146, 147, 248, 264 n.3
Boyd, Quinn, 146
Buck, Neil, 193, *plate 40, plate 41,* 239, 240, 243, 248
Bui. *See* Harris, Carmela
Burden, Douglas, 9, 260 n.14
Burns, Barney, 13–14, 21, 39, 52, 53, *plate 4,* 63, 64, 70, 71, 72, 84, 85, 86, 96, *plate 11,* 122, 126, 137–38, 161, 171, 185, 201, 206; and Chita Hueca camp, 132, 135, 136; and Las Piedras camp, 162, 163, 164, 166, 175, 176
burro train: attack on, 39–41, 247
Burrule, John E., 218
Bye, Bill, 100, 198, 199, 200
Bylas, 120, 192

camps: Apache, 38–39, 48, 63, 64, 92, 122, 126, 127–28, 154, 226, 246; at El Paso Púlpito, 68–69, 102; mining, 133–34; on Sierra Chita Hueca, 65–66, 91, 99, 103, 132, 134, 135–36, 137, 138–40, 142–46, 147–49, *plate 16, plate 17, plate 18, plate 19, plate 20,* 227, 248, 251–54; in Sierra las Espuelas, 153, 156–57, 164, 167–68, 169–70, 172–81, *plate 24, plate 25, plate 26, plate 27, plate 28, plate 29, plate 30, plate 32, plate 33,* 247, 255–58
Cananea, 112, 246
Cananea Copper Company, 77, 112, 246
Cañon de los Embudos, 153
Canyon of the Caves, 91
captives, 43, 245: Apache, 44, 47, 93, 94–95, 96, 125, 126–27, 128–29, 194, 195–203, 208–9, 213–14, 226, 235; Mexican, xv, 21–22, 41–42, 45–46, 55, 129–30, 246. *See also* Harris, Carmela; Lupe; Medina, Julio; Tasahuinora, Julia
Carillo, Colonel, 27

Carmela. *See* Harris, Carmela
Carranza, Venustiana, 77, 78
Carrera Ranch, 218
Carretas, 77
Carretas Pass, 40–41, 77, 247
Carretas Plains, 155, 161–62, 163–64
Carretas Ranch, 139, 140, 146, 248, 264 n.3
Casas Grandes, 84, 132, 200, 235
Casas Grandes culture, 86
caves, 69, 125–26; at Chita Hueca, 99, 139–40, 251; at El Paso Púlpito, 74, 75, 101, 102, 130–31, 186; storage, 36, 37–38
Cave Valley, 117–19, 159, 245, 246
Central Apaches, 4
Cerro del Caballo, 128
Chafino, Jesús, 199–200, 270 n.14
Chafino, Manuela, 199, 200
Chamberlain, Chy, 78, 91, 131, 132, 264 n.7
Chaparo, Tacha, 171
Chappo, *plate 34*
Chesoko, 90
Chi, Chis, 129, 130
Chihé nde, 5
Chihuahua City, 199, 232
Chihuahua plains, 104, 105
children: as captives, 93, 94, 96, 194, 195–203, 208–9, 213; kidnappings of, xv, 1, 21–22, 41–43, 47, 248
Chinese, 90, 95
Chiricahuas, 4–5, 153, 186, 221, 248, 263 n.1, 270 n.2; with Apache Kid, 115, 116; and Geronimo, 31–32, 82, 231; and Charley McComas, 26–27; in Mexico, 194, 232–34, 235–36, 264 n.1, 264 n.3; renegade, 192–93; and Sierra Madre Apaches, 212–13, 217, 224, 225, 229, 230
Chiricahua Mountains, 31, 246, 260 n.3
Chita Hueca. *See* Sierra Chita Hueca
Chua, Josefina, 88–89
Chuhuichupa, 71, 114, 157, 158, 172, 182, 245, 246, 247
Ch'uk'ane nde, 5
Cibecue, 192, 193, 248
Cibecue Apaches, 4, 31, 120
Ciudad Juárez, 232, 249

Cleghorn, Mildred, 236
Cloudcroft, 220–21
Coahuila: Kickapoos in, 87, 88
Cochise, 5, 92, 130
Colonia Diaz, 71, 245
Colonia Dublán, 71, 131, 245, 246
Colonia García, 71, 245; Apache attack on, 117–19
Colonia Hernandez Jovales, 43
Colonia Juárez, 42, 71, 91, 118, 120, 157, 245
colonial period, 79, 80, 265 n.29
Colonia Morelos, 50, 62, 63, 64–65, 246, 265 n.23; Mexican raid on, 71–72, 78
Colonia Oaxaca, 64, 65–66, 71, 72, 92, 99, 122, 123, 132, 151–52, 186–87, 245
Colonia Pacheco, 42, 43, 71, 114, 219–20, 245, 246, 248
Colonia San José, 246
Columbus, 66, 247, 262 n.2
Coma, Jose Ben, 140
Comanches, 4
concealment, 103, 110, 145–46, 148, 154
Cordoba, Rita, 88
Corral, José, 171
Correador, Major, 92
Cortés, Loreta, 94, 95
Crawford, Captain, 92
Cremony, John, 2
Cristero Rebellion, 123, 248, 263 n.1, 269 n.2
Crook, George, 27, 82, 83, 153, 235
Cummings, Byron, 9, 260 n.3
Cumpas, 52, 197
Curley, Sherman, 33, 245, 262 n.11
Curtis, Bill, 13, 37–38, 39, 46, 47, 48, 51, 61, 66, 75, 91, 92, 98, 99, 122, 132, 150, 151, 152, 155, 187, 202; and El Paso Púlpito, 68–69, 102, 186; life of, 49–50; and Nácori Chico, 105–6; and Sierra las Espuelas, 153, 157, 174, 175, 178, 184, plate 27, 247, 256; smuggling by, 123–24
Curtis, Horace, 49–50
Curtis, Martha Jane, 49–50

Daklugie, Asa, 32
Darrow, Ruey, 26–27, 261 n.5

Davis, Britton, 2
Davis, Bryan, 158
Davis, Chester, 143
Davis, Lloyd, 143, 158–59, 182
depression, 182–83, 248
Desouches Gabilondo, Aïda, 91–92
Desperation Ranch, 260 n.3
Di Peso, Charles, 181
Dja'okin, 245
Doherty, Kathy, 14, 163, 164, 165, 166, 185, plate 23
Dórame, 42–43, 248
Douglas, 24–25, 28, 61
Douglas Daily Dispatch (newspaper), 27, 28, 36, 219
Dowdle, James, 39
drug trafficking, 53–54, 162
Durango, 4

earthquake of 1887, 78, 81
Eastern Apaches, 4
Ecochi, 90
economy, 182–83, 184
El Cajon del Salto, 127
El-cha-nache, 33
El Gato Negro, 96
Elias, Governor, 29
Elias, José Maria. See Natculba·ye
El Oso, 146
El Paso Púlpito, 68–69, 99, plate 6, 129, 132, 186, 251, 263 n.1; caves at, 74, 75, 101, 102, 130–31
Embudos canyon, 153
Enriquez, 77
extermination policies, 80–81

Fenn, Alvah, 61, 62, 83–84
Fenn, Carmen, 61
Fenn, Joe, 111, 146, 170, 268 n.2
Fenn, Moroni, 61, 62, 91, 110, 111, 154, 155, 157, 174, 175, 178
feuds, 41, 194–95
Figueroa family, 47
Fimbres, Cayetano, 45, 56, 109
Fimbres, Francisco, 10, 21, plate 3, 109, 178, 268 n.1; Lupe's advice to, 45–46; manhunt by, 22–23, 36, 37, 46–47, 51–52, 55–56, 57, 62, 141–42, 248; and punitive expedition, 27–28, 29–30, 91

Fimbres, Gerardo, 36, 46, 55; kidnapping of, xv, 1, 21–22, 45, 112, 248; killing of, 57, 61, 68, 201, 248
Fimbres, Maria, xiii
Fimbres, Maria Dolores: murder of, xv, 1, 21–22, 45, 112, 201
Fimbres, Reyes, xiii, xiv
Fimbres, Vicki, 21
Fimbres expedition, 23, 36, 37, 46–47, 51–52, 55–56, 57, 62, 141–42, 248; Americans and, 27–28, 29–30, 91
Fimbres family, xiii–xv, 43; ambush of, 1, 10, 20–22, 247
folklore, 5–6, 26; of Apache captives, 195–96, 197–98; of Apache Juan, 185–86; of Apache Kid, 115–17; of Sierra Madre Apaches, 24–25, 218–19, 232
Fort Apache Reservation, 30, 101, 109, 115, 143, 181, 182, 192, 212, 232, 139, 248
Fort Huachuca, 270 n.5
Frenchmen, 155–56, 245, 268 n.4
Fronteras, 186
Fuentes, Dolores, 55, 109, 209
Fuentes, Jesús, 54–55, 204
Fun, *plate 34*

Gabilondo, Liolito, 65, 92, 99, 139, 148, 266 n.1
Gabilondo Ranch, 72, 92, 100, 133, 134, 146, 268 n.2
Galvez, Bernardo de, 80
Galvez peace policy, 80
García, Aristeo, 201–2
García, Lorenzo, 96, 264 n.3
Gatewood, Charles, 65
Gatliff, Leslie, 26, 29, 36
Gereque, María, 246
Geronimo, 5, 32, 129, 235, *plate 34*; people associated with, 31, 33, 101–2, 231; surrender of, 65, 245; U.S. army pursuit of, 82–83, 92–93, 153
Goddard, Pliny, 3, 259 n.5
gold prospecting, 155–56
Gómez, Alfonso, 164, 165, 167, 177
Gomez family, 76
González, Agustín, 97, 100, 150, 181, 268 n.5
Gonzalez family, 233

Goodwin, Anne Stockton, 238
Goodwin, Elizabeth Sage (Elizabeth Sage Hare), 7, 8
Goodwin, Grenville, 14, *plate 1, plate 8, plate 39, plate 40,* 246, 247, 248; death of, 241, 242–43, 249; diary of, 11–12; family of, 7–8; fieldwork by, 1–2, 30, 192; gravesite of, 137–38; marriage of, 238–39; in Southwest, 8–10
Goodwin, Henry Sage, 238
Goodwin, Jan, *plate 39,* 237, 240, 241–42, 243–44; marriage of, 238–39
Goodwin, Margot, 14, 65, 163, 164, 166, 167, 168, 171, 176, 185, *plate 15,* 235
Goodwin, Neil, *plate 22, plate 31*
Goodwin, Seth, 14, 21, 52, 53, 161, 163, 164, 165, 166, 167, 168, 172, 175, 185, *plate 23,* 201
Goodwin, Walter Lippincott, 7
Goulding's Trading Post, 34
Grajeda, Felipe, 109
Grajera, Louis, 140
Greene, William, 112, 246
Guerrero, 4
Guyanopa, 234, 247

Hachita, 66, 266 n.1
Hachita Hueca. *See* Sierra Chita Hueca
haciendas, 112, 133
Hands, Alfred, 29, 245
Hands, John, 20, 29, *plate 1,* 260 n.3
Haouzous, Sam, 32
Hardy, Bullets, 34–35
Hare, Meredith, 7
Hare, Elizabeth Sage (Goodwin), 7, 8
Harris, Ann, 206–8, 209–10, 211
Harris, Carmela (Bui), 202–5, 206, 207, 208, 209–11, 229, *plate 36, plate 37, plate 38,* 248, 271 n.1, 272 n.3
Harris, Dixie, 202, 206, 207, 208–9, 210, 211
Harris, Enrique, 206
Harris, Jack, 201, 202, 206, 207, 208, 209
Harris, Magdalena de, 206
Harris, Martin, 159
Hatch, Herman, 42, 43
Hatch, Roy, 42

Haynie, Ether, 49
Hearst, George, 112
Hermosillo, 209, 271 n.1
Hinton, Tom, 196, 197, 233, 234
Hoffman, John, 9, 19, 66, 67, 247, 260 n.1
Hoijer, Harry, 3
horses, 121, 243–44; at Chita Hueca camp, 147–48; theft of, 124, 125, 128, 140, 146, 157, 186, 247
Houghton, Henry, 138
Houser, Allan, 33, 229
houses, 226; at Chita Hueca, *plate 17, plate 18*, 252–54; at Sierra las Espuelas, *plate 24, plate 25, plate 26, plate 27, plate 28, plate 33*, 255
Huachinera, 79, 84, 88, 92, 93–94, 126, 228, 246, 247
Huachuca Mountains, 193, 248, 270 n.5
Hunt, José, 124
Hunt, Stewart, 89, 124–26, 129, 141, 181, 247, 267 n.5
hunting, 8, 176–77. *See also* manhunts
Hurtado, Geronimo, 195–96
Hurtado, Ramon, 195
Hurtado, Rosa, 195–96

Ingstad, Helge, 223–24, 249; expedition of, 228–30, 272 n.8; and Carmela Harris, 202–3; and Lupe, 109–11, 121

Janos, 96, 162, 170, 235, 265 n.29
jerky, 182
Jicarilla, 4
José, 123, 132
Juan, xiii, xiv
Juh, 32, 92, 130
Julia. *See* Tasahuinora, Julia
Julio. *See* Medina, Julio

Kanseah, Aryliss, 235–36
Kanseah, Berle, 101, 102, 130, 235–36
Kanseah, Jasper, 102, 235
Kayenta, 34
Kenoi, Sam, 32, 33, 193, 194, 217, 220, 229, 230
Kickapoos, 61, 76, 84–85, 87–88, 89–90, 246, 263 n.2

kidnappings, 20, 246; by Apache Kid, 115, 116, 120, 121, 245; of children, 41–43, 47, 219, 248; of Gerardo Fimbres, xv, 1, 21–22, 45–46, 112
Kietah, 65
killings. *See* murders
King, Barbara Buck, *plate 42*, 239–40
Kiowa Apaches, 4
Kiowas, 4
Kirker, James, 80–81, 265 n.13
Kroeber, Alfred L., 3

La Cueva de la India, 128
Langford family, 71, 72
La Nopalera Ranch, 185
Las Piedras Canyon, 155, 157, 166, 226, 247; Apache camp in, 167–68, 169–70, 172–81, 187, *plate 24, plate 25, plate 26, plate 27, plate 28, plate 29, plate 30, plate 32, plate 33*, 255; post-cutting in, 159–60, 247; ranches at, 162–65; smuggling through, 184–85. *See also* Sierra las Espuelas
Las Varas, 99, 131, 138, 154, 247, 253
leather, 182
Lillywhite, Layne, 71–72
Lipan Apaches, 4, 246, 263 n.1
logging, 112, 246
Lola. *See* Barela, Lola
looting, 78
Los Angeles, 242–43
Los Laureles, 201–2
Los Otates ranch, 267 n.5
Los Pozos, 112
Lumholtz, Carl, 245; *Unknown Mexico*, 114
Lummis, Charles, 2
Lupe, xiii, xiv–xv, 20–21, *plate 2*, 100, 121, 127, 143, 202, 214, 215–16, 226, 229, 246, 247, 271 n.1, 271 n.2, 272 n. 3; Mexicanization of, 43–44; and Apaches, 45–46, 47; family of, 56–57; interview with, 109–11
Lynd, Charles (Charlie), 82, 88, 89
Lynd family, 88–89

Machichi, Pablo, 172, 269 n.2
Mack, J. D., 246
MacMurray, Gordon, 233, 247

MacNeil, Beula Fenn, 111, 131, 268 n.2
MacNeil, Wayne, 131, 154, 247, 268 n.2
MacNeil family, 268 n.2
Madero, Francisco, 77
Madrid, Manuel, 195, 196
Madrid Fimbres, Estolano, 55, *plate 5*
Malanoche, Rancho, 234
Mal-shua-pie. *See* Natculba·ye
Mangas Coloradas, 4–5, 92
manhunts, 62; by Francisco Fimbres,
    22–23, 29–30, 36, 37, 46–47, 51–52,
    55–57, 248; from Nácori Chico, 194–
    95. *See also* punitive expeditions
Marcos, 130, 132, 139, 140, 143, 251
marijuana, 184
Marsil, 115
Martine, 65
Martineau, J. H., 219
Massai, 214, 246
Matepuya, 90
Mayos, 79, 263 n.1
McComas, Charley, 26–27
McComas, Judge Hamilton, 26, 27
McComas family, 26–27
McCullough, Billy, 65, 235
Medina, Julio, 196–97, 198, 228, 229,
    *plate 35*, 248
Medina family, 197
Mendoza, Francesca, 143
Merrill, H. H., 245
Mesa, 117
Mesa Blanca, 199–200
Mesa de Tres Ríos, 113, 247
Mescalero Reservation, 186, 229, 246;
    and Sierra Madre Apaches, 193,
    212–13, 215, 216, 217, 220, 225,
    230–31, 232, 249
Mescaleros, 4, 213
mescal pits, 175
Metz, Don, 21, 52, 53, 161, 201
Mexican-American War, 81
Mexican Revolution, 41, 62, 63–64,
    66, 113, 246–47; lawlessness and,
    77–78; and Mormon colonies,
    71–72
Mexicans, 93; as informants, 13–14;
    perceptions of Apaches by, 72–73,
    112; with Sierra Madre Apaches, 99,
    103, 129–30

Mexico, 3–4, 28, 70; extermination
    policy of, 80–81. *See also various
    towns; topographic features*
Miller Ranch, 248
Mineral de Dolores, 246
mines, mining, 89, 112, 113, 246, 245,
    247; folklore about, 83–84
missionaries, 79
Mochopa, 81
Moctezuma, 125, 126–27, 129, 246, 267
    n.5, 269–70 n.2
Molina, Isabel, 171
Molina, Leonardo, 171
Molina, Nacho, 171
Molina, Socorro, 171
Molina family: murders of, 170–72,
    247
Mora, Ysidro (Isidro), 57, 228
Mormons, 13, 37; and Mexican Revo-
    lution, 66, 71–72, 78, 247; in Mex-
    ico, 42, 49–50, 64, 65, 112, 117–18,
    157, 219–20, 229, 245, 246
Morris, Curtis, 146
Morrow, Ralph, 219
Mountain Pimas, 233–34, 249, 263 n.1
Muñoz, Perfecto, 43
Muñoz, Roberto, 43
murders, 29, 54, 115, 194, 245, 246, 247,
    249; of Apaches, 36, 46–47, 51–52,
    56, 97, 124, 194, 195, 201, 202, 208,
    271 n.1; of Gerardo Fimbres, 57, 61,
    68; of Maria Dolores Fimbres, xv, 1,
    21–22, 45, 47, 112; of Molina family,
    170–72; of Thompson family,
    118–19
myths. *See* folklore

Nácori Chico, 20, 44, 55, 70, 79, 105–6,
    228, 247, 248; Apaches and, 45, 52,
    81, 92, 103–4, 178, 198, 201–3,
    208–9, 218, 249; drug trafficking in,
    53–54; Fimbres kidnapping and
    murder in, 21–22; manhunts from,
    29–30, 141–42, 194–95
Nacozari, 112, 132, 246
Naiche, 33, 65
Namasica, 90
Nana, 233
Na-pi-a, 33

Natcułba·ye (Mal-shua-pie; José Maria Elias), 32, 33, 104, 262 n.8, 272 n.11
Navajo, 35
Navajo Reservation, 34, 238, 248, 260 n.1
Naylor, Tom, 63, 64, 70, 71, 72, 132, 136, 161
Nde, 3
Ndéndaa'i, 5, 32–33, 193, 216
New Mexico, 25, 48
New Spain, 79–80
newspaper reports, 20, 36; of Fimbres murder and kidnapping, 13, 23, 29; and punitive expedition, 27–28
Nogales Ranch, 269 n.6
Noriega Calles, José, 51
Northern Tonto Apaches, 4

Obregón, Álvaro, 77
Ojos Azules Ranch, 134, 135, 139, 148
Olivas, Leonardo, 40, 51, 247
Opata, 47, 79, 92, 96, 265 n.24
Opler, Morris, 2, 3, 197, 212–13, 214–15, 230, 231, 263 n.1
Oputo, 84, 125
oral histories, 13
Orozco, Becky, 65

Pacheco. See Colonia Pacheco
Palmilla gathering, xiv
Palomas Land and Cattle Company, 25, 48, 176, 268 n.3, 269 n.6
Pancho Villa Museum, 66
Paquimé, 86
Parker, Neil, 233, 249
Patroncito, 139, 140
peace policy: Galvez's, 80
Pedregón, Jesús (father), 40, 41, 247
Pedregón, Jesús (son), 40
Peloncillo Mountains, 221–22
Perez, Cirilo, 57, 128
Perico, 217, 248, 272 n.6
Peridot, 115
Pershing, John J., 37, 39, 262 n.2
Perugia, 211
Pespichi, 90
petroglyphs. See rock art
Pico de la India, 143
Piedra Volada, 171

Pimas. See Mountain Pimas
Piños Altos, xiii, 44, 45, 113
Pitacachi Mountains, 64
Pomerene, 61–62
Portillo, Juan, 185
Portillo family, 185, 247
post cutting, 159–60, 247
Potawatomis, 88
presidios, 80, 97
Price, Anna, 192, 193, 248, 273 n.3
Prohibition, 184
prospectors, 155–56, 245, 247
Puerto de los Guacamayos, 127
Pulpit Creek, 69, 99, 132
Pulpit Pass. See El Paso Púlpito
Pulpit Rock, 73
punitive expeditions, 262 n.2; Francisco Fimbres's, 55–56, 91; governments and, 28–29; Mexican, 23, 26; Nácori Chico's, 29–30; recruitment for, 27–28

Quequechi, 90
Quesada, Guadalupe, 136, *plate 14*

raiding, 3–4, 31, 217, 218, 245, 256; by Apache Kid, 115, 116, 120–21; on Apaches, 76, 140, 149, 156; on McComas family, 26–27; in Mexico, 80–81, 89; and Sierra Madre Apaches, 39–40, 47, 48, 100, 127, 224, 229–30, 247
railroads, 246
Ramirez, Mrs. Jacinto, 214
Ramsey, Walter, 141, 218–19, 248
rancherias. See camps
ranches, ranching, 48, 92, 112, 113, 124–25, 127, 131; on Carretas Plains, 161–62; at Las Piedras Canyon, 162–65
Rascón, Maria, 198
Rascón, Rodolfo, 47, 54, 55, *plate 5*, 201, 204
Reciprocal Border Crossing Agreement (1891–1896), 245, 262 n.11
renegades: Apache, 115, 116, 181, 192–93, 233; white, 100, 101
Reyes, ranch foreman, 99, 103, 140, 149
Rios, Efrain, 166, 167

Rios, Maria, 166
Robles, Lorenzo, 196
rock art, 101, 102, *plate 7*, 264 n.1
Rodriguez, Audutio, 126
Rodriguez, Simon, 126–28
Rope, John, 32, 153
Rowe, Jack, 201
Rufkey, Bert, 10, 24, 29, 260 n.1
Ruiz, Rafaela, 44–45, 56, 101
Ruiz, Reyes, 44, 45
Ruiz Norberto Aguillar, 55, *plate 4,
    plate 5*
rustling, 181, 229
Rusvayo, 246

Sahuaripa, 47
Salome, 129
Salto, Rancho el, 127
Samaniego, Amiglia, 198, 199, 218, 248
Samaniego, Angelica, 93
Samaniego, Antonia, 93
Samaniego, Juan Jose, 93
Samaniego, Maria, 93, 94–95, 245
Samaniego, Miguel, 77
Samaniego Bruda de Davila, Natalia,
    93
San Bernardino Ranch. *See* Slaughter
    Ranch
San Bernardino Valley, 70–71, 186
San Carlos Apaches, 4, 10, 19
San Carlos Reservation, 10, 29, 30, 31,
    37, 101, 121, 182–83, 237, 239, 260 n.1;
    Apache Kid at, 115–16; economic
    depression at, 182–83; fieldwork at,
    191, 192, 212, 219, 248; Lupe at, 109–
    10; outbreaks from, 245, 262 n.10;
    and Sierra Madre Apaches, 24, 114,
    141, 178, 181, 232, 247, 260 n.2, 262 n.1
San Luis pass, 263 n.2
San Miguel, 41, 76–77, 78, 247
San Pedro Ojitos ranch, 112, 146
Santa Anaute, Rancho, 128
Santa Anita, Rancho, 133
Satachi, 81
Satsinistu, 33, 272 n.11
scalping, 80–81, 196
Schrader, Art, 69, 123, 130–31, 132, 142,
    147, 150, 151–52, 153, 184, 186, 201
Serva, 81

Sevey family, 119
Shaffer, Doug, 65
*shis inday*, 130
Sierra Azules, 136. *See also* Sierra Chita
    Hueca
Sierra Chita Hueca (Hachita Hueca;
    Azules), 75, 76, 104–5; Apache camp
    in, 65–66, 91, 99, 103, 130, 132, 133–
    134, 135–37, 138–39, 142–46, 147–
    49, 178, 179, 180, *plate 16, plate 17,
    plate 18, plate 19, plate 20*, 193, 226,
    227, 248, 251–54
Sierra de Huachinera, 96
Sierra de la Nutria, 128
Sierra Durarno, 91
Sierra el Medio, 105
Sierra el Tigre, 65, 91, 127, 247
Sierra las Espuelas, 37–38, 62, 68, 69,
    99, 105, 169, 180, *plate 22*, 245, 248;
    Apache camp in, 153, 154, 156–57,
    169–70, 171, 226, 247, 255–58; pros-
    pecting in, 155–56, 247; ranches in,
    161–62; trails in, 181, 182. *See also*
    Las Piedras Canyon
Sierra Madre, 91, 105, 233, 246; Apaches
    in, xiii–xiv, 1, 5–6, 10, 17, 19, 20,
    32–33; Geronimo in, 31–32; Gren-
    ville Goodwin's diary of, 11–12;
    roads through, 132–33; settlements
    in, 112–13. *See also various ranges;
    topographic features; towns*
Sierra Madre Apaches, xiii–xiv, 1,
    5–6, 10, 17, 19, 20, 37, 47, 106, 113,
    114, 115, 141, 191–92, 203, 215, 222,
    231, 235, 245, 248, 260 n.2, 262 n.1,
    272 n.3; attack on, 194–95; attack on
    Colonia García by, 117–19; camps
    of, 38–39, 99; capture of, 125,
    126–27; efforts to contact, 216–17,
    223–27; folklore of, 24–25, 103–4,
    218–19; Stewart Hunt and, 124–26;
    identity of, 32–33; Ingstad and,
    229–30; kidnappings by, 41–42;
    killings of, 51–52, 56–57; Lupe and,
    110–11; and Mescalero Reservation,
    193, 212–13, 230–31, 249; Mexican-
    ization of, 232–33; and Mexicans,
    45, 129–30; movements of, 177–78;
    and Pacheco, 219–20; raiding by,

246, 247; raids on, 76, 140; smuggling by, 181–82; trade with, 100, 181; whites with, 100–101
Sierra San Luis, 153
Sierra Tasahuinora, 100, 178, 198, 200
Sierra Tobacco, 128
silver smuggling, 131
Sixth Mexican Infantry, 96
Skeleton Canyon, 65
skunks, 186–87
Slaughter, John, 246, 270 n.3
Slaughter Ranch, 186, 270 n.3
slaves: Apaches as, 93, 95, 96
Smith, Hooke, 116
Smith, Misse, 63, 70, 122, 137, 138, 161
smuggling, 123–24, 131, 181–83; by Americans, 184–85, 186
Snake Tanks, 220
Sobarzo, Abelardo, 142
Solomonville, 245, 246
Southern Tonto Apaches, 4
Spanish, 79, 265 n.29
Speedy, 27
Spencer, Dr., 88, 98, 265 n.22
Spicer, Edward (Ned), 2, 243
strikes, mining, 77, 246
Swanson, Charles Walter, 85, 89–90
Swanson, John, 84, 85–86, 89, 247

Tamichopa, 87–88
Tamuqua, 90
Tapila Ranch, 124, 141, 181, 199, 247
Tarahumaras, 263 n.1
Tasahuinora, Julia, 198–199, 200, 248, 271 n.2
Taylor, Russell, 24–25, 221
Tayopa mine, 83–84
Tepaia, 90
The 31 Ranch, 201–2
Thomas, Sr., 101
Thompson, Annie, 118, 119
Thompson, Annie MacNeil, 117
Thompson, Elmer, 117, 118, 119
Thompson, Hans, 118, 119–20
Thompson, Hiram, 118, 119
Thompson, Jensine, 118, 119, 120
Thompson, Karen, 118, 119
Thompson family, 117–20, 245
Tigre mine, 37

tobacco train: attack on, 39–41
Tonto Apaches, 115, 261 n.2
Topete, Ricardo, 22, 248
Torazon, Miguel, 97, 98, 99, 102
toys, 111–12, 173
trade, 100, 181, 265 n.29
trails, 181, 182, 254
Tres Rios, 113
*trincheras*, 86
Tuetaque, 90
Tujunga, 210
Turnbull, Mt., 120
Tutuaca, 94, 95

United States, 4, 28, 66, 81, 87. *See also* U.S. army
U.S. army, 81, 82–83, 92–93, 153, 262 n.11
U.S. State Department, 28
University of Arizona, 9, 10, 29, 109, 247, 248
*Unknown Mexico* (Lumholtz), 114
Ures, 129
Urquijo, Pedro, 22, 57

Vacas, 155
Valencia, Cruz, 93
Valenzuela, Gilberto, 22
Valenzuela, rancher, 103–4
Vance, Marion, 157, 247
Vance, Robert, 119, 247
Van Orden, Jay, 65
Vegas, Ramon, 103, 129, 130
Victorio, 5, 92
Villa, Nelda, 14, 21, 40, 42, 52, 53, 54, 84, 96, *plate 11*, 126, 130, 143, 185, 201
Villa, Pancho, 37, 39, 66, 77, 78, 247, 262 n.2, 263 n.1
Villas, Rancho de las, 128

Warihios, 47
Welch, John, 143
Western Apaches, 2, 4, 30, 31, 83, 110, 204, 215, 264 n.2, 267 n.4, 272 n.2
White Mountain Apaches, 4
whites: with Apaches, 6, 26, 100–101, 103, 110
Willcox, 246

Yanozha (Ya-no-ja), 217, 228, 229, 230,
  *plate 34*, 248, 249, 272 n.6
Yaqui revolts, 77
Yaquis, 102, 197, 263 n.1
Yuzos, Melferd, 103

Zozaya, Francisco, 96, 97–98, 100, 103,
  130, 150, 178, 198–99, 268 n.5
Zozaya, Jesús, 98
Zozaya ranch, 87